The Red-Blooded Heroes of the Frontier

"Burning brush dropped from above failed to lodge
before the recess"

The Red-Blooded Heroes of the Frontier

of the Frontier

Cowboys, Indians, Outlaws, Lawmen, Bounty
Hunters and Six-Gun Killers of the Old West

Edgar Beecher Bronson

LEONAUR

The Red-Blooded Heroes of the Frontier
Cowboys, Indians, Outlaws, Lawmen, Bounty Hunters and Six-Gun Killers
of the Old West
by Edgar Beecher Bronson

First published under the title
The Red-Blooded Heroes of the Frontier

Leonaur is an imprint of Oakpast Ltd

Copyright in this form © 2012 Oakpast Ltd

ISBN: 978-0-85706-986-3 (hardcover)
ISBN: 978-0-85706-987-0 (softcover)

http://www.leonaur.com

Publisher's Notes

Contents

Contents

CHAPTER 1

Loving's Bend

From San Antonio to Fort Griffin, Joe Loving's was a name to conjure with in the middle sixties. His tragic story is still told and retold around camp-fires on the Plains.

One of the thriftiest of the pioneer cow-hunters, he was the first to realize that if he would profit by the fruits of his labour he must push out to the north in search of a market for his cattle. The Indian agencies and mining camps of northern New Mexico and Colorado, and the Mormon settlements of Utah, were the first markets to attract attention. The problem of reaching them seemed almost hopeless of solution. Immediately to the north of them the country was trackless and practically unknown. The only thing certain about it was that it swarmed with hostile Indians. What were the conditions as to water and grass, two prime essentials to moving herds, no one knew. To be sure, the old overland mail road to El Paso, Chihuahua, and Los Angeles led out west from the head of the Concho to the Pecos; and once on the Pecos, which they knew had its source indefinitely in the north, a practicable route to market should be possible.

But the trouble was to reach the Pecos across the ninety intervening miles of waterless plateau called the *Llano Estacado*, or Staked Plain. This plain was christened by the early Spanish explorers who, looking out across its vast stretches, could note no landmark, and left behind them driven stakes to guide their return. An elevated tableland averaging about one hundred miles wide and extending four hundred miles north and south, it presents, approaching anywhere from the east or the west, an endless line of sharply escarped bluffs from one hundred to two hundred feet high that with their buttresses and re-entrant angles look at a distance like the walls of an enormous fortified town. And indeed it possesses riches well worth fortifying.

7

While without a single surface spring or stream from Devil's River in the south to Yellow House Cañon in the north, this great mesa is nevertheless the source of the entire stream system of central and south Texas. Absorbing thirstily every drop of moisture that falls upon its surface, from its deep bosom pours a vitalizing flood that makes fertile and has enriched an empire,—a flood without which Texas, now producing one-third of the cotton grown in the United States, would be an arid waste. Bountiful to the south and east, it is niggardly elsewhere, and only two small springs, Grierson and Mescalero, escape from its western escarpment.

A driven herd normally travels only twelve to seventeen miles a day, and even less than this in the early Spring when herds usually are started. It therefore seemed a desperate undertaking to enter upon the ninety-mile "dry drive," from the head of the Concho to the Horsehead Crossing of the Pecos, wherein two-thirds of one's cattle were likely to perish for want of water.

Joe Loving was the first man to venture it, and he succeeded. He traversed the Plain, fought his way up the Pecos, reached a good market, and returned home in the Autumn, bringing a load of gold and stories of hungry markets in the north that meant fortunes for Texas ranchmen. This was in 1866. It was the beginning of the great "Texas trail drive," which during the next twenty years poured six million cattle into the plains and mountains of the Northwest. Of this great industrial movement, Joe Loving was the pioneer.

At this time Fort Sumner, situated on the Pecos about four hundred miles above Horsehead Crossing, was a large Government post, and the agency of the Navajo Indians, or such of them as were not on the war-path. Here, on his drive in the Summer of 1867, Loving made a contract for the delivery at the post the ensuing season of two herds of beeves. His partner in this contract was Charles Goodnight, later for many years the proprietor of the Palo Duro ranch in the Pan Handle.

Loving and Goodnight were young then; they had helped to repel many a Comanche assault upon the settlements, had participated in many a bloody raid of reprisal, had more than once from the slight shelter of a buffalo-wallow successfully defended their lives, and so they entered upon their work with little thought of disaster.

Beginning their round-up early in March as soon as green grass began to rise, selecting and cutting out cattle of fit age and condition, by the end of the month they reached the head of the Concho with two herds, each numbering about two thousand head. Loving was in

8

charge of one herd and Goodnight of the other.

Each outfit was composed of eight picked cowboys, well drilled in the rude school of the Plains, a "horse wrangler," and a cook. To each rider was assigned a mount of five horses, and the loose horses were driven with the herd by day and guarded by the "horse wrangler" by night. The cook drove a team of six small Spanish mules hitched to a mess wagon. In the wagon were carried provisions, consisting principally of bacon and jerked beef, flour, beans, and coffee; the men's blankets and "war sacks," and the simple cooking equipment. Beneath the wagon was always swung a "rawhide"—a dried, untanned, unscraped cow's hide, fastened by its four corners beneath the wagon bed. This rawhide served a double purpose: first, as a carryall for odds and ends; and second, as furnishing repair material for saddles and wagons. In it were carried pots and kettles, extra horseshoes, farriers' tools, and firewood; for often long journeys had to be made across country which did not furnish enough fuel to boil a pot of coffee. On the sides of the wagon, outside the wagon box, were securely lashed the two great water barrels, each supplied with a spigot, which are indispensable in trail driving. Where, as in this instance, exceptionally long dry drives were to be made other water kegs were carried in the wagons.

Such wagons were rude affairs, great prairie schooners, hooded in canvas to keep out the rain. Some of them were miracles of patchwork, racked and strained and broken till scarcely a sound bit of iron or wood remained, but, all splinted and bound with strips of the cowboy's indispensable rawhide, they wabbled crazily along, with many a shriek and groan, threatening every moment to collapse, but always holding together until some extraordinary accident required the application of new rawhide bandages. I have no doubt there are wagons of this sort in use in Texas today, (as at time of first publication), that went over the trail in 1868.

The men need little description, for the cowboy type has been made familiar by Buffalo Bill's most *truthful* exhibitions of plains life. Lean, wiry, bronzed men, their legs cased in leather *chaparejos*, with small boots, high heels, and great spurs, they were, despite their loose, slouchy seat, the best rough-riders in the world.

Cowboy character is not well understood. Its most distinguishing trait was absolute fidelity. As long as he liked you well enough to take your pay and eat your grub, you could, except in very rare instances, rely implicitly upon his faithfulness and honesty. To be sure, if he got the least idea he was being misused he might begin throwing lead at

"The loose horses were guarded by the
'horse wrangler' by night

you out of the business end of a gun at any time; but so long as he liked you, he was just as ready with his weapons in your defence, no matter what the odds or who the enemy. Another characteristic trait was his profound respect for womanhood. I never heard of a cowboy insulting a woman, and I don't believe any real cowboy ever did. Men whose nightly talk around the camp-fire is of home and "mammy" are apt to be a pretty good sort.

And yet another quality for which he was remarkable was his patient, uncomplaining endurance of a life of hardship and privation equalled only among seafarers. Drenched by rain or bitten by snow, scorched by heat or stiffened by cold, he passed it all off with a jest. Of a bitterly cold night he might casually remark about the quilts that composed his bed: "These here durned huldys ain't much thicker 'n hen skin!" Or of a hot night: "Reckon ole mammy must 'a stuffed a hull bale of cotton inter this yere ole huldy." Or in a pouring rain: "'Pears like ole Mahster's got a durned fool idee we'uns is web-footed." Or in a driving snow storm: "Ef ole Mahster had to *git rid* o' this yere damn cold stuff, he might 'a dumped it on fellers what's got more firewood handy."

Vices? Well, such as the cowboy had, someone who loves him less will have to describe. Perhaps he was a bit too frolicsome in town, and too quick to settle a trifling dispute with weapons; but these things were inevitable results of the life he led.

In driving a herd over a known trail where water and grass are abundant, an experienced trail boss conforms the movement of his herd as near as possible to the habit of wild cattle on the range. At dawn the herd rises from the bed ground and is "drifted" or grazed, without pushing, in the desired direction. By nine or ten o'clock they have eaten their fill, and then they are "strung out on the trail" to water. They step out smartly, two men—one at either side—"pointing" the leaders; and "swing" riders along the sides push in the flanks, until the herd is strung out for a mile or more, a narrow, bright, parti-coloured ribbon of moving colour winding over the dark green of hill and plain. In this way they easily march off six to nine miles by noon.

When they reach water they are scattered along the stream, drink their fill and lie down. Dinner is then eaten, and the boys not on herd doze in the shade of the wagon, until, a little after two o'clock, the herd rise of their own accord and move away, guided by the riders. Rather less distance is made in the afternoon. At twilight the herd is rounded up into a close circular compact mass and "bedded down" for the night; the first relief of the night guard riding slowly round, singing softly and turning back stragglers. If properly grazed, in less than a half-hour the herd is quiet and at rest; and, barring an occasional wild or hungry beast trying to steal away into the darkness, so they lie till dawn unless stampeded by some untoward incident.

Every two or three hours a new "relief" is called and the night guard changed. Round and round all night ride the guards, jingling their spurs and droning some low monotonous song, recounting through endless *stanzas* the fearless deeds of some frontier hero, or humming some love ditty rather too passionate for gentle ears.

But when a ninety-mile drive across the Staked Plain is to be done, all this easy system is changed. In order to make the journey at all the pace must be forced to the utmost, and the cattle kept on their legs and moving as long as they can stand.

Therefore, when Loving and Goodnight reached the head of the Concho, two full days' rest were taken to recuperate the "drags," or weaker cattle. Then, late one afternoon, after the herd had been well grazed and watered, the water barrels and kegs filled, the herd was thrown on the trail and driven away into the west, without halt or rest, throughout the night. Thus, driving in the cool of the night and of the early morning and late evening, resting through the heat of mid-day when travel would be most exhausting, the herd was pushed on westward for three nights and four days.

On these dry drives the horses suffer most, for every rider is forced, in his necessary daily work, to cover many times the distance travelled by the herd, and therefore the horses, doing the heaviest work, are refreshed by an occasional sip of the precious contents of the water barrels—as long as it lasts. By night of the second day of this drive every drop of water is consumed, and thereafter, with tongues parched and swollen by the clouds of dust raised by the moving multitude, thin, drawn, and famished for water, men, horses, and cattle push madly ahead.

Come at last within fifteen miles of the Pecos, even the leaders, the strongest of the herd, are staggering along with dull eyes and drooping heads, apparently ready to fall in their tracks. Suddenly the whole appearance of the cattle changes; heads are eagerly raised, ears pricked up, eyes brighten; the leaders step briskly forward and break into a trot. Cow-hunters say they smell the water. Perhaps they do, or perhaps it is the last desperate struggle for existence. Anyway, the tide is resistless.

Nothing can check them, and four men gallop in the lead to control and handle them as much as possible when they reach the stream. Behind, the weaker cattle follow at the best pace they can. In this way over the last stage a single herd is strung out over a length of four or five miles.

Great care is needed when the stream is reached to turn them in at easy waterings, for in their maddened state they would bowl over one another down a bluff of any height; and they often do so, for men and horses are almost equally wild to reach the water, and indifferent how they get there.

However, the Pecos was reached and the herds watered with comparatively small losses, and both Loving's and Goodnight's outfits lay at rest for three days to recuperate at Horsehead Crossing. Then the drive up the wide, level valley of the Pecos was begun, through thickets of *tornilla* and *mesquite*, horses and cattle grazing belly-deep in the tall, juicy *zacaton*.

The perils of the *Llano Estacado* were behind them, but they were now in the domain of the Comanche and in hourly danger of ambush or open attack. They found a great deal of Indian "sign," their trails and camps; but the "sign" was ten days or two weeks old, which left ground for hope that the war parties might be out on raids in the east or south. After travelling four days up the Pecos without encountering any fresh "sign," they concluded that the Indians were off on some foray; therefore it was decided that Loving might with reasonable safety proceed ahead of the herds to make arrangements at Fort Sumner for their delivery, provided he travelled only by night, and lay in concealment during the day.

In Loving's outfit were two brothers, Jim and Bill Scott, who had accompanied his two previous Pecos drives, and were his most experienced and trusted men. He chose Jim Scott for his companion on the dash through to Fort Sumner. When dark came, Loving mounted a favourite mule, and Jim his best horse; then, each well armed with a Henry rifle and two six-shooters, with a brief "So long, boys!" to Goodnight and the men, they trotted off up the trail. Riding rapidly all night, they hid themselves just before dawn in the rough hills below Pope's Crossing, ate a snack, and then slept undisturbed till nightfall. As soon as it was good dusk they slipped down a ravine to the river, watered their mounts, and resumed the trail to the north. This night also was uneventful, except that they rode into, and roused, a great herd of sleeping buffalo, which ran thundering away over the Plain.

13

Dawn came upon them riding through a level country about fifteen miles below the present town of Carlsbad, without cover of any sort to serve for their concealment through the day. They therefore decided to push on to the hills above the mouth of Dark Cañon. Here was their mistake. Had they ridden a mile or two to the west of the trail and dismounted before daylight, they probably would not have been discovered. It was madness for two men to travel by day in that country, whether fresh sign had been seen or not. But, anxious to reach a hiding place where both might venture to sleep through the day, they pressed on up the trail. And they paid dearly the penalty of their foolhardiness.

Other riders were out that morning, riders with eyes keen as a hawk's, eyes that never rested for a moment, eyes set in heads cunning as foxes and cruel as wolves. A war party of Comanches was out and on the move early, and, as is the crafty Indian custom, was riding out of sight in the narrow valley below the well-rounded hills that lined the river. But while hid themselves, their scouts were out far ahead, creeping along just beneath the edge of the Plain, scanning keenly its broad stretches, alert for quarry. And they soon found it.

Loving and Jim hove in sight!

To be sure they were only two specks in the distance, but the trained eyes of these savage sleuths quickly made them out as horsemen, and white men.

Halting for the main war party to come up, they held a brief council of war, which decided that the attack should be delivered two or three miles farther up the river, where the trail swerved in to within a few hundred yards of the stream. So the scouts mounted, and the war party jogged leisurely northward and took stand opposite the bend in the trail.

On came Loving and Jim, unwarned and unsuspecting, their animals jaded from the long night's ride. They reached the bend. And just as Jim, pointing to a low round hill a quarter of a mile to the west of them, remarked, "Thar'd be a blame good place to stan' off a bunch o' Injuns," they were startled by the sound of thundering hoofs off on their right to the east. Looking quickly round they saw a sight to make the bravest tremble.

Racing up out of the valley and out upon them, barely four hundred yards away, came a band of forty or fifty Comanche warriors, crouching low on their horses' withers, madly plying quirt and heel to urge their mounts to their utmost speed.

14

"LOVING AND JIM WERE TWO MERE SPECKS IN THE DISTANCE, BUT THE SAVAGE SLEUTHS MADE THEM OUT AS HORSEMEN—AND WHITE MEN"

Their own animals worn out, escape by running was hopeless. Cover must be sought where a stand could be made, so they whirled about and spurred away for the hill Jim had noted. Their pace was slow at the best. The Indians were gaining at every jump and had opened fire, and before half the distance to the hill was covered a ball broke Loving's thigh and killed his mule. As the mule pitched over dead, providentially he fell on the bank of a buffalo-wallow—a circular depression in the prairie two or three feet deep and eight or ten feet in diameter, made by buffalo wallowing in a muddy pool during the rains.

Instantly Jim sprang to the ground, gave his bridle to Loving, who lay helpless under his horse, and turned and poured a stream of lead out of his Henry rifle that bowled over two Comanches, knocked down one horse, and stopped the charge.

While the Indians temporarily drew back out of range, Jim pulled Loving from beneath his fallen mule, and, using his neckerchief, applied a tourniquet to the wounded leg which abated the haemorrhage, and then placed him in as easy a position as possible within the shelter of the wallow, and behind the fallen carcass of the mule. Then Jim led his own horse to the opposite bank of the wallow, drew his bowie knife and cut the poor beast's throat: they were in for a fight to the death, and, outnumbered twenty to one, must have breastworks. As the horse fell on the low bank and Jim dropped down behind him, Loving called out cheerily:

"Reckon we're all right now, Jim, and can down half o' them before they get us. Hell! Here they come again!"

A brief "Bet yer life, ole man. We'll make 'em settle now," was the only reply.

Stripped naked to their waist-cloths and *moccasins*, with faces painted black and bronze, bodies striped with vermilion, with curling buffalo horns and streaming eagle feathers for their war bonnets, no warriors ever presented a more ferocious appearance than these charging Comanches. Their horses, too, were naked except for the bridle and a hair rope loosely knotted round the barrel over the withers.

On they came at top speed until within range, when with that wonderful dexterity no other race has quite equalled, each pushed his bent right knee into the slack of the hair rope, seized bridle and horse's mane in the left hand, curled his left heel tightly into the horse's flank, and dropped down on the animal's right side, leaving only a hand and a foot in view from the left. Then, breaking the line of their charge, the whole band began to race round Loving's entrenchment in single file, firing beneath their horses' necks and gradually drawing nearer as they circled.

Loving and Jim wasted no lead. Lying low behind their breastworks until the enemy were well within range, they opened a fire that knocked over six horses and wounded three Indians. Balls and arrows were flying all about them, but, well sheltered, they remained untouched. The fire was too hot for the Comanches and they again withdrew.

Twice again during the day the Indians tried the same tactics with no better result. Later they tried sharpshooting at long range, to which Loving and Jim did not even reply. At last, late in the afternoon, they resorted to the desperate measure of a direct charge, hoping to ride over and shoot down the two white men. Up they came at a dead run five or six abreast, the front rank firing as they ran. But, badly exposed in their own persons, the fire from the buffalo-wallow made such havoc in their front ranks that the savage column swerved, broke, and retreated.

Night shut down. Loving and Jim ate the few biscuits they had baked and some raw bacon. Then they counselled with one another. Their thirst was so great, it was agreed they must have water at any cost. They knew the Indians were unlikely to attempt another attack until dawn, and so they decided to attempt to reach the stream shortly after midnight. Although it was scarcely more than fifteen hundred yards, that was a terrible journey for Loving. Compelled to crawl noiselessly to avoid alarming the enemy, Jim could give him little assistance. But going slowly, dragging his shattered leg behind him without a murmur, Loving followed Jim, and they reached the river safely and drank.

It was now necessary to find new cover. For long distances the banks of the Pecos are nearly perpendicular, and ten to twenty feet high. At flood the swift current cuts deep holes and recesses in these banks. Prowling along the margin of the stream, Jim found one of these recesses wide enough to hold them both, and deep enough to afford good defence against a fire from the opposite shore, Above them the bank rose straight for twenty feet. Thus they could not be attacked by firing, except from the other side of the river; and while the stream was only thirty yards wide, the opposite bank afforded no shelter for the enemy.

In the gray dawn the Indians crept in on the first entrenchment and sprang inside the breastworks with upraised weapons, only to find it deserted. However, the trail of Loving's dragging leg was plain, and they followed it down to the river, where, coming unexpectedly in range of the new defences, two of their number were killed outright.

Throughout the day they exhausted every device of their savage cunning to dislodge Loving, but without avail. They soon found the opposite bank too exposed and dangerous for attack from that direction. Burning brush dropped from above failed to lodge before the recess, as they had hoped it might. The position seemed impregnable, so they surrounded the spot, resolved to starve the white men out.

Loving and Jim had leisure to discuss their situation. Loving was losing strength from his wound. They had no food but a little raw bacon. Without relief they must inevitably be starved out. It was therefore agreed that Jim should try to reach Goodnight and bring aid. It was a forlorn hope, but the only one. The herds must be at least sixty miles back down the trail. Jim was reluctant to leave, but Loving urged it as the only chance.

As soon as it was dark, Jim removed all but his underclothing, hung his boots round his neck, slid softly into the river, and floated and swam downstream for more than a quarter of a mile. Then he crept out on the bank. On the way he had lost his boots, which more than doubled the difficulty and hardship of his journey. Still he struck bravely out for the trail, through cactus and over stones. He travelled all night, rested a few hours in the morning, resumed his tramp in the afternoon, and continued it well-nigh through the second night.

Near morning, famished and weak, with feet raw and bleeding, totally unable to go farther, Jim lay down in a rocky recess two or three hundred yards from the trail, and went to sleep.

It chanced that the two outfits lay camped scarcely a mile farther down the trail. At dawn they were again *en route*, and both passed Jim without rousing or discovering him. Then a strange thing happened. Three or four horses had strayed away from the "horse wrangler" during the night, and Jim's brother Bill was left behind to hunt them. Circling for their trail, he found and followed it, followed it until it brought him almost upon the figure of a prostrate man, nearly naked, bleeding, and apparently dead. Dismounting and turning the body over, Bill was startled to find it to be his brother Jim. With great difficulty Jim was roused; he was then helped to mount Bill's horse, and hurried on to overtake the outfit. Coffee and a little food revived him so that he could tell his story.

Neither danger nor property was considered where help was need-

"The figure of a prostrate man, apparently dead"

ed, in those days. Goodnight instantly ordered six men to shift saddles to their strongest horses, left the outfits to get on as best they might, and spurred away with his little band to his partner's relief.

Loving had a close call the day after Jim left. The Comanches had other plans to carry out, or perhaps they were grown impatient. In any event, they crossed the river and raced up and down the bluff, firing beneath their horses' necks. It was a miracle Loving was not hit; but, lying low and watching his chance, he returned such a destructive fire that the Comanches were forced to draw off. The afternoon passed without alarm. As a matter of fact, the remaining Comanches had given up the siege as too dear a bargain, and had struck off southwest toward Guadalupe Peak.

When night came, Loving grew alarmed over his situation. Jim might be taken and killed. Then no chance would remain for him where he lay. He must escape through the Indians and try to reach the trail at the crossing in the big bend four miles north. Here his own outfits might reach him in time. Therefore, he started early in the night, dragged himself painfully up the bluff, and reached the plain. He might have lain down by the trail nearby; but supposing the Comanches still about, he set himself the task of reaching the big bend.

Starving, weak from loss of blood, his shattered thigh compelling him to crawl, words cannot describe the horror of this journey. But he succeeded. Love of life carried him through. And so, late the next afternoon, the afternoon of the day Goodnight started to his relief, Loving reached the crossing, lay down beneath a mesquite bush near the trail, and fell into a swoon. Ever since, this spot has been known as Loving's Bend. It is half a mile below the present town of Carlsbad.

At dusk of the evening on which Loving reached the ford, a large party of Mexican freighters, travelling south from Fort Sumner to Fort Stockton, arrived and pitched their camp near where he lay, but Loving did not hear them. He was far into the dark valley and within the very shadow of Death. Help must come to him; he could not go to it. Luckily it came.

While some were unharnessing the teams, others went out to fetch firewood. In the darkness one Mexican, thinking he saw a big mesquite root, seized it and gave a tug. It was Loving's leg. Startled and frightened, the Mexican yelled to his mates:

"*Que vienen, hombres! Que vienen por el amor de Dios! Aqui esta un muerto.*"

Others came quickly, but it was not a dead man they found, as their mate had called. Dragged from under the mesquite and carried to the fire, Loving was found still breathing. The spark of life was very low, however, and the mescal given him as a stimulant did not serve to rouse him from his stupor. But the next morning, rested somewhat from his terrible hardships and strengthened by more mescal, he was able to take some food and tell his story. The Mexicans bathed and dressed his wound as well as they could, and promised to remain in camp until his friends should come up.

Before noon Goodnight and his six men galloped in. They had reached his entrenchment that morning, guided by the Indian sign around about it, and had discovered and followed his trail. Goodnight hired a party of the Mexicans to take one of their *carretas* and convey Loving through to Fort Sumner. With the fort still more than two hundred miles away, there was small hope he could survive the journey, but it must be tried. A rude hammock was improvised and slung beneath the canvas cover of the *carreta*, and, placed within it, Loving was made as comfortable as possible. After a nine days' forced march, made chiefly by night, the Mexicans brought their crazy old *carreta* safely into the post.

While with rest and food Loving had been gaining in strength, the heat and the lack of proper care were telling badly on his wound. Goodnight had returned to the outfits, and, after staying with them a week, he had brought them through as far as the Rio Penasco without further mishap. Then placing the two herds in charge of the Scott brothers, he himself made a forced ride that brought him into Sumner only one day behind Loving.

Goodnight found his partner's condition critical. Gangrene had attacked the wound. It was apparent that nothing but amputation of the wounded leg could save him. The medical officer of the post was out with a scouting cavalry detail, and only a hospital steward was available for the operation. To trust the case to this man's inexperience seemed murder. Therefore, Goodnight decided to send a rider through to Las Vegas, the nearest point where a surgeon could be obtained.

Here arose what seemed insuperable difficulties. From Fort Sumner to Las Vegas the distance is one hundred and thirty miles. Much travelled by freight teams carrying government supplies, the road was infested throughout with hostile Navajos, for whom the freight trains were the richest spoils they could have. Offer what he would, Goodnight could find no one at the Fort bold enough to ride through alone and fetch a surgeon. He finally raised his offer to a thousand dollars for anyone who would make the trip. It was a great prize, but the danger was greater than the prize. No one responded. To go himself was impossible; their contract must be fulfilled.

At this juncture a hero appeared. His name was Scot Moore. Moore was the contractor then furnishing wood and hay to the post. Coming in from one of his camps and learning of the dilemma, himself a friend of Loving, he instantly went to Goodnight.

"Charlie," he said, "why in the world did you not send for me before? Joe shall not die here like a dog if I can save him. I've got a young Kentucky saddle mare here that's the fastest thing on the Pecos. I'll be in Vegas by sun-up tomorrow morning, and I'll be back here sometime tomorrow night with a doctor, if the Navajos don't get us. Pay? Pay be damned. I'm doin' it for old Joe; he'd go for me in a minute. If I'm not back by nine o'clock tomorrow night, Charlie, send another messenger and just tell old Joe that Scot did his best."

"It's mighty good of you, Scot," replied Goodnight, "I never will forget it, nor will Joe. You know I'd go myself if I could."

"That's all right, pardner," said Scot. "Just come over to my camp a spell and look over some papers I want you to attend to if I don't show up."

And they strolled away. Officers and other bystanders shook their heads sadly.

"Devilish pity old Scot had to come in."

"Might 'a known nobody could hold him from goin'."

"He'll make Vegas all right in a night run if the mare don't give out, but God help him when he starts back with a doctor in a wagon; ain't one chance in a thousand he'll get through."

"Well, if any man on earth can make it, bet your *alce* Scot will."

These were some of the comments. Scot Moore was known and loved from Chihuahua to Fort Lyon. One of the biggest-hearted, most amiable and generous of men, he was known as the coolest and most utterly fearless in a country where few men were cowards.

At nightfall, the mare well fed and groomed and lightly saddled, Scot mounted, bearing no arms but his two pistols, called a careless "*Hasta luego, amigos*" to his friends, and trotted off up the road. For two hours he jogged along easily over the sandy stretches beyond the Bosque Redondo. Then getting out on firmer ground, the mare well warmed, he gave her the rein and let her out into a long, low, easy lope that scored the miles off famously. And so he swept on throughout the night, with only brief halts to cool the mare and give her a mouthful

22

of water, through Puerta de Luna, past the Cañon Pintado, up the Rio Gallinas, past sleeping freighters' camps and Mexican *placitas*. Twice he was fired upon by alarmed campers who mistook him for a savage marauder, but luckily the shots flew wild.

The last ten miles the noble mare nearly gave out, but, a friend's life the stake he was riding for, Scot's quirt and spurs lifted her through.

Half an hour after sunrise, before many in the town were out of bed, Scot rode into the *plaza* of Las Vegas and turned out the doctor, whom he knew.

Dr. D—— was no coward by any means, but it took all Scot's eloquence and persuasiveness to induce him to consent to hazard a daylight journey through to Sumner, for he well knew its dangers. Scarcely a week passed without news of some fearful massacre or desperate defence. But, stirred by Scot's own heroism or perhaps tempted by the heavy fee to be earned, he consented.

Having breakfasted and gotten the best team in town hitched to a light buckboard, Scot and the doctor were rolling away into the south on the Sumner trail before seven o'clock, over long stretches of level grassy mesa and past tall black volcanic buttes.

Driving on without interruption or incident, shortly after noon they approached the head of the Arroyo de los Enteros, down which the trail descended to the lower levels of the great Pecos Valley. Enteros Cañon is about three miles long, rarely more than two hundred yards wide, its sides rocky, precipitous, and heavily timbered, through which wound the wagon trail, exposed at every point to a perfect ambuscade. It was the most dreaded stretch of the Vegas–Sumner road, but Scot and the doctor drew near it without a misgiving, for no sign of the savage enemy had they seen.

Just before reaching the head of the *cañon*, the road wound round a high butte. Bowling rapidly along, Scot half dozing with fatigue, the doctor, unused to the plains, alert and watchful, they suddenly turned the hill and came out upon the immediate head of the *cañon*, when suddenly the doctor cried, seizing Scot's arm:

"Good God Scot, look! For God's sake, look!"

And it was time. There on either hand, to their right and to their left, tied by their lariats to drooping *piñon* bough, stood fifty or sixty Navajo ponies. The ponies were bridled and saddled. Upon some were tied lances and on others arms. All were dripping with sweat and heaving of flank, their knife-marked ears drooping with fatigue; not more than five minutes could have elapsed since their murderous riders had left them. Apparently it was an ambush laid for them, and they were already surrounded. Even the cool Scot shook himself in surprise to find that he was still alive.

Overcome with terror, the doctor cried: "Turn, Scot! Turn, for Heaven's sake! It's our only chance to pull for Vegas."

But Scot had been reflecting. With wits sharpened by a thousand perils and trained in scores of desperate encounters, he answered: "Doc, you're wrong; dead wrong. We're safe as if we were in Fort Union. If they were laying for us we'd be dead now. No, they are after bigger game. They have sighted a big freight outfit coming up from the Pecos, and are laying for that in the *cañon*. We can slide through without seeing a buck or hearing a shot. We'll go right on down Enteros, old boy."

"Scot, you're crazy," said the doctor. "I will not go a step. Let's run for Vegas. Any instant we may be attacked. Why, damn your fool soul, they've no doubt got a bead on us this minute."

With a sharp stroke of his whip, Scot started the team into a smart trot down into the *cañon*. Then he turned to the doctor and quietly answered: "Doc, you seem to forget that Joe Loving is dying, and that I *promised* to fetch you. Reckon you'll have to go!" And down they went into what seemed the very jaws of death.

But Scot was right. It was a triumph of logic. The Navajos were indeed lying for bigger game.

And so it happened that, come safely through the *cañon*, out two miles on the plain they met a train of eight freight teams travelling toward Vegas. They stopped and gave the freighters warning, told what they had seen, begged them to halt and corral their wagons. But it was no use. The freighters thought themselves strong enough to repel any attack, and drove on into the *cañon*.

None of them came out.

And to this day the traveller through Enteros may see pathetic evidence of their foolhardiness in a scattered lot of weather-worn and rusted wheel tyres and hub bands.

Before midnight Scot and the doctor reached Sumner, having changed teams twice at Mexican *placitas*. Covering two hundred and sixty miles in less than thirty hours, Scot Moore had kept his word! Unhappily, however, Joe Loving had become so weak that he died under the shock of the operation. Now Scot Moore himself is dead and gone, but the memory of his heroic ride should live as long as noble deeds are sung.

Chapter 2

A Cow-Hunters' Court

The recent death, (as at time of first publication), of Shanghai Rhett, at Llano, Texas, makes another hole in the rapidly thinning ranks of the pioneer Texas cow-hunters. Cow-hunting in early days was the industry upon which many of the greatest fortunes of the State were founded, and from it sprang the great cattle-ranch industry that between the years 1866 and 1885 converted into gold the rich wild grasses of the tenantless plains and mountains of Texas, New Mexico, the Indian Territory, Kansas, Nebraska, Colorado, Wyoming, Dakota, and Montana.

The economic value of this great industrial movement in promoting the settlement and development of that vast region of the West lying between the ninety-eighth and one hundred and twentieth meridians, and embracing half the total area of the United States, is comprehended by few who were not personally familiar with the conditions of its rise and progress. There can be no question that the ranch industry hastened the occupation and settlement of the Plains by at least thirty years. Farming in those wilds was then an impossibility. Remote from railways, unmapped, and untrod by white men, it was under the sway of hostile Indians, before whose attacks isolated farming settlements, with houses widely scattered, would have been defenceless,—alike in their position and in their inexperience in Indian warfare. Then, moreover, there was neither a market nor means of transportation or the farmer's product. All these conditions the Texas cow-hunters changed, and they did it in little more than a decade.

In Texas were bred the leaders and the rank and file of that great army of cow-hunters whose destiny it was to become the pioneers of this vast region. Pistol and knife were the treasured toys of their childhood; they were inured to danger and to hardship; they were expert horsemen, trained Indian-fighters, reckless of life but cool in its defence; and thus they were an ideal class for the pacification of the Plains.

Shanghai Rhett's death removed one of the comparatively few survivors of this most interesting and eventful past.

In Texas after the war, when Shang was young, a pony, a lariat, a six-shooter, and a branding iron were sufficient instruments for the acquisition of wealth. A trained eye and a practised hand were necessary for the effective use of pistol and lariat; the running iron anybody could wield; therefore, while a necessary feature of equipment, the iron was a secondary affair. The pistol was useful in settling annoying questions of title; the horse and the lariat, in taking possession after title was settled; the iron, in marking the property with a symbol of ownership. The property in question was always cattle.

Before the war, cattle were abundant in Texas. Fences were few. Therefore, the cattle roamed at will over hill and plain. To determine ownership each owner adopted a distinctive "mark and brand." The owner's mark and brand were put upon the young before they left their mothers, and upon grown cattle when purchases were made. Thus the broad sides and quarters of those that changed hands many times were covered over with this barbarous record of their various transfers.

The system of marking and branding had its origin among the Mexicans. Marking consists in cutting the ears or some part of the animal's hide in such a way as to leave a permanent distinguishing mark. One owner would adopt the "swallow fork," a V-shaped piece cut out of the tip of the ear; another, the "crop," the tip of the ear cut squarely off; another, the "under-half crop," the under half of the tip of the ear cut away; another, the "over-half crop," the reverse of the last; another, the "under-bit," a round nick cut in the lower edge of the ear; another, the "over-bit," the reverse of the last; another, the "under-slope," the under half of the ear removed by cutting diagonally upward; another, the "over-slope," the reverse of the last; another, the "grub," the ear cut off close to the head; another, the "wattle," a strip of the hide an inch wide and two or three inches long, either on forehead, shoulder, or quarters, skinned and left hanging by one end, where before healing it leaves a conspicuous lump; another, the "dewlap," three or four inches of the loose skin under the throat skinned down and left hanging.

Branding consists in applying a red-hot iron to any part of the animal for six or eight seconds, until the hide is seared. Properly done, hair never again grows on the seared surface and the animal is "brand-ed for life." A small five-inch brand on a young calf becomes a great twelve-to-eighteen-inch mark by the time the beast is fully grown.

In Mexico the art of branding dates back to the time when few men were lettered and most men used a *rubrica* mark or flourish in-stead of a written signature. Thus, in Mexico the brand is always a device, whatever complex combination of lines and circles the whim of the owner may conceive. In this country the brand was usually a combination of letters or numerals, though sometimes shapes and forms are represented. Branding and marking cattle and horses is cer-tainly a most cruel practice, but under the old conditions of the open range, where individual ownerships numbered thousands of head, no other means existed of contradistinguishing title.

During the war these vast herds grew and increased unattended, neglected by owners, who were in the field with the armies of the Confederacy. So it happened that hundreds of thousands of cattle ranged the plains of Texas after the war, unmarked and unbranded, wild as the native game, to which no man could establish title. This situation afforded an opportunity which the hard-riding and desper-ate men who found themselves stranded on this far frontier after the wreck of the Confederacy were quick to seize. Shang Rhett was one of them. From chasing Federal soldiers they turned to chasing un-branded steers, and found the latter occupation no less exciting and much more profitable than the former.

First, bands of free companions rode together and pooled their gains. Then the thrift of some and the improvidence of others set in motion the immutable laws of distribution. Soon a class of rich and powerful individual owners was created, who employed great outfits of ten to fifty men each, splendidly mounted and armed. These out-fits were in continually moving camps, and travelled light, without wagons or tents. The climate being mild even in winter, seldom more than two blankets to the man were carried for bedding. The cooking paraphernalia were equally simple, at the most consisting of a coffee pot, a frying-pan, a stew kettle, and a Dutch oven.

Each man carried a tin cup tied to his saddle. Plates, knives, and forks were considered unnecessary luxuries, as every man wore a bowie knife at his belt, and was dexterous in using his slice of bread as a plate to hold whatever delicacy the frying-pan or kettle might con-tain. Sometimes even the Dutch oven was dispensed with, and bread was baked by winding thin rolls of dough round a stick and planting the stick in the ground, inclined over a bed of live coals. Often the frying-pan was left behind, and the meat roasted on a stick over the fire; and no meat in the world was ever so delicious as a good fat side of ribs so roasted.

The wild, unbranded cattle were everywhere—in the cross-timbers of the Palo Pinto, in the hills and among the post oaks of the Concho and the Llano, on the broad savannas of the Lower Guadalupe and the Brazos, in the plains and mesquite thickets of the Nueces and the Frio. And through these wild regions, on the outer fringe of settlement, ranged the cow-hunters, as merry and happy a lot as ever courted adventure, careless of their lives.

Of adventure and hazard the cow-hunters had quite enough to keep the blood tingling. They had to deal with wild men as well as wild cattle. Comanches and Kiowas, the old lords of the manor, were bitterly disputing every forward movement of the settler along the whole frontier. No community, from Griffin to San Antonio, escaped their attacks and depredations. Indeed, these incursions were regular monthly visitations, made always "in the light of the moon." A war party of naked bucks on naked horses, the lightest and most dexterous cavalry in the world, would slip softly near some isolated ranch or lonely camp by night. The cleverest and cunningest would dismount and steal swiftly in upon their quarry.

Slender, sinewy, bronze figures creeping and crouching like panthers, crafty as foxes, fierce and merciless as maddened bulls, their presence was rarely known until the blow fell. Sometimes they were content to steal the settlers' horses, and by daylight be many miles away to the west or north. Sometimes they fired buildings and shot down the inmates as they ran out. Sometimes they crept silently into camps, knifed or tomahawked one or more of the sleepers, and stole away, all so noiselessly that others sleeping near were undisturbed. Sometimes they lay in ambush about a camp till dawn, and then with mad war-whoops charged among the sleepers with their deadly arrows and tomahawks.

Against these wily marauders the cow-hunters could never abate their guard. And it was these same cow-hunters the Indians most dreaded, for they were tireless on a trail and utterly reckless in attack. It was not often the Indians got the best of them, and then only by ambush, or overwhelming numbers. Better armed, of stouter hearts in a stand-up fight, little bands of these cow-hunters often soundly thrashed war parties outnumbering them ten to one.

"Slender, sinewy bronze figures creeping and crouching like panthers, crafty as foxes, their presence was rarely known until the blow fell"

Then it not infrequently fell out that collisions occurred between rival outfits of cow-hunters, disputes over territory or cattle, which led to bitter feuds not settled till one side or the other was killed off or run out of the country. Battles royal were fought more than once in which a score or more of men were killed, wherein the *casus belli* was a difference as to the ownership of a brindle steer.

These men were a law unto themselves. Courts were few and far between on the line of the outer settlements. Powder and lead came cheaper than attorneys' fees, and were, moreover, found to be more effective. Thus the rifle and pistol were almost invariably the cow-hunters' court of first and last resort for disputes of every nature. Except in rare instances where there happened to be survivors among the families of the original plaintiff and defendant, this form of litigation was never prolonged or tiresome. When there were any survivors the case was sure to be re-argued.

Occasionally, of course, in the immediate settlements a case would be brought to formal trial before a judge and jury. While, as a rule, the procedure of these courts conformed to the statutes and was formal enough, rather startling informalities sometimes characterized their sessions. A case in point, of which Shang Rhett was the hero, occurred at Llano.

At that time the town of Llano could boast of only one building, a big rough stone house, loop-holed for defence against the Indians. Under this one roof the enterprising owner assembled a variety of industries and performed a variety of functions that would dismay the most versatile man of any older community. Here he kept a general store, operated blacksmith and wheelwright shops, served as post-master, ran a hotel, and sat as justice of the peace. Indeed, he got so much in the habit of self-reliance in all emergencies, that in more than one instance he subjected himself to some criticism by calmly sitting as both judge and jury in cases wherein he had no jurisdiction. Getting a jury at Llano was no easy task. Often the country for miles around might be scoured without producing a full panel.

Llano being the county seat, and this the only house in town, it somewhat naturally from time to time enjoyed temporary distinction as a court house, when at long intervals the Llano County court met. The accommodations, however, were inconveniently limited—so limited in fact that on one occasion at least they were responsible for a sad miscarriage of justice.

A murder trial was on. One of the earliest settlers, a man well known and generally liked, had killed a newcomer. It was felt that he had given his victim no chance for his life, else he probably would not have been brought to trial at all. And even in spite of the prevailing disapproval, there was an undercurrent of sympathy for him in the community.

However, court met and the case was called. Several settlers were witnesses in the case. It was, therefore, considered a remarkable and encouraging evidence of Llano County's growth in population when the district attorney succeeded in raking together enough men for a jury. At noon of the second day of the trial the evidence was all in, arguments of counsel finished, and the case given to the jury. The prisoner's case seemed hopeless. A clearly premeditated murder had been proved, against which scarcely any defence was produced.

Judge, jury, prisoner, and witnesses all had dinner together in the "court-room," which was always demeaned from its temporary dignity as a hall of justice, to the humble rank of a dining-room as soon as court adjourned. Directly after dinner the jury withdrew for deliberation, in custody of two bailiffs.

The house was large, to be sure, but its capacity was already so far taxed that it could not provide a jury room. It was therefore the custom of the bailiffs to use as a jury room an open, mossy glade shaded by a great live oak tree on the farther bank of the Llano, and distant two or three hundred yards from the court house. Here, therefore, the jury were conducted, the bailiffs retired to some distance, and discussion of a verdict was begun. In spite of the weight of evidence against him, two or three were for acquittal. The others said they were "damned sorry; Jim was a mighty good feller, but it 'peared like they'd have to foller the evidence." So the discussion pro and con ran on into the mid-afternoon without result.

It was an intensely hot afternoon, the air close and heavy with humidity, an hour when all Texans who can do so take a siesta. Judge and counsel were snoozing peacefully on the gallery of the distant court house, and the two bailiffs guarding the "jury room," overcome by habit and the heat, were stretched at full length on the ground, snoring in concert. This situation made the opportunity for a friend at court. Shang Rhett was the friend awaiting this opportunity. Stepping lightly out of the brush where he had been concealed, a few paces brought him among the jurors.

"Howdy! boys?" Shang drawled. "Pow'ful hot evenin', ain't it! Moseyin' roun' sort o' lonesome like, I thought mebbe so you fellers 'd be tired o' talkin' law, an' I'd jes' step over an' pass the time o' day an' give you a rest."

A rude diplomat, perhaps, Shang was nevertheless a cunning one. Several jurors expressed their appreciation of his sympathy and one answered: "Tired o' talkin'! Wall, I reckon so. I'm jes' tireder an' dryer 'n if I'd been tailin' down beef steers all day. My ol' tongue's been a-floppin' till thar ain't nary 'nother flop left in her 'nless I could git to ile her up with a swaller o' red-eye, an—"regretfully—"I reckon thar ain't no sort o' chanst o' that."

"Thar ain't, hey?" replied Shang, producing a big jug from the brush nearby. "'Pears like, 'nless I disremember, thar's some red-eye in this yere jug."

Upon examination the jug was found to be nearly full; but, passed and repassed around the "jury room," it was not long before the jug was empty, and the jury full.

Shrewdly seizing the proper moment before the jurors got drunk enough to be obstinate and combative, Shang made his appeal. "Fellers," he said, "I allows you all knows that Jim's my friend, an' I reckon you cain't say but what he 's been a mighty good friend to more'n one o' you. Course, I know he got terrible out o' luck when he had t' kill this yer Arkinsaw feller. But then, boys, Arkinsawyers don't count fer much nohow, do they? Pow'ful onery, no account lot, sca'cely fit to practise shootin' at. We fellers ain't a-goin' to lay that up agin Jim, air we? We ain't a-goin' to help this yer jack-leg prosecutin' attorney send ol' Jim up. Why, fellers, we knows well enough that airy one o' us might 'a done the same thing ef we'd been out o' luck, like Jim was, in meetin' up with this yer Arkinsawyer afore we'd had our mornin' coffee. What say, boys? Bein' as how any o' us might be in Jim's boots mos' any day, reckon we'll have to turn him loose?"

Shang's pathetic appeal for Jim's life clearly won outright more than half the jury, but there were several who, while their sympathies were with Jim, "'lowed they'd have to bring a verdic' accordin' to the evidence."

"Verdic'? Why, fellers," retorted Jim's advocate, "whar's the use of a fool verdic'? 'Sposin' we fellers was goin' to be verdicked? This is a time for us fellers to stan' together, shua'. I'll tell you what le's do; le's all slip off inter th' brush, cotch our hosses an' pull our freight fer home. This yer court ain't goin' to git airy jury but us in Llano 'till a new one's growed, an' if we skip I reckon they'll have to turn Jim loose."

"'Nless I disremember, thar's some red-eye in this yere jug"

This alternative met all objections. In a moment the "jury room" was empty.

Shortly thereafter the two bailiffs, awakened by a clatter of hoofs over the rocky hills behind them, were doubly shocked to find the only tenant of the "jury room" an empty jug.

One of the bailiffs sighted some of the escaping jurors and opened fire; the other hastened to alarm the court. The latter, running toward the house, met the judge and counsel who had been roused by the firing, and yelled out: "Jedge, the hull jury's stampeded! Bill's winged two o' them. Gi' me a fast hoss an' a lariat an' mebbe so I'll cotch some more."

Two or three jurors who were too much fuddled with drink to saddle and mount were quickly captured. The rest escaped. Of course, the court was outraged and indignant, but it was powerless. So Jim was released, thanks to Shang's diplomacy and eloquence. And, by the way, in the dark days that came to ranchmen in 1885, Jim, risen to be a well-known and powerful banker in ———— City, furnished the ready money necessary to save Shang's imperilled fortune; and when at length he heard that Shang was at death's door, Jim found the time to leave his large affairs and come all the way up from ———— to Llano to bid his old friend farewell.

For two or three years after the war the cow-hunters were busy accumulating cattle. From Palo Pinto to San Diego great outfits were working incessantly, scouring the wilds for unbranded cattle.

Directly an animal was sighted, one or two of these riders would spur in pursuit, rope him by horns or legs, and throw him to the ground. Then dismounting and springing nimbly upon the prostrate beast, they quickly fastened the beast's feet with a "hogtie" hitch so that he could not rise, a fire was built, the short saddle iron heated, and the beast branded. The feet were then unbound and the cow-hunter made a flying leap into his saddle, and spurred away to escape the infuriated charge sure to be delivered by his maddened victim.

In this work horses were often fatally gored and not a few men lost their lives. Notwithstanding the fact that it was such a downright desperate task, the men became so expert that they did not even hesitate to tackle, alone and single-handed, great bulls of twice the weight of their small ponies; they roped, held, threw, and branded them. The least accident or mistake, a slip of the foot, a stumble by one's horse, a breaking cinch, a failure to maintain full tension on the lariat, slowness in dismounting to tie an animal or in mounting after it was untied—

any one of these things happening meant death, unless the cow-hunter could save himself with a quick and accurate shot. Indeed the boys so loved this work and were so proud of their skill, that when an unusually vicious old "mossback" was encountered, each strove to be the first catch and master him. And God knows they should have loved it, as must any man with real red blood coursing through his veins, for it was not work; I libel it to call it work; it was rather sport, and the most glorious sport in the world. Riding to hounds over the stiffest country, or hunting grizzly in juniper thickets, is tame beside cow-hunting in the old days.

The happiest period of my life was my first five years on the range in the early seventies. Indeed it was a period so happy that memory plays me a shabby trick to recall its incidents and fire me with longings for pleasures I may never again experience. Its scenes are all before me now, vivid as if of yesterday.

The night camp is made beside a singing stream or a bubbling spring; the night horses are caught and staked; there is a roaring, merry fire of fragrant cedar boughs; a side of fat ribs is roasting on a spit before the fire, its sweet juices hissing as they drop into the flames, and sending off odours to drive one ravenous; the rich amber contents of the coffee pot is so full of life and strength that it is well-nigh bursting the lid with joy over the vitality and stimulus it is to bring you. Supper eaten, there follow pipe and cigarette, jest and badinage over the day's events; stories and songs of love, of home, of mother; and rude impromptu epics relating the story of victories over vicious horses, wild beasts, or savage Indians. When the fire has burnt low and become a mass of glowing coals, voices are hushed, the camp is still, and each, half hypnotized by gazing into the weirdly shifting lights of the dying embers, is wrapped in introspection. Then, rousing, you lie down, your canopy the dark blue vault of the heavens, your mattress the soft, curling buffalo grass.

After a night of deep refreshing sleep you spring at dawn with every faculty renewed and tense. Breakfast eaten, you catch a favourite roping-horse, square and heavy of shoulder and quarter, short of back, with wide nervous nostrils, flashing eyes, ears pointing to the slightest sound, pasterns supple and strong as steel, and of a nerve and temper always reminding you that you are his master only by sufferance. Now begins the day's hunt. Riding softly through cedar brake or mesquite thicket, slipping quickly from one live oak to another, you come upon your quarry, some great tawny yellow monster with sharp-pointed,

"The great loop of your lariat circling and hissing about your head"

wide-spreading horns, standing startled and rigid, gazing at you with eyes wide with curiosity, uncertain whether to attack or fly. Usually he at first turns and runs, and you dash after him through timber or over plain, the great loop of your lariat circling and hissing about your head, the noble horse between your knees straining every muscle in pursuit, until, come to fit distance, the loop is cast. It settles and tightens round the monster's horns, and your horse stops and braces himself to the shock that may either throw the quarry or cast horse and rider to the ground, helpless, at his mercy. Once he is caught, woe to you if you cannot master and tie him, for a struggle is on, a struggle of dexterity and intelligence against brute strength and fierce temper, that cannot end till beast or man is vanquished!

Thus were the great herds accumulated in Texas after the war. But cattle were so abundant that their local value was trifling. Markets had to be sought. The only outlets were the mining camps and Indian agencies of the Northwest, and the railway construction camps then pushing west from the Missouri River. So the Texans gathered their cattle into herds of two thousand to three thousand head each, and struck north across the trackless Plains. Indeed this movement reached such proportions that, excepting in a few narrow mining belts, there is scarcely one of the greater cities and towns between the ninety-eighth and one hundred and twentieth meridians which did not have its origin as a supply point for these nomads. Figures will emphasize the magnitude of the movement. The cattle-drive northward from Texas between the years 1866 and 1885 was approximately as follows:

1866	260,000	1877	201,000
1867	35,000	1878	265,649
1868	75,000	1879	257,927
1869	350,000	1880	394,784
1870	350,000	1881	250,000
1871	600,000	1882	250,000
1872	350,000	1883	265,000
1873	404,000	1884	416,000
1874	166,000	1885	350,000
1875	151,618		———
1876	321,998	Total	5,713,976

The range business on a large and profitable scale was long since practically done and ended. In Texas there remain very few open ranges capable of turning off fair grass beef. With the good lands farmed and the poor lands exhausted, the ranges have become narrower every year; and every year the cost of getting fat grass steers has been eating deeper and deeper into the rangeman's pocket. Of course, there are still isolated ranges where the rangemen still hang on, but they are not many, and most of them must soon fall easy prey to the ploughshare.

When the rangeman was forced to lease land in Texas, or buy water fronts in the Territories and build fences, his fate was soon sealed. With these conditions, he soon found that the sooner he reduced his numbers, improved his breed, and went on tame feed, the better. A corn shock is now a more profitable close herder than any cowpuncher who ever wore spurs. This is a sad thing for an old rangeman to contemplate, but it is nevertheless the simple truth. Soon the merry crack of the six Footer will no more be heard in the land, its wild and woolly manipulator being driven across the last divide, with faint show of resistance, by an unassuming granger and his all-conquering hoe.

The rangeman, like many another in the past, has served his purpose and survived his usefulness. His work is practically done, and few realize what a noble work it has been, or what its cost in hardship and danger.

I refer, of course, not alone to the development of a great industry, which in its time has added millions to the material wealth of the country, but to its collateral results and influence. But for the venturesome rangeman and his rifle, millions of acres, from the Gulf in the South to Bow River in the far Canadian Northwest, now constituting the peaceful, prosperous homes of hundreds of thousands of thrifty farmers, would have remained for many years longer what it had been from the beginning—a hunting and battle ground for Indians, and a safe retreat for wild game.

What was the hardship, and what the personal risk with which this great pioneer work was accomplished, few know except those who had a hand in it, and they as a rule, were modest men who thought little of what they did, and now that it is done, say less.

CHAPTER 3

A Self-Constituted Executioner

Some think it fair to give a man warnin' you intend to kill him on sight, an' then get right down to business as soon as you meet. But that ain't no equal chance for both. The man that sees his enemy first has the advantage, for the other is sure to be more or less rattled.

"Others consider it a square deal to stan' back to back with drawn pistols, to walk five paces apart an' then swing and shoot. But even this way is open to objections. While both may be equally brave an' determined, one may be blamed nervous, like, an' excitable, while the other is cool and deliberate; one may be a better shot than the other, or one may have bad eyes.

"I tell you, gentlemen, none o' these deals are fair; they are murderous. If you want to kill a man in a neat an' gentlemanly way that will give both a perfectly equal show for life, let both be put in a narrow hole in the ground that they can't git out of, their left arms securely tied together, their right hands holdin' bowie knives, an' let them cut, an' cut an' cut till one is down."

His heavy brow contracted into a fierce frown; his black eyes narrowed and glittered balefully; his surging blood reddened the bronzed cheeks.

"Let them cut, I say, cut to a finish. That's fightin', an' fightin' dead fair. Ah!" and the hard lines of the scarred face softened into a look of infinite longing and regret, "if only I could find another man with nerve enough to fight me that way!"

The speaker was Mr. Clay Allison, formerly of Cimarron, later domiciled at Pope's Crossing. His listeners were cowboys. The scene was a round-up camp on the banks of the Pecos River near the mouth of Rocky Arroyo. Mr. Allison was not dilating upon a theory. On the contrary, he was eminently a man of practice, especially in the matters of which he was speaking. Indeed he was probably the most expert taker of human life that ever heightened the prevailing dull colours of a frontier community. Early in his career the impression became general that his favourite tint was crimson.

And yet Mr. Allison was in no sense an assassin. I never knew him to kill a man whom the community could not very well spare. While engaged as a ranchman in raising cattle, he found more agreeable occupation for the greater part of his time in thinning out the social weeds that are apt to grow quite too luxuriantly for the general good in new Western settlements. His work was not done as an officer of the law either. It was rather a self-imposed task, in which he performed, at least to his own satisfaction, the double functions of judge and executioner. And in the unwritten code governing his decisions all offences had a common penalty—death.

Mr. Allison was born with a passion for fighting, and he indulged the passion until it became a mania. The louder the bullets whistled, the redder the gleaming blades grew, the more he loved it.

Yet no knight of old that rode with King Arthur was ever a more chivalrous enemy. He hated a foul blow as much as many of his contemporaries loved "to get the drop," which meant taking your opponent unawares and at hopeless disadvantage. In fact in most cases he actually carried a chivalry so far as to warn the doomed man, a week or two in advance, of the precise day and hour when he might expect to die. And as Mr. Allison was known to be most scrupulous in standing to his word, and as the victim knew there was no chance of a reprieve, this gave him plenty of time to settle up his affairs and to prepare to cross the last divide. Thus the estates of gentlemen who happened to incur Mr. Allison's disapproval were usually left in excellent condition and gave little trouble to the probate courts.

Of course the gentlemen receiving these warnings were under no obligations to await Mr. Allison's pleasure. Some suddenly discovered that they had imperative business in other and remote parts of the country. Others were so anxious to save him unnecessary trouble that they frequented trails he was known to travel, and lay sometimes for hours and days awaiting him, making themselves as comfortable as possible in the meantime behind some convenient boulder or tall *nopal*, or in the shady recesses of a mesquite thicket. But they might as well have saved all this bother, for the result was the same. Mr. Allison could always spare the time to journey even from New Mexico to Montana where it was necessary to the fulfilment of a promise to do so.

To those who were impatient and sought him out in advance, he was ever obliging and proved ready to meet them where and when and how they pleased. It was all the same to him. To avoid annoying legal complications, he was known to have more than once deliberately given his opponent the first shot.

In the early eighties a band of horse rustlers were playing great havoc among the saddle stock in north-eastern New Mexico. It was chiefly through Mr. Allison's industry and accurate marksmanship that their numbers were reduced below a convenient working majority. The leader vowed vengeance on Allison. One day they met unexpectedly in the stage ranch at the crossing of the Cimarron.

Mr. Allison invited the rustler to take a drink. The invitation was accepted. It was remarked by the bystanders that while they were drinking neither seemed to take any especial interest in the brazen pictures that constituted a feature of the Cimarron bar and were the pride of its proprietor. The next manoeuvre in the game was a proposition by Mr. Allison that they retire to the dining-room and have some oysters. Unable to plead any other engagement to dine, the rustler accepted. As they sat down at table, both agreed that their pistols felt heavy about their waists, and each drew his weapon from the scabbard and laid it on his knees.

While the Cimarron ranch was noted for the best cooking on the trail, other gentlemen at dinner seemed oddly indifferent to its delicacies, nervously gulped down a few mouthfuls and then slipped quietly out of the room, leaving loaded plates.

Presently Mr. Allison dropped a fork on the floor—perhaps by accident—and bent as if to pick it up. An opening in his enemy's guard the rustler could not resist: he grabbed the pistol lying in his lap and raised it quickly, but in doing so he struck the muzzle beneath the edge of the table, causing an instant's delay. It was, however, enough; Allison had pitched sideways to the floor, and, firing beneath the table, converted a bad rustler into a good one.

Dodge City used to be one of the hottest places on the Texas trail. It was full of thugs and *desperadoes* of the worst sort, come to prey upon the hundreds of cowboys who were paid off there. This money had to be kept in Dodge at any cost. Usually the boys were easy game. What money the saloons failed to get was generally gambled off against brace games of *faro* or *monte*. And those who would neither drink nor play were waylaid, knocked down, and robbed.

On one occasion when the Hunter and Evans "Jinglebob" outfits were in town, they objected to some of these enforced levies as unreasonably heavy. A pitched battle on the streets resulted. Many of the boys were young and inexperienced, and they were getting quite the worst of it, when Clay Allison happened along and took a hand.

The fight did not last much longer. When it was over, it was discovered that several of Dodge's most active citizens had been removed from their field of usefulness. For the next day or two, "Boot Hill" (the local graveyard) was a scene of unusual activity.

From all this it fell out that a few days later when Clay Allison rode alone out of Dodge returning home, he was ambushed a few miles from town by three men and shot from his horse. Crippled too badly to resist, he lay as if dead. Thinking their work well done, the three men came out of hiding, kicked and cursed him, shot two or three more holes in him, and rode back to town. But Allison, who had not even lost consciousness, had recognized them. A few hours later the driver of a passing wagon found him and hauled him into town. After lingering many weeks between life and death, Allison recovered. As soon as they heard that he was convalescing, the three who had attacked him wound up their affairs and fled the town.

When able to travel Allison sold his ranch. Questioned by his friends as to his plans, he finally admitted that he felt it a duty to hunt down the men who had ambushed him; remarked that he feared they might bushwhack someone else if they were not removed.

Number One of the three men he located in Cheyenne, Wyoming. Cheyenne was then a law-abiding community, and Allison could not afford to take any chances of court complications that would interfere with the completion of his work. He therefore spent several days in covertly watching the habits of his adversary. From the knowledge thus gained he was able one morning suddenly to turn a street corner and confront Number One. Without the least suspicion that Allison was in the country, the man, knowing that his life hung by a thread, jerked his pistol and fired on the instant. As Allison had shrewdly calculated, his enemy was so nervous that his shot flew wild. Number One did not get a second shot. At the inquest several witnesses of the affray swore that Allison did not even draw until after the other had fired.

Several weeks later Number Two was found in Tombstone, Arizona, a town of the good old frontier sort that had little use for coroners and juries, so the fighting was half fair. Half an hour after landing from the stagecoach, Allison encountered his man in a gambling-house. Number Two remained in Tombstone—permanently—while Mr. Allison resumed his travels by the evening coach.

The hunt for Number Three lasted several months. Allison followed him relentlessly from place to place through half a dozen States and Territories, until he was located on a ranch near Spearfish, Dakota.

They met at last, one afternoon, within the shadow of the Devil's Tower. In the duel that ensued, Allison's horse was killed under him. This occasioned him no particular inconvenience, however, for he found that Number Three's horse, after having a few hours' rest, was able to carry him into Deadwood, where he caught the Sidney stage.

With this task finished, Mr. Allison was able to return to commercial pursuits. He settled at Pope's Crossing on the Pecos River, in New Mexico, bought cattle, and stocked the adjacent range. Pecos City, the nearest town, lay fifty miles to the south.

Started as a "front camp" during the construction of the Texas Pacific Railway in 1880, for five or six years Pecos contrived to rock along without any of the elaborate municipal machinery deemed essential to the government and safety of urban communities in the effete East. It had neither council, mayor, nor peace officer. An early experiment in government was discouraging.

In 1883 the Texas Pacific station-agent was elected mayor. His name was Ewing, a little man with fierce whiskers and mild blue eyes. Two nights after the election a gang of boys from the "Hash Knife" outfit were in town; fearing circumscription of some of their privileges, the election did not have their approval. Gleaming out of the darkness fifty yards away from the Lone Wolf Saloon, the light of Mayor Ewing's office window offered a most tempting target. What followed was very natural—in Pecos.

The mayor was sitting at his table receiving train orders, when suddenly a bullet smashed the telegraph key beside his hand and other balls whistled through the room bearing him a message he had no trouble in reading. Rushing out into the darkness, he spent the night in the brush, and toward morning boarded an east-bound freight train. Mayor Ewing had abdicated. The railway company soon obtained another station-agent, but it was some years before the town got another mayor.

On Pecos carnival nights like this, when some of the cowboys were in town, prudent people used to sleep on the floor of Van Slyke's store with bags of grain piled round their blankets two tiers deep, for no Pecos house walls were more than inch boards.

At this early period of its history the few wandering advance agents of the Gospel who occasionally visited Pecos were not well received. They were not abused; they were simply ignored. When not otherwise occupied, the average Pecosite had too much whittling on hand to find time to "'tend meetin:'" of this every pine drygoods box in the town bore mute evidence, its fair sides covered with innumerable rude carvings cut by aimless hands.

This prevailing indifference to religion shocked Mr. Allison. As opportunity offered he tried to remedy it, and as far as his evangelical work went it was successful. One Tuesday morning about ten o'clock he walked into the Lone Wolf Saloon, laid two pistols on the end of the bar next the front door, and remarked to Red Dick, the bartender, that he intended to turn the saloon into a church for a couple of hours and did not want any drinks sold or cards thrown during the services.

Taking his stand just within the doorway, pistol in hand, Mr. Allison began to assemble his congregation. The first comer was Billy Jansen, the leading merchant of the town. As he was passing the door Clay remarked:

"Good-mornin', Mr. Jansen, won't you please step inside? Religious services will be held here shortly an' I reckon you'll be useful in the choir."

The only reply to Billy's protest of urgent business was a gesture that made Billy think going to church would be the greatest pleasure he could have that morning.

Mr. Allison never played favourites at any game, and so all passers were stopped: merchants, railway men, gamblers, thugs, cowboys, freighters—all were stopped and made to enter the saloon. The least furtive movement to draw a gun or to approach the back door received prompt attention from the *impromptu* evangelist that quickly restored order in the congregation. When fifty or sixty men had been brought into this improvised fold, Mr. Allison closed the door and faced about.

"Fellers," he said, "this meetin' bein' held on the Pecos, I reckon we'll open her by singin' 'Shall We Gather at the River?' Of course we're already gathered, but the song sort o' fits. No gammon now, fellers; everybody sings that knows her."

The result was discouraging. Few in the audience knew any hymn, much less this one. Only three or four managed to hoarsely drawl through two verses.

The hymn finished—as far as anybody could sing it—Mr. Allison said:

"Now, fellers, we'll pray. Everybody down!"

Only a few knelt. Among the congregation were some who regarded the affair as sacrilegious, and others of the independent frontier type were unaccustomed to dictation. However, a slight narrowing of the cold black eyes and a significant sweep of the six-shooter brought every man of them to his knees, with heads bowed over faro lay-outs and on monte tables.

"O Lord!" began Allison, "this yere's a mighty bad neck o' woods, an' I reckon You know it. Fellers don' think enough o' their souls to build a church, an' when a pa'son comes here they don' treat him half white. O Lord! make these fellers see that when they gits caught in the final round-up an' drove over the last divide, they don' stan' no sort o' show to git to stay on the heavenly ranch 'nless they believes an' builds a house to pray an' preach in. Right here I subscribes a hundred dollars to build a church, an' if airy one o' these yere fellers don' tote up accordin' to his means, O Lord, make it Your pers'n'l business to see that he wears the Devil's brand and ear mark an' never gits another drop o' good spring water.

"Of course, I allow You knows I don' sport no wings myself, but I want to do what's right ef You'll sort o' give a shove the proper way. An' one thing I want You to understan'; Clay Allison's got a fast horse an' is tol'able handy with his rope, and he's goin' to run these fellers into Your corral even if he has to rope an' drag 'em there. Amen. Everybody git up!"

While he prayed in the most reverent tone he could command, and while his attitude was one of simple supplication, Mr. Allison never removed his keen eyes from the congregation.

"Reckon we'll sing again, boys, an' I want a little more of it. Le's see what you-all knows."

At length six or eight rather sheepishly owned knowing "Old Hundred," and it was sung.

Then the sermon was in order.

"Fellers," he began, "my ole mammy used to tell me that the only show to shake the devil off your trail was to believe everythin' the Bible says. What yer mammy tells you 's bound to be right, dead right, so I think I'll take the sentiment o' this yere round-up on believin'. O' course, as a square man I'm boun' to admit the Bible tells some pow'ful queer tales, onlike anythin' we-'uns strikes now days. Take

45

that tale about a fish swallerin' a feller named Jonah; why, a fish 't could swaller a man 'od have to be as big in the barrel as the Pecos River is wide an' have an openin' in his face bigger'n Phantom Lake Cave. Nobody on the Pecos ever see such a fish. But I wish you fellers to distinctly understan' it's a *fact*. I believes it. Does you? Every feller that believes a fish swallered Jonah, hold up his right hand!"

It is sad to have to admit that only two or three hands were raised.

"Well, I'll be durned," the evangelist continued, "you *air* tough cases. That's what's the matter with you; you are shy on faith. You fellers has got to be saved, an' to be saved you got to believe, an' believe hard, an' I'm agoin' to make you. Now hear *me*, an' mind you don' forget it's Clay Allison talkin' to you: I tells you that when that thar fish had done swallerin' Jonah, he swum aroun' fer a hull hour lookin' to see if thar was a show to pick up any o' Jonah's family or friends. Now what I tells you I reckon you're all bound to believe. Every feller that believes that Jonah was jes' only a sort of a snack fer the fish, hold up his right hand; an' if any feller don' believe it, this yere ol' gun o' mine will finish the argiment."

Further exhortation was unnecessary; all hands went up.

And so the sermon ran on for an hour, a crude homily full of rude metaphor, with little of sentiment or pleading, severely didactic, mandatory as if spoken in a dungeon of the Inquisition. When Red Dick passed the hat among the congregation for a subscription to build a church, the contribution was general and generous. Many who early in the meeting were full of rage over the restraint, and vowing to themselves to kill Allison the first good chance they got, finished by thinking he meant all right and had taken about the only practicable means "to git the boys to 'tend meetin'."

In the town of Toyah, twenty miles west of Pecos, a gentleman named Jep Clayton set the local spring styles in six-shooters and bowie knives, and settled the hash of anybody who ventured to question them. A reckless bully, he ruled the town as if he owned it.

One day John McCullough, Allison's brother-in-law and ranch foreman, had business in Toyah. Clayton had heard of Allison but knew little about him. Drunk and quarrelsome, he hunted up McCullough, called him every abusive name he could think of before a crowd, and then suggested that if he did not like it he might send over his brother-in-law Allison, who was said to be a gun fighter. A mild and peaceable man himself, McCullough avoided a difficulty and returned to Pecos.

Two days later a lone horseman rode into Toyah, stopped at Young-bloods' store, tied his horse, and went in. Approaching the group of loafers curled up on boxes at the rear of the store, he inquired:

"Can any of you gentlemen tell me if a gentleman named Clayton, Jep Clayton, is in town, an' where I can find him?"

They replied that he had been in the store an hour before and was probably nearby.

As the lone horseman walked out of the door, one the loungers remarked:

"I believe that's Clay Allison, an' ef it is it's all up with Jep."

He slipped out and gave Jep warning, told him Allison was in town, that he had known him years before, and that Jep had better quit town or say his prayers. Concluding, he said, "You done barked up the wrong tree this time, sure."

Allison went on from one saloon to another, at each making the same polite inquiry for Mr. Clayton's whereabouts. At last, out on the street Allison met a party of eight men, a crowd Clayton had gathered, and repeated his inquiry. A man stepped out of the group and said: "My name's Clayton, an' I reckon yours is Allison. Look here, Mr. Allison, this is all a mistake. I——"

"Why, what's a mistake? Didn't you meet Mr. McCullough the other day?"

"Yes."

"Didn't you abuse him shamefully?"

"Well, yes, but——"

"Didn't you send me an invite to come over here?"

"Well, yes, I did, but it was a mistake, Mr. Allison; I was drunk. It was whiskey talkin'; nothin' more. I'm terrible sorry. It was jes' whiskey talk."

"Whiskey talk, was it? Well, Mr. Clayton, le's step in the saloon here and get some whiskey an' see if it won't set you goin' again. I believe I'd enjoy hearin' jes' a few words o' your whiskey talk."

They entered a saloon. For an hour Clayton was plied with whiskey, taunted and jeered until those who had admired him slunk away in disgust, and those who had feared him laughed in enjoyment of his humiliation. But no amount of whiskey could rouse him that day.

Allison's scarred, impassive face, low, quiet tones, and glittering black eyes held him cowed. The terror of Toyah had found his master, and knew it.

47

At last, in utter disgust, Allison concluded:

"Mr. Clayton, your invitation brought me twenty miles to meet a gun fighter. I find you such a cur that if ever we meet again I'll lash you into strips with a bull whip."

A month later Mr. Clayton was killed by his own brother-in-law, Grant Tinnin, one of the quiet good men of the country, who never failed to score in any real emergency.

"I wonder how it will all end!" Allison used often to remark while lying idly staring into the camp-fire. "Of course I know I can't keep up this sort o' thing; some one's sure to get me. An' I'd jes' give anything in the world to know *how* I'm goin to die—by pistol or knife."

It turned out that Fate had decreed other means for his removal.

One day Allison and his brother-in-law John McCullough had a serious quarrel. Allison left the ranch and rode into town to think it over. In his later years killing had become such a mania with him that his best friend could never feel entirely safe against his deadly temper; the least difference might provoke a collision. McCullough was therefore not greatly surprised to get a letter from Allison a few days later, sent out by special messenger, telling him that Allison would reach the ranch late in the afternoon of the next day and would kill him on sight.

Early in the morning of the appointed day Allison left town in a covered hack. He had been drinking heavily and had whiskey with him. About half-way between town and the ranch he overtook George Larramore, a freighter, seated out in the sun on top of his heavy load.

"Hello, George!" called Allison; "mighty hot up there, ain't it?"

"Howd'y, Mr. Allison. I don' mind the heat; I'm used to it," answered Larramore.

"George," called Allison, after driving on a short distance, "'pears to me the good things o' this world ain't equally divided. I don't see why you should sit up there roasting in the sun an' me down here in the shade o' the hack. We'll jes' even things a little right here. You crawl down off that load an' jump into the hack an' I'll get up there an' drive your team."

"Pow'ful good o' you, Mr. Allison, but——"

"Crawl down, I say, George, it's Clay tellin' you!"

And the change was made without further delay.

Five miles farther up the road John McCullough and two friends lay in ambush all that day and far into the night, with ready Winchesters, awaiting Allison. But he never came.

Shortly after taking his seat on top of the high load in the broiling sun, plodding slowly along in the dust and heat, Allison was nodding drowsily, when suddenly a protruding mesquite root gave the wagon a sharp jolt that plunged Clay headlong into the road, where, before he could rise, the great wheels crunched across his neck.

Triggerfingeritis

On the Plains thirty years ago there were two types of man-killers; and these two types were subdivided into classes.

The first type numbered all who took life in contravention of law. This type was divided into three classes: A, Outlaws to whom blood-letting had become a mania; B, Outlaws who killed in defence of their spoils or liberty; C, Otherwise good men who had slain in the heat of private quarrel, and either "gone on the scout" or "jumped the country" rather than submit to arrest.

The second type included all who slew in support of law and order. This type included six classes: A, United States marshals; B, Sheriffs and their deputies; C, Stage or railway express guards, called "messengers;" D, Private citizens organized as Vigilance Committees—these often none too discriminating, and not infrequently the blind or willing instruments of individual grudge or greed; E, Unorganized bands of ranchmen who took the trail of marauders on life or property and never quit it; F, "Inspectors" (detectives) for Stock Growers' Associations.

Throughout the seventies and well into the eighties, in Wyoming, Dakota, western Kansas and Nebraska, New Mexico, and west Texas, courts were idle most of the time, and lawyers lived from hand to mouth. The then state of local society was so rudimentary that it had not acquired the habit of appeal to the law for settlement of its differences. And while it may sound an anachronism, it is nevertheless the simple truth that while life was far less secure through that period, average personal honesty then ranked higher and depredations against property were fewer than at any time since.

---

1. Triggerfingeritis is an acute irritation of the sensory nerves of the index finger of habitual gun-packers; usually fatal—to someone.

As soon as society had advanced to a point where the victim could be relied on to carry his wrongs to court, judges began working overtime and lawyers fattening. But of the actual pioneers who took their lives in their hands and recklessly staked them in their everyday goings and comings (as, for instance, did all who ventured into the Sioux country north of the Platte between 1875 and 1880) few long stayed—no matter what their occupation—who were slow on the trigger: it was back to Mother Earth or home for them.

Of the supporters of the law in that period Boone May was one of the finest examples any frontier community ever boasted. Early in 1876 he came to Cheyenne with an elder brother and engaged in freighting thence overland to the Black Hills. Quite half the length of the stage road was then infested by hostile Sioux. This meant heavy risks and high pay. The brothers prospered so handsomely that, toward the end of the year, Boone withdrew from freighting, bought a few cattle and horses, and built and occupied a ranch at the stage-road crossing of Lance Creek, midway between the Platte and Deadwood, in the very heart of the Sioux country. Boone was then well under thirty, graceful of figure, dark-haired, wore a slender downy moustache that served only to emphasize his youth, but possessed that reserve and repose of manner most typical of the utterly fearless.

The Sioux made his acquaintance early, to their grief. One night they descended on his ranch and carried off all the stage horses and most of Boone's. Although the "sign" showed there were fifteen or twenty in the party, at daylight Boone took their trail, alone. The third day thereafter he returned to the ranch with all the stolen stock, besides a dozen split-eared Indian ponies, as compensation for his trouble, taken at what cost of strategy or blood Boone never told.

Learning of this exploit from his drivers, Al. Patrick, the superintendent of the stage line, took the next coach to Lance Creek and brought Boone back to Deadwood, enlisted in his corps of "messengers"; he was too good timber to miss.

At that time every coach south-bound from Deadwood to Cheyenne carried thousands in its mail-pouches and express-boxes; and once a week a treasure coach armoured with boiler plate, carrying no passengers, and guarded by six or eight "messengers" or "sawed-off shotgun men," conveyed often as high as two hundred thousand dollars of hard-won Black Hills gold bars.

Thus it naturally followed that, throughout 1877 and 1878, it was the exception for a coach to get through from the Chugwater to

Jenny's stockade without being held up by bandits at least once.

Any that happened to escape Jack Wadkins in the south were likely to fall prey to Dune Blackburn in the north—the two most desperate bandit-leaders in the country.

In February, 1878, I had occasion to follow some cattle thieves from Fort Laramie to Deadwood. Returning south by coach one bitter evening we pulled into Lance Creek, eight passengers inside, Boone May and myself on the box with 'Gene Barnett the driver; Stocking, another famous messenger, roosted behind us atop of the coach, fondling his sawed-off shotgun.

From Lance Creek southward lay the greatest danger zone. At that point, therefore, Boone and Stocking shifted from the coach to the saddle, and, as 'Gene popped his whip and the coach crunched away through the snow, both dropped back perhaps thirty yards behind us.

An hour later, just as the coach got well within a broad belt of plum bushes that lined the north bank of Old Woman's Fork, out into the middle of the road sprang a lithe figure that threw a snap shot over 'Gene's head and halted us.

Instantly six others surrounded the coach and ordered us down. I already had a foot on the nigh front wheel to descend, when a shot out of the brush to the west, (Boone's, I later learned) dropped the man ahead of the team.

Then followed a quick interchange of shots for perhaps a minute, certainly no more, and then I heard Boone's cool voice:

"Drive on, 'Gene!"

"Move an' I'll kill you!" came in a hoarse bandit's voice from the thicket east of us.

"Drive on, 'Gene, or *I'll kill* you," came then from Boone, in a tone of such chilling menace that 'Gene threw the bud into the leaders, and away we flew at a pace materially improved by three or four shots the bandits sent singing past our ears and over the team! The next down coach brought to Cheyenne the comforting news that Boone and Stocking had killed four of the bandits and stampeded the other three.

Within six months after Boone was employed, both Dune Blackburn and Jack Wadkins disappeared from the stage road, dropped out of sight as if the earth had opened and swallowed them, as it probably had. Boone had a way of absenting himself for days from his routine duties along the stage road. He slipped off entirely alone after this new quarry precisely as he had followed the Sioux horse-raiders and, while

"Into the middle of the road sprang a lithe figure"

he never admitted it, the belief was general that he had run down and "planted" both. Indeed it is almost a certainty this is true, for beasts of their type never change their stripes, and sure it is that neither were ever seen or heard of after their disappearance from the Deadwood trail.

Late in the Autumn of the same year, 1878, and also at or near the stage-crossing of Old Woman's Fork, Boone and one companion fought eight bandits led by a man named Tolle, on whose head was a large reward. This was earned by Boone at a hold-up of a U. P. express train near Green River.

This band was, in a way, more lucky, for five of the eight escaped; but of the three otherwise engaged one furnished a head which Boone toted in a gunny sack to Cheyenne and exchanged for five thousand dollars, if my memory rightly serves.

This incident was practically the last of the serious hold-ups on the Cheyenne road. A few pikers followed and "stood up" a coach occasionally, but the strong organized bands were extinct.

Throughout 1879 Boone's activities were transferred to the Sidney-Deadwood road, where for several months before Boone's coming, Curly and Lame Johnny had held sway. Lame Johnny was shortly thereafter captured, and hanged on the lone tree that gave the Big Cottonwood Creek its name. A few months later, Curly was captured by Boone and another, but was never jailed or tried: when nearing Deadwood, he tried to escape from Boone, and failed.

With the Sioux pushed back within the lines of their new reservation in southern Dakota and semi-pacified, and with the Sidney road swept clean of road-agents, life in Boone's old haunts became for him too tame. Thus it happened that, while trapping was then no better within than without the Sioux reservation, the Winter of 1879-80 found Boone and four mates camped on the Cheyenne River below the mouth of Elk Creek, well within the reserve, trapping the main stream and its tributaries. For a month they were undisturbed, and a goodly store of fur was fast accumulating. Then one fine morning, while breakfast was cooking, out from the cover of an adjacent hill and down upon them charged a Sioux war party, one hundred and fifty strong.

Boone's four mates barely had time to take cover below the hard-by river bank—under Boone's orders—before fire opened. Down straight upon them the Sioux charged in solid mass, heels kicking and quirts pounding their split-eared ponies, until, having come within a hundred yards, the mass broke into single file and raced past the camp, each warrior lying along the off side of his pony and firing beneath its neck—the usual but utterly stupid and suicidal Sioux tactics, for accurate fire under such conditions is of course impossible.

Meantime Boone stood quietly by the camp-fire, entirely in the open, coolly potting the enemy as regularly and surely as a master wing-shot thinning a flight of ducks. Three times they so charged and Boone so received them, pouring into them a steady, deadly fire out of his Winchester and two pistols. And when, after the third charge, the war party drew off for good, forty-odd ponies and twenty-odd warriors lay upon the plain, stark evidence of Boone's wonderful nerve and marksmanship. Shortly after the fight one of his mates told me that while he and three others were doing their best, there was no doubt that nearly all the dead fell before Boone's fire.

A type diametrically opposite to that of the debonair Boone May was Captain Jim Smith, one of the best peace-officers the frontier ever knew. Of Captain Smith's early history nothing was known, except that he had served with great credit as a captain of artillery in the Union Army. He first appeared on the U. P. during construction days in the late sixties. Serving in various capacities as railroad detective, marshal, stock inspector, and the like, for eighteen years Captain Smith wrote more red history with his pistol (barring May's work on the Sioux) than any two men of his time.

The last I knew of him he had enough dead outlaws to his credit—thirty-odd—to start, if not a respectable, at least, a fair-sized graveyard. Captain Jim's mere look was almost enough to still the heart-beat and paralyze the pistol hand of any but the wildest of them all. His great burning black eyes, glowering deadly menace from cavernous sockets of extraordinary depth, were set in a colossal grim face; his straight, thin-lipped mouth never showed teeth; his heavy, tight-curling black moustache and stiff black imperial always had the appearance of holding the under lip closely glued to the upper. In years of intimacy, I never once saw on his lips the faintest hint of a smile. He had tremendous breadth of shoulders and depth of chest; he was big-boned, lean-loined, quick and furtive of movement as a panther. In short, Captain Jim was altogether the most fearsome-looking man I ever saw, the very incarnation of a relentless, inexorable, indomitable, avenging Nemesis.

Like most men lacking humour, Captain Jim was devoid of vices; like all men lacking sentiment, he cultivated no intimacies. Throughout those years loved nothing, animate or inanimate, but his guns—the full length "45" that nestled in its breast scabbard next his heart, and the short "45," sawed off two inches in front of the cylinder, that he always carried in a deep side-pocket of his long sack coat. This was often a much patched pocket, for Jim was a notable economist of time, and usually fired from within the pocket. That he loved those guns I know, for often have I seen him fondle them as tenderly as a mother her first-born.

In 1879 Sidney, Neb., was a hell-hole, filled with the most desperate toughs come to prey upon overland travellers to and from the Black Hills. Of these toughs McCarthy, proprietor of the biggest saloon and gambling-house in town, was the leading spirit and boss. Nightly, men who would not gamble were drugged or slugged or leaded. Town marshals came and went—either feet first or on a keen run.

So long as its property remained unmolested the U. P. management did not mind. But one night the depot was robbed of sixty thousand dollars in gold bullion. Of course, this was the work of the local gang. Then the U. P. got busy. Pete Shelby summoned Captain Jim to Omaha and committed the Sidney situation to his charge. Frequenting haunts where he knew the news would be wired to Sidney, Jim casually mentioned that he was going out there to clean out the town, and purposed killing McCarthy on sight. This he rightly judged would stampede, or throw a chill into, many of the pikers—and simplify his task.

Arrived in Sidney, Jim found McCarthy absent, at North Platte, due to return the next day. Coming to the station the next morning, Jim found the express reported three hours late, and returned to his room in the railway House, fifty yards north of the depot. He doffed his coat, shoulder scabbard, and boots, and lay down, shortly falling into a doze that nearly cost him his life. Most inconsiderately the train made up nearly an hour of its lost time. Jim's awakening was sudden, but not soon enough. Before he had time to rise at the sound of the softly opening door, McCarthy was over him with a pistol at his head.

Jim's left hand nearly touched the gun pocket of his coat, and his right lay in reach of the other gun; but his slightest movement meant instant death.

"Heerd you come to hang my hide up an' skin the town, but you're under a copper and my open play wins, Black Jim! See?" growled McCarthy.

"Well, Mac," coolly answered Jim, "you're a bigger damn fool than I allowed. Never heard of you before makin' a killin' there was nothin' in. What's the matter with you and your gang? I'm after that bullion, and I've got a straight tip: Lame Johnny's the bird that hooked onto it. If you're standing in with him, you better lead me aplenty, for if you don't I'll sure get him."

"Honest? Is that right, Jim? Ain't lyin' none?" queried McCarthy, relieved of the belief that his gang were suspected.

"Sure, she's right, Mac."

"But I heerd you done said you was comin' to do me," persisted McCarthy.

"Think I'm fool enough to light in diggin' my own grave, by sendin' love messages like that to a gun expert like you, Mac?" asked Captain Jim.

Whether it was the subtle flattery or Jim's argument, Mac lowered his gun, and while backing out of the room, remarked: "Nothin' in mixin' it with you, Jim, if you don't want me."

But Mac was no more than out of the room when Jim slid off the bed quick as a cat; softly as a cat, on his noiseless stockinged feet he followed Mac down the hall; crafty as a cat, he crept down the creaking stairs, tread for tread, a scant arm's length behind his prey—why, God alone knows, unless for a savage joy in longer holding another thug's life in his hands. So he hung, like a leech to the blood it loves, across the corridor and to the middle of the trunk room that lay between the hall and the hotel office. There Jim spoke:

"Oh! Mr. McCarthy!"

Mac whirled, drawing his gun, just in time to receive a bullet squarely through the heart.

During the day Jim got two more scalps. The rest of the McCarthy gang got the impression that it was up to them to pull their freight out of Sidney, and acted on it.

★★★★★★

In 1882 the smoke of the Lincoln County War still hung in the timber of the Ruidoso and the Bonito, a feud in which nearly three hundred New Mexicans lost their lives. Depredations on the Mescalero Reservation were so frequent that the Indians were near open revolt.

Needing a red-blooded agent, the Indian Bureau sought and got one in Major W. H. H. Llewellyn, since Captain of Rough Riders, Troup H, then a United States marshal with a distinguished record.

The then Chief of the Bureau offered the Major two troops of cavalry to preserve order among the Mescaleros and keep marauders off the reservation, and was astounded when Llewellyn declined and said he would prefer to handle the situation with no other aid than that of one man he had in mind.

Captain Jim Smith was the man. And pleased enough was he when told of the turbulence of the country and the certainty of plenty doing in his line.

But by the time they reached the Mescalero Agency, the feud was ended; the peace of exhaustion after years of open war and ambush had descended upon Lincoln County, and the Mescaleros were glad enough quietly to draw their rations of flour and coffee, and range the Sacramentos and Guadalupes for game. For Jim and the band of Indian police which he quickly organized there was nothing doing.

Inaction soon cloyed Captain Jim. It got on his nerves. Presently he conceived a resentment toward the agent for bringing him down there under false pretences of daring deeds to be done, that never materialized. One day Major Llewellyn imprudently countermanded an order Jim had given his chief of police, under conditions which the Captain took as a personal affront. The next thing the Major knew, he was covered by Jim's gun listening to his death sentence.

"Major," began Captain Jim, "right here is where you cash in. Played me for a big fool long enough. Toted me off down here on the guarantee of the best show of fightin' I've heard of since the war— here where there ain't a man in the Territory with nerve enough left to tackle a prairie dog, 's far 's I can see. Lied to me a plenty, didn't you? Anything to say before you quit?"

Since that time Major Llewellyn has become (and is now) a famous pleader at the New Mexican bar, but I know he will agree that the most eloquent plea he has this day made was that in answer to Captain Jim's arraignment. Luckily it won.

A month later Jim called on me at El Paso. At the time I was President of the West Texas Cattle Growers' Association, organized chiefly to deal with marauding rustlers.

"Howd'y, Ed," Jim began, "I've jumped the Mescalero Reservation, headed north. Nothin' doin' down here now. But, say, Ed, I hear they're crowdin' the rustlers a plenty up in the Indian Territory and the Pan Handle, and she's a cinch they'll be down on you thick in a few months. And, say, Ed, don't forget old Jim; when the rustlers come, send for him. You know he's the cheapest proposition ever—never any lawyers' fees or court costs, nothin' to pay but just Jim's wages."

That was the last time we ever met, and lucky it will probably be for me if we never meet again; for if Jim still lives and there is aught in this story he sees occasion to take exception to, I am sure to be due for a mix-up I can very well get on without.

******

From 1878 to 1880 Billy Lykins was one of the most efficient inspectors of the Wyoming Stock Growers' Association, a short man of heavy muscular physique and a round, cherubic, pink and white face, in which a pair of steel-blue glittering eyes looked strangely out of place. A second glance, however, showed behind the smiling mouth a set of the jaw that did not belie the fighting eyes. So far as I can now recall, Billy never failed to get what he went after while he remained in our employ.

Probably the toughest customer Billy ever tackled was Doc Middleton. As an outlaw, Doc was the victim of an error of judgment. When he first came among us, hailing from Llano County, Texas, Doc was as fine a puncher and jolly, good-tempered range-mate as any in the Territory. Sober and industrious, he never drank or gambled. But he had his bit of temper, had Doc, and his chunk of good old Llano nerve. Thus, when a group of carousing soldiers, in a Sidney saloon, one night lit in to beat Doc up with their six-shooters for refusing to drink with them, the inevitable happened in a very few seconds; Doc killed three of them, jumped his horse, and split the wind for the Platte.

And therein lay his error.

The killing was perfectly justifiable; surrendered and tried, he would surely have been acquitted. But his breed never surrender, at least, never before their last shell is emptied. Flight having made him an outlaw, the government offered a heavy reward for him, dead or alive. For a time he was harboured among his friends on the different ranches; indeed was a welcome guest of my Deadman Ranch for several days; but in a few weeks the hue and cry got so hot that he had to jump for the Sand Hills south of the Niobrara.

Ever pursued, he found that honest wage-earning was impossible. Presently he was confronted with want, not of much, indeed of very little, but that want was vital—he wanted cartridges. At this time the Sand Hills were full of deer and antelope; and therefore to him cartridges meant more even than defence of his freedom, they meant food. It was this want that drove him into his first actual crime, the

59

stealing of Sioux ponies, which he ran into the settlements and sold.

The downward path of the criminal is like that of the limpid, clean-faced brook, bred of a bubbling spring nestled in some shady nook of the hills, where the air is sweet and pure, and pollution cometh not. But there it may not stay; on and yet on it rushes, as helpless as heedless, till one day it finds itself plunged into some foul current carrying the off-scourings of half a continent. So on and down plunged Doc; from stealing Indian ponies to lifting ranch horses was no long leap in his new code.

Then our stock association got busy and Billy Lykins took his trail. Oddly, in a few months the same type of accident in turn saved the life of each. Their first encounter was single-handed. With the better horse, Lykins was pressing Doc so close that Doc raced to the crest of a low conical hill, jumped off his mount, dropped flat on the ground and covered Lykins with a Springfield rifle, meantime yelling to him:

"Duck, you little Dutch fool; I don't want to kill you;" for they knew each other well, and in a way were friends.

But Billy never knew when to stop. Deeper into his pony's flank sank the rowels, and up the hill on Doc he charged, pistol in hand. At thirty yards Doc pulled the trigger, when—wonder of wonders—the faithful old Springfield missed fire. Before Doc could throw in another shell or draw his pistol, Billy was over him and had him covered.

If my memory rightly serves, the Sidney jail held Doc almost a fortnight. A few weeks later Doc had assembled a strong gang about him, rendezvoused on the Piney, a tributary of the lower Niobrara. There he was far east of Lykins's bailiwick, but a good many degrees within Lykins's disposition to quit his trail. Accompanied by Major W. H. H. Llewellyn and an Omaha detective (inappropriately named Hassard), Lykins located Doc's camp, and the three lay near for several days studying their quarry.

One morning Llewellyn and Hassard started up the creek, mounted, on a scout, leaving Lykins and his horse hidden in the brush near the trail. At a sharp bend of the path the two ran plunk into Doc and five of his men. Both being unknown to Doc's gang, and the position and odds forbidding hostilities, they represented themselves as campers hunting lost stock, and turned and rode back down the trail with the outlaws, alert for any play their leader might make.

Recognizing his man, Billy lay with his "45" and "70" Sharps comfortably resting across a log; and when the band were come within twenty yards of him, he drew a careful bead on Doc's head and pulled

"At a sharp bend of the trail they ran into Doc and five of his men"

the trigger. By strange coincidence his Sharps missed fire, precisely as had Doc's Springfield a few weeks before.

Hearing the snap of the rifle hammer, with a curse Doc jerked his gun and whirled his horse toward the brush just as Billy sprang out into the open and threw a pistol shot into Doc that broke his thigh. Swaying in saddle, Doc cursed Hassard for leading him into a trap, and shot him twice before himself pitching to the ground. Hassard stood idly, stunned apparently by a sort of white-hot work he was not used to, and received his death wound without any effort even to draw. Meantime, the firm of Lykins and Llewellyn accounted for two more before Doc's mates got out of range. Thus, like the brook, Doc had drifted down the turbid current of crime till he found himself impounded in the Lincoln penitentiary with the off-scourings of the state.

While it is true that back into such impounding most who once have been there soon return, Doc turned out to be one of the rare exceptions proving the rule; for the last I heard of him, he was the lame but light-hearted and wholly honest proprietor of a respectable Rushville saloon.

★★★★★★

When in the early eighties the front camps of the Atchison, Topeka, and Santa Fe and the Texas Pacific met at El Paso, then a village called Franklin, within a few weeks the population jumped from a few hundred to nearly three thousand. Speculators, prospectors for business opportunities, mechanics, miners, and tourists poured in—a chance-taking, high-living, free-spending lot that offered such rich pickings for the predatory that it was not long before nearly every fat pigeon had a hungry, merciless vulture hovering near, watching for a chance to fasten its claws and gorge itself.

The low one-storey *adobes*, fronted by broad, arched *portals*, that then lined the west side of El Paso Street for several blocks, was a long solid row of variety theatres, dance halls, saloons, and gambling-houses, never closed by day or by night. They were packed with a roistering mob that drifted from one joint to another, dancing, gambling, carousing, fighting. Naturally, at first the predatory confined their attentions to the roisterers.

Of course every lay-out was a brace game, from which no player arose with any notable winning except occasionally when the "house" felt it a good bit of advertising to graduate a handsome winner—and then it was usually a "capper," whose gains were in a few minutes passed back into the till.

The *faro* boxes were full of springs as a watch; faro decks were carefully cut "strippers." An average good dealer would shuffle and arrange as he liked the favourite cards of known high-rollers. These had been neatly split on either edge and a minute bit of bristle pasted in, which no ordinary touch would feel, but which the sand-papered finger tips of an expert dealer would catch and slip through on the shuffle and place where they would do (the house) the most good. The "tin horns" gave out few but false notes; the roulette balls were kicked silly out of the boxes representing heavily played numbers. Not content with the "Kitty's" rake-off, every stud poker table had one or more "cappers" sitting in, to whom the dealers could occasionally throw a stiff pot. The backs of poker decks were so cunningly marked that while the wise ones could read their size and suit across the table, no untaught eye could detect their guile. And wherever a notable roll was once flashed, greedy eyes never left it until it was safe in the till of some game, or its owner "rolled" and relieved of it by force.

For months orgy ran riot and the predatory band grew bolder and cruder in their methods. Killings were frequent. Few nights passed without more or less street hold-ups—usually more. Respectable citizens took the middle of the street, literally gun in hand, when forced to be out of nights. The mayor and City Council were powerless. City marshals and deputies they hired in bunches, but all to no purpose. Each fresh lot of appointees were short-lived, literally or officially— mostly literally. Finally, a vigilance committee was formed, made up of good citizens not a few of whom were gun experts with their own bit of red record. But nothing came of it. The predatories openly flouted and defied them.

On one notable night when the committee were assembled in front of the old Grand Central Hotel, a mob of two hundred toughs lined up before the thirty-odd of the committee and dared them to open the ball; and it was a miracle the little *plaza* was not then and there turned into a slaughter pen bloody as the Alamo. It really looked as if nothing short of martial law and a strong body of troops could pacify the town.

But one night, into the chamber of the City Council stalked a man, the man of the hour, unheralded and unknown. He gave the name of Bill Stoudenmayer. About all that was ever learned of him was that he hailed from Fort Davis. His type was that of a course, brutal, Germanic gladiator, devoid of strategy; a bluff, stubborn, give-and-take fighter, who drove bull-headed at whatever opposed him. But El Paso soon learned that he could handle his guns with as deadly dexterity as did his forebears their nets and tridents.

Asked his business with the council, he said he had heard they had failed to find a marshal who could hold the town down, and allowed he'd like to try the job if the council would make it worth his while. Questioned as to his views, he explained that he was there to make some good money for himself and save the city more; if they would pay him five hundred dollars a month for two months, they could discharge all their deputies and he would go it alone and agree to clear the town of toughs or draw no pay. The Mayor and Council were paralyzed in a double sense: by the wild audacity of this proposal, and by their memory of recent threats of the thug-leaders that they would massacre the council to a man if any further attempts were made to circumscribe their activities. Some were openly for declining the offer, but in the end a majority gained heart of Stoudenmayer's own hardihood sufficiently to hire him.

The rest of the night Stoudenmayer employed in quietly familiarizing himself with the personnel of the enemy. He lost no time. At daylight the next morning, several notices, manually written in a rude hand and each bearing the signature of the rude hand that wrote it, were found conspicuously posted between Oregon Street and the *plaza*. The signature was, "Bill Stoudenmayer, City Marshal."

The notice was brief but pointed:

"Any of the hold-ups named below I find in town after three o'clock today, I'm going to kill on sight."

Then followed seventy names. The list was carefully chosen: all "pikers" and "four-flushers" were omitted; none but the *élite* of the gun-twirling, black-jack swinging toughs was included. Hardly a single man was named in the list lacking a more or less gory record.

By the toughs Stoudenmayer was taken as a jest, by respectable citizens as a lunatic. Heavy odds were offered that he would not last till noon, with few takers. And yet throughout the morning Stoudenmayer quietly walked the streets, unaccompanied save by his two guns and his conspicuously displayed marshal's star.

Nothing happened until about two o'clock, when two men sprang out from ambush behind the big cottonwood tree that then stood on the northeast corner of El Paso and San Antonio Streets, one armed with a shotgun and the other with a pistol, and started to "throw down" on Stoudenmayer, who was approaching from the other side of the street. But before either got his artillery into action, the marshal jerked his two pistols and killed both, then quietly continued his stroll, over their prostrate bodies, and past them, up the street. It was such an obviously workmanlike job that it threw a chill into the hardiest of the sixty-eight survivors,—so much of a chill that, though Stoudenmayer paraded streets and threaded saloon and dance-hall throngs all the rest of the afternoon, seeking his prey, not a single man of them could he find; all stayed close in their dens.

But that the thug-leaders were not idle Stoudenmayer was not long learning. In the last moments of twilight, just before the pall of night fell upon the town, the marshal was standing on the east side of El Paso Street, midway between Oregon and San Antonio Streets, no cover within reach of him. Suddenly, without the slightest warning, a heavy fusillade opened on him from the opposite side of the street, a fusillade so heavy it would have decimated a company of infantry. At least a hundred men fired at him at the word, and it was a miracle he did not go down at the first volley. But he was not even scathed. Drawing his pistols, Stoudenmayer marched upon the enemy, slowly but steadily, advancing straight, it seemed, into the jaws of death, but firing with such wonderful rapidity and accuracy that seven of his foes were killed and two wounded in almost as many seconds, although all kept close as possible behind the shelter of the *portal* columns. And every second he was so engaged, at least a hundred guns, aimed by cruel trained eyes, that scarce ever before had missed whatever they sought to draw a bead on, were pouring out upon him a hell of lead that must have sounded to him like a flight of bees.

But stand his iron nerve and fatal snap-shooting the thugs could not. Before he was half way across the street, the hostile fire had ceased, and his would-be assassins were flying for the nearest and best cover they could find. Out of the town they slipped that night, singly and in squads, boarding freight trains north and east, stages west and south, stealing teams and saddle stock, some even hitting the trails afoot, in stark terror of the man. The next morning El Paso found herself evacuated of more than two hundred men who, while they had been for a time her most conspicuous citizens, were such as she was glad enough to spare. In twenty-four hours Bill Stoudenmayer had made his word good and fairly earned his wages; indeed he had accomplished single-handed what the most hopeful El Pasoites had despaired of seeing done with less authority and force than two or three troops of regular cavalry.

Then El Paso settled down to the humdrum but profitable task of laying the foundations for the great metropolis of the Farther Southwest. Since then, an occasional sporadic case of *triggerfingeritis* has developed in El Paso, usually in an acute form; but never once since the night Stoudenmayer turned the El Paso Street Portals into a shambles has it threatened as an epidemic.

Unluckily, Bill Stoudenmayer did not last long to enjoy the glory of his deed. He was a marked man, merely from motives of revenge harboured by friends of the departed (dead or live), but as a man with a reputation so big as to hang up a rare prize in laurels for any with the strategy and hardihood to down him. It was therefore matter of no general surprise when, a few weeks after his resignation as City Marshal, he fell the victim of a private quarrel.

★★★★★★

A few years later, Hal Gosling was the U. S. Marshall for the Western District of Texas. Early in Gosling's regime, Johnny Manning became one of his most efficient and trusted deputies. The pair were wide opposites: Gosling, a big, bluff, kindly, rollicking dare-devil afraid of nothing, but a sort that would rather chaff than fight; Manning a quiet, reserved, slender, handsome little man, not so very much bigger than a full-grown "45," who actually sought no quarrels but would rather fight than eat. Each in his own way, the pair made themselves a holy terror to such of the desperadoes as ventured any liberties with Uncle Sam's belongings.

One of their notable captures was a brace of road-agents who had appropriated the Concho stage road and about everything of value that travelled it. The two were tried in the Federal Court at Austin and sentenced to hard labour at Huntsville. Gosling and Manning started to escort them to their new field of activity. Handcuffed but not otherwise shackled, the two prisoners were given a seat together near the middle of a day coach. By permission of the marshal, the wife of one and the sister of the other sat immediately behind them—dear old Hal Gosling never could resist any appeal to his sympathies. The seat directly across the aisle from the two prisoners was occupied by Gosling and Manning. With the car well filled with passengers and their men ironed, the marshal and his deputy were off their guard. When out of Austin barely an hour, the train at full speed, the two women slipped pistols into the hands of the two convicted bandits, unseen by the officers. But others saw the act, and a stir of alarm among those nearby caused Gosling to whirl in his seat next the aisle, reaching for the pistol in his breast scabbard. But he was too late. Before he was half risen to his feet or his gun out, the prisoners fired and killed him.

Then ensued a terrible duel, begun at little more than arm's length, between Manning and the two prisoners, who presently began backing toward the rear door. Quickly the car filled with smoke, and in it pandemonium reigned, women screaming, men cursing, all who had not dropped in a faint ducking beneath the car seats and trying their best to burrow in the floor. When at length the two prisoners reached the platform and sprang from the moving train, Johnny Manning, shot full of holes as a sieve, lay unconscious across Hal Gosling's body; and the sister of one of the bandits hung limp across the back of the seat the prisoners had occupied, dead of a wild shot.

But Johnny had well avenged Hal's death and his own injuries; one of the prisoners was found dead within a few yards of the track, and the other was captured, mortally wounded, a half-mile away.

After many uncertain weeks, when Manning's system had successfully recovered from the overdose of lead administered by the departed, he quietly resumed his star and belt, and no one ever discovered that the incident had made him in the least gun-shy.

★★★★★★

Whenever the history of the Territory of New Mexico comes to be written, the name of Colonel Albert J. Fountain deserves and should have first place in it. Throughout the formative epoch of her evolution from semi-savagery to civilization, an epoch spanning the years from 1866 to 1896, Colonel Fountain was far and away her most distinguished and most useful citizen. As soldier, scholar, dramatist, lawyer, prosecutor, Indian fighter, and desperado-hunter, his was the most picturesque personality I have ever known. Gentle and kindhearted as a woman, a lover of his books and his ease, he nevertheless was always as quick to take up arms and undergo any hazard and hardship in pursuit of murderous rustlers as he was in 1861 to join the California Column (First California Volunteers) on its march across the burning deserts of Arizona to meet and defeat Sibley at Val Verde. A face fuller of the humanities and charities of life than his would be hard to find; but, roused, the laughing eyes shone cold as a wintry sky. He despised wrong, and hated the criminal, and spent his whole life trying to right the one and suppress or exterminate the other. In this work, and of it, ultimately, he lost his life.

In the early eighties, while the New Mexican courts were wellnigh idle, crime was rampant, especially in Lincoln, Dona Ana, and

Grant Counties. To the east of the Rio Grande the Lincoln County War was at its height, while to the west the Jack Kinney gang took whatever they wanted at the muzzle of their guns; and they wanted about everything in sight. County peace officers were powerless.

At this stage Fountain was appointed by the Governor "Colonel of State Militia," and given a free hand to pacify the country. As an organized military body, the militia existed only in name. And so Fountain left it. Serious and effective as was his work, no man loved a grand-stand play more than he. He liked to go it alone, to be the only thing in the spot light. Thus most of his work as a desperado-hunter was done single-handed.

On only one occasion that I can recall did he ever have with him on his raids more than one or two men, always Mexicans, temporarily deputized. That was when he met and cleaned out the Kinney gang over on the Miembres, and did it with half the number of the men he was after. Among those who escaped was Kinney's lieutenant. A few weeks later Colonel Fountain learned that this man was in hiding at Concordia, a *placita* two miles below El Paso. He was one of the most desperate Mexican outlaws the border has ever known, a man who had boasted he would never be taken alive, and that he would kill Fountain before he was himself taken dead, a human tiger, whom the bravest peace officer might be pardoned for wanting a great deal of help to take. Yet Fountain merely took his armoury's best and undertook it alone: and by mid-afternoon of the very next day after the information reached him he had his man safely manacled at the El Paso depot of the Santa Fe Railway.

While waiting for the train, Colonel George Baylor, the famous captain of Texas Rangers, chided Fountain for not wearing a cord to fasten his pistol to his belt, as then did all the Rangers, to prevent its loss from the scabbard in a running fight; and he finished by detaching his own cord, and looping one end to Fountain's belt and the other to his pistol. Then Fountain bade his old friend goodbye and boarded the train with his prisoner, taking a seat near the centre of the rear car.

When well north of Canutillo and near the site of old Fillmore, Fountain rose and passed forward to speak to a friend who was sitting a few seats in front of him, a safe enough proceeding, apparently, with his prisoner handcuffed and the train doing thirty-five miles an hour. But scarcely had he reached his friend's side, when a noise behind him caused him turn—just in time to see his Mexican running for the rear door. Instantly Fountain sprang after him, before he got to

68

the door the man had leaped from the platform. Without the slightest hesitation, Fountain jumped after him, hitting the ground only a few seconds behind him but thirty or forty yards away, rolling like a tumbleweed along the ground. By the time Fountain had regained his feet, his prisoner was running at top speed for the mesquite thickets lining the river, in whose shadows he must soon disappear, for it was already dusk. Reaching for his pistol and finding it gone—lost evidently in the tumble—and fearing to lose his prisoner entirely if he stopped to hunt for it, Fountain hit the best pace he could in pursuit. But almost at the first jump something gave him a thump on the shin that nearly broke it, and, looking down, there, dangling on Colonel Baylor's pistol-cord, he saw his gun.

Always a cunning strategist, Fountain dropped to the ground, sky-lined his man on the crest of a little hillock he had to cross, and took a careful two-handed aim which enabled Rio Grande ranchers thereafter to sleep easier of nights.

★★★★★★

And now, just as I am finishing this story, (as at time of first publication), the wires bring the sad news that dear old Pat Garrett, the dean and almost the last survivor of the famous man-hunted of west Texas and New Mexico, has gone the way of his kind—"died with his boots on." I cannot help believing that he was the victim of a foul shot, for in his personal relations I never knew him to court a quarrel or fail to get an adversary. Many a night we have camped, eaten, and slept together. Barring Colonel Fountain, Pat Garrett had stronger intellectuality and broader sympathies than any of his kind I ever met. He could no more do enough for a friend than he could do enough to an outlaw. In his private affairs so easy-going that he began and ended a ne'er-do-well, in his official duties as a peace officer he was so exacting and painstaking that he ne'er did ill. His many intrepid deeds are too well known to need recounting here.

All his life an atheist, he was as stubbornly contentious for his unbelief as any Scotch Covenanter for his best-loved tenets.

Now, laid for his last rest in the little burying-ground of Las Cruces, a tiny, white-paled square of sandy, hummocky bench land where the pink of fragile *nopal* petals brightens the graves in Spring and the mesquite showers them with its golden pods in Summer; where the sweet scent of the *juajilla* loads the air, and the sun ever shines down out of a bright and cloudless sky; where a diminutive forest of crosses of wood and stone symbolize the faith he in life refused to accept—

now, perhaps, Pat Garrett has learned how widely he was wrong. Peace to his ashes, and repose to his dauntless spirit!

CHAPTER 5

A Juggler With Death

This is the story of a man, a virile, strong, resourceful man, all of whose history from his youth to his untimely death thrills one at the reading and points lessons worth learning.

The most careful study and the most just comparison would doubtless concede to Washington Harrison Donaldson the high rank—high, indeed, in a double sense—of having been the greatest aeronaut the world has ever known.

While a few men have done some great deeds in aeronautics which he did not accomplish, nevertheless Donaldson did more things never even undertaken by any other aeronaut that any man who has ever lived. Indeed, much of his work would be deemed by mankind at large downright absurd, hair-brained, foolhardy, and reckless to the point of actual madness; and yet no man ever possessed a saner mind than Donaldson; no man was ever more fond of family, friends, and life in general, or normally more reluctant to undertake what he regarded as a needlessly hazardous task. His boldest and most seemingly reckless feats were to him no more than the every-day work of a man of a strong mind, of a stout heart, and of a perfectly trained body, who had so completely mastered every detail of his profession as gymnast, acrobat, and aeronaut, that he had come to have absolute faith in himself, downright abiding certainty that within his sphere of work not only must he succeed, but that, in the very nature of things it was quite impossible for him to fail.

Donaldson's story may well serve as an inspiration, as does that of every man who, with a cool head and high courage, takes his life in his hands for adventure into the world's untrodden fields. While he was regarded by average onlookers as little better than a "Merry Andrew," a public shocker, doing feats before the multitude to still the heart and

71

freeze the blood, those whose fortune it was to know him intimately realized him to be a man of the most serious purpose, with a great faith in the future of aerial navigation. He seemed to be possessed by the conviction that it was one day to become wholly practicable and generally useful; for he was keen to do all he could to popularize and advance it, and to demonstrate its large measure of safety where practised under reasonable conditions.

To many still living his memory is dear—to all indeed who ever knew him well, and it is to his memory and to the surviving friends who held him dear I dedicate this little story.

Washington Harrison Donaldson was the son of David Donaldson, an artist of no mean ability of Philadelphia, where the boy was born October 10, 1840. The mother, of straight descent from a line of patriots active during the Revolution, gave the boy the name of Washington; the father, an ardent worker for General Harrison's candidacy for the presidency in the "Tippecanoe-and-Tyler-too" campaign, added the name of Harrison. It is not conceivable that this christening with two names so closely linked with notable deeds of high emprise in the early history of this country, had its influence upon the boy.

As a mere youth he showed the most adventurous spirit and ardent ambition to excel his mates, to do deeds of skill and dexterity that others could not do. When still a child he was running up an unsupported eight-foot ladder, and balancing himself upon the topmost round in a way to startle the cleverest professional athletes. A little later, getting hold of any old rope, stretching it in any old way as a "slack-rope," he was busy perfecting himself as a slack-rope walker. Naturally, school held him only a very few years, for his type of mind obviously was not that of a student.

While still in early youth, he got his father's consent to work in the parental studio, and persevered long enough to acquire some ability in sketching. Later he employed this art in illustrating some of his aerial voyages. During these studio days he studied legerdemain and ventriloquism, and became one of the most expert sleight-of-hand wizards and ventriloquial entertainers of his time.

Donaldson's first appearance before the public was at the old Long's Varieties on South Third Street in Philadelphia. His feats as a rope-walker have probably never been surpassed. In 1862 a rope twelve hundred feet long was stretched across the Schuylkill River at Philadelphia at a height of twelve hundred feet above the water. After passing back and forth repeatedly over this rope, he finished his exhibition by leaping from a rope into the river from a height of approximately ninety feet. Two years later he successfully walked a rope eighteen hundred feet long and two hundred feet high, stretched across the Genesee Falls at Rochester, N.Y. Five years later he was riding a velocipede on a tight-wire from stage to gallery of a Philadelphia theatre, the first to do this performance.

Thus his years were spent between 1857 and 1871; and great as were the dangers and severe the tasks incident to this period of his career, to him it was not work but the play he loved. While the work in itself was not one to emulate—for there are perhaps few less useful tasks than those that made up his occupation—nevertheless, he was training himself for his career; and the absolute mastery over it which he accomplished, the boldness with which he did it, the readiness, certainty, and complete success with which he carried out everything he undertook make a lesson worth studying.

Donaldson's career as an aeronaut was brief. His first ascent was made August 30, 1871; his last, July 15, 1875. The story of the first is characteristic of the man. In his lexicon there was no such word as "fail." His balloon was small, holding only eight thousand cubic feet of gas. The gas was of poor quality, and when ready to rise he found it impossible even to make a start until all ballast had been thrown from the basket; and when at length the start was made, it was only to alight in a few minutes on the roof of a neighbouring house. Bent upon winning and doing at all hazards what he had undertaken, Donaldson quickly cast overboard all loose objects in the basket—ropes, anchors, provisions, even down to his boots and coat. Thus relieved of weight, he was able to make a voyage of about eighteen miles.

There are two essentials to safe ballooning: first, the easy working of the cord which controls the safety valve at the top of the netting, by which descent may be effected when the balloon is going too high; and surplus ballast, which may be thrown out to lighten the balloon when approaching the ground, to avoid striking the earth at dangerously rapid speed. Hence it followed that, his car having been stripped of every bit of weight to obtain the ascent, Donaldson's descent was so violent that he was not a little bruised before he got his balloon safely anchored again upon the earth.

The difficulties and risks of this first trip, arising from the poor appliances he had, were enough to discourage, if not deter, a heart less bold than his, but to him a new difficulty only meant the letting out of another reef in his resolution to conquer it. Thus it was that immediately upon his return from this, his first trip, he not only announced that he would make another ascent the ensuing week, but that he would undertake something never previously undertaken in aerial navigation, namely, that he would dispense with the basket or car swung beneath the concentrating ring of every normal balloon, and in its place would have nothing but a simple trapeze bar suspended beneath the ring, upon which in mid-air, at high altitude, he proposed to perform all feats done by then most highly trained gymnasts in trapeze performances.

His experience on this first trip, to quote his own phraseology, was "so glorious that I decided to abandon the tight-rope forever."

The second ascent was made in a light breeze. When approximately a mile in height, to quote a chronicler:

> Suddenly the aeronaut threw himself backward and fell, catching with his feet on the bar, thus sending a thrill through the crowd; but with another spring he was upstanding on the bar, and then followed one feat after another—hanging by one hand, one foot, by the back of his head, etc., until the blood ceased to curdle in the veins of the awe-stricken crowd, and they gave vent to their feelings in cheer after cheer. His glittering dress sparkled in the sun long after his outline was lost to the naked eye.

Intending no long journey, Donaldson climbed from the trapeze into the concentrating ring, where he seized the cord operating the safety valve and sought to open the valve. But the valve stuck and did not open readily, thus when Donaldson gave a more violent tug at the cord in his effort to open the valve, a great rent was torn in the top of the gas bag, through which the gas poured, causing the balloon to fall with appalling rapidity. Long afterwards Donaldson said that this was the first time in his life that he had ever felt actually afraid. Luckily he dropped into the top of a large tree, which broke his fall sufficiently to enable him to land without any serious injury.

Donaldson's sincerity and downright joy in his work, and the poetic temperament, which in him was always struggling for utterance, are pointed out by a chronicler in the words added by him to the description Donaldson gave of his trip after his return to Norfolk in 1872:

> The people of Norfolk cannot form the remotest conception of the grand appearance of Norfolk from a balloon. The city

"I CLIMBED HALFWAY UP THE NETTING, OPENED MY
KNIFE WITH MY TEETH, AND CUT A HOLE ABOUT TWO
FEET LONG"

looks almost surrounded by water, and the various tributaries to the Elizabeth River appear magnificently beautiful, looking like streams of silver. Floating over a field of foliage, the trees appear all blended together like blades of grass.

The chronicler adds:

Donaldson seemed to be perfectly enraptured by his subject, as was evinced by the beaming expression of his countenance while relating his experience. The motion of the balloon he describes as delightful, particularly in ascent, as it appears to be perfectly motionless, and any object within view beneath looks as if it were receding from you.

As a token of appreciation of this particular exploit, a handsome gold medal was given to Donaldson by the citizens of Norfolk.

A later ascent from Norfolk resulted in one of the most perilous experiences ever endured by any aeronaut, and indeed developed conditions from which none could possibly have hoped to escape with life except a perfectly trained and fearless aeronaut. His experience on this trip he told as follows:

After cutting the basket loose, the balloon shot up very rapidly. I pulled the valve cord and the gas escaped too freely. I was then almost at the water's edge, and going at the rate of one mile a minute. Quick work must be done, or a watery grave. I had either to cut a hole in the balloon or go to sea, and as there were no boats in sight, I chose the lesser evil. Seizing three of the cords, I swung out of the ring, into the netting, the balloon careening on her side. I climbed half way up the netting, opened my knife with my teeth, and cut a hole about two feet long. The instant I cut the hole the gas rushed out so fast that could scarcely get back to the ring.

After reaching the ring I lashed myself fast to it with a rope. While I was climbing up the rigging to cut the hole in the side of the balloon, my cap fell off, and so fast did I descend that before I got half way down I caught up with and passed the cap. Continuing to descend, I struck the ground in a large corn field, and was dragged nearly a thousand feet, the wind blowing a perfect gale. Crashing against a rail fence, I was rendered insensible. When I came to, I found myself hanging to one side of a tree, and the balloon to the other side, ripped to shreds. This was the *last tree*. I could have thrown a stone into the ocean from where I landed. On this trip I travelled ten miles in seven minutes.

Many want to know if the wind blows hard up there. They do not stop to think that I am carried by the wind, and whether I am in a dead calm or sailing at the rate of one hundred miles an hour, I am perfectly still; and when I went the ten miles in seven minutes I did not feel the slightest breeze; and when I cannot see the earth it is impossible to tell whether I am going or hanging still.

Just as Donaldson was a bit of an artist and left many sketches illustrating his experiences, so also he was a bit of a poet and left many pieces describing in lofty thought, but crude versification, the sentiments inspired by his ascents. The following is one of them:

There's pleasure in a lively trip when sailing through the air,
The word is given, 'Let her go!' To land I know not where.
The view is grand, 'tis like a dream, when many miles from home.
My castle in the air, I love above the clouds to roam.

In prose Donaldson was very much more at home than in verse; indeed many of his descriptions equal in clearness and beauty anything ever written of the impressions that come to fliers in cloudland. Take, for example, the following:

It's a pleasure to be up here, as I sit and look at the grand cloud pictures, the most splendid effects of light, unknown to all that cling to the surface of the earth. The ever-shifting scenes, the bright, dazzling colours, the soft roseate and purple hues, the sudden light and fiery sun . . . and on I go as if carried by spiritual wings, far above the diminutive objects of a Lilliputian world. We rise in the midst of splendour, where light and silence combine to make one wish he never need return.

Donaldson was a many-sided man—among other things, in no small measure a philosopher, as when he commented as follows:

I have noticed on different occasions a class of people who were only half alive and who find fault with my exercise, which to them looks frightful. Their nervous system is not properly balanced. They have too much nerves for their system, which is caused by want of a little moderate exercise up where the air is pure, instead of which they spend hours in a place which they call their office. They sit themselves in a dark corner, hidden from the sun's rays, and in one position remain for hours, inhaling the poisonous air with the room full of carbonic acid gas, which is as poisonous to man as arsenic is to rats; and in addition to this, will fill their lungs with tobacco smoke, and to steady their nerves require a stimulation of perhaps eight or ten brandies a day. If I were as helpless as this class of people, then my life would be swinging by a thread, and I would wind up with a broken neck.

About as sound philosophy and scientific hygiene as could well be found.

And yet another side to his character: the kindly nature, the gentleness and generous thought for others, reluctance to cause needless injury or pain, which is always the characteristic of any man of real courage. This beautiful side of his nature he once hinted at as follows:

I cannot look at a person cutting a chicken's head off, and as for shooting a poor, innocent bird for sport, I think it is a great wrong and should not be allowed. Did you ever think what a barbarous set we were—worse than Indians or Fiji Islanders! There is nothing living but what we torture and kill. As for fear … my candid opinion is that the only time one is out of danger is when sailing through the air in a balloon.

Early in 1873, after having made twenty-five or thirty ascents, and well-nigh exhausted people's capacity for sensations and excitements afforded by ballooning over *terra firma*, Donaldson began making plans for a balloon of a capacity and equipment adequate, in his judgment, to enable him to make a successful crossing of the Atlantic to England or the Continent. So soon as his plans became publicly known, Professor John Wise, who as early as 1843 had done his best to raise the funds necessary for a transatlantic journey by balloon, joined forces with Donaldson, and together they made application to the authorities of the city of Boston for an adequate appropriation. This was voted by one Board but vetoed by another. Thereupon, *The Daily Graphic* took up their proposition, and undertook the financing of the expedition under a formal contract executed June 27, 1873.

As a consequence of this contract, Donaldson proceeded to build the largest balloon ever constructed, of a gas capacity of 600,000 cubic feet, and a lifting power of 14,000 pounds. The total weight of the balloon, including its car, lifeboat, and equipment, was 7,100 pounds, thus leaving approximately 6,000 pounds surplus lifting capacity for ballast, passengers, etc.

Of course, a liberal supply of provisions was to be carried, with tools, guns, and fishing tackle, to be available for meeting any emergency arising from a landing in a wild, unsettled region. Moreover, a carefully selected set of scientific instruments was embraced in the equipment for making observations and records of changing conditions *en route*.

The inflation of this aerial monster began in Brooklyn at the Capitoline Grounds September 10, 1873. A high wind prevailed, and after the bag had received 100,000 cubic feet of gas, she became so nearly uncontrollable, notwithstanding 300 men and 100 sacks of ballast, each sack weighing 200 pounds, were holding her down, that Donaldson and his associates decided to empty her.

On the twelfth of September inflation was again undertaken, although a high wind again prevailed. When something more than half full, the bag burst, and the aeronauts concluded that she was of a size impossible to handle. The bag and rigging were thereupon taken in hand, and she was reduced one-half; that is, to a capacity of 300,000 cubic feet of gas.

The remodelling was finished early in October, and inflation of this new balloon was begun at 1 p.m. on Sunday, October 6, and by 10.30 p.m. of that day the inflation was completed, the life-boat was attached, and she was firmly secured for the night.

At nine the next morning the crew took their places in the boat. Donaldson as aeronaut; Alfred Ford as correspondent for the *Graphic*; George Ashton Lunt, an experienced seaman, as navigator. Ascent was made, without incident, the balloon drifting first to the north, and then to the southward toward Long Island Sound.

Unhappily this voyage was brief, and very nearly tragical in its finish. About noon the balloon entered the field of a storm of wind and rain of extraordinary violence, and before long the cordage, etc., was so heavily loaded with moisture, that although practically all available ballast was disposed of, the balloon descended in spite of them. The speed of the balloon was so great that Donaldson did not dare hazard a dash against some house, or into some forest or other obstacle, but selected a piece of open ground, and advised his companions to hang by their hands over the side of the boat and drop at the word. The word at length given by Donaldson, both he and Ford dropped—a distance of about thirty feet, happily without serious injury other than a severe shaking up. Lunt, curious about the distance and the effect of such a fall, as well as unfamiliar with the action of a balloon when relieved of weight, hung watching the descent of his companions—only to realise quickly that he was shooting up into the air like a rocket. Then he clambered back into the boat. However, it was not long before, again weighted and beaten down by the continuing rain, the balloon descended upon a forest, where Lunt swung himself into a tree-top, whence he dropped through its branches to the earth, practically unhurt.

Thus ended the transatlantic voyage of the *Graphic* balloon, a voyage that constitutes the only serious failure I can recall of anything in the line of his profession as an aeronaut that Donaldson ever undertook to do. This failure is not to be counted to his discredit, for precisely as a good soldier does not surrender until his last round of ammunition is spent, so Donaldson did not give in until his last pound of ballast was exhausted.

In all respects the most brilliant aerial voyage ever made by Donaldson was his sixty-first ascension, on July 24, 1874, a voyage which continued for twenty-six hours. This was the longest balloon voyage in point of hours ever made up to that time, and indeed it remained a world's record for endurance up in the air until 1900, and the endurance record in the United States, until the recent St. Louis Cup Race.

The ascent was made from Barnum's "Great Roman Hippodrome," which for some years occupied the site of what is now Madison Square Garden, in a balloon built by Mr. Barnum to attempt to break the record for time and distance of all previous balloon voyages. An account of this thrilling trip is given in the following chapter of this book.

The history of the ascent Donaldson made from Toronto, Canada, on June 23, 1875, is in itself a sufficient refutation of the charges made less than a month later, that on his last trip he sacrificed his passenger, Grimwood, to save his own life. On his Toronto trip he was accompanied by Charles Pirie, of the *Globe*; Mr. Charles, of the *Leader*; and Mr. Devine, of the *Advertiser*. On this occasion Donaldson accepted the three passengers under the strongest protest, after having told them plainly that the balloon was leaky, the wind blowing out upon the lake, and that the ascent must necessarily be a peculiarly dangerous one. Nevertheless, they decided to take the hazard. Later they regretted their temerity.

Husbanding his ballast as best he could, nevertheless, the loss of gas through leakage was such that by midnight, when well over the centre of Lake Ontario, the balloon descended into a rough, tempestuous sea, and was saved from immediate destruction only by the cutting away of both the anchor and the drag rope. This gave them a temporary lease of life, but at one o'clock the car again struck the waters and dragged at a frightful speed through the lake, compelling the passengers to stand on the edge of the basket and cling to the ropes, the cold so intense they were well-nigh benumbed. At length they were rescued by a passing boat, but this was not until after three o'clock in the morning.

Of Donaldson's conduct in these hours of terrible extremity, a passenger wrote:

> But for his judicious use of the ballast, his complete control of the balloon as far as it could be controlled, his steady nerve, kindness, and coolness in the hour of danger, the occupants would never have reached land. . . . The party took no provisions with them excepting two small pieces of bread two inches square, which Mr. Devine happened to have in his pocket. At eleven at night, the Professor, having had nothing but a noon lunch, was handed up the bread. . . . About three o'clock in the morning, when the basket was wholly immersed in the water, and the inmates clinging almost lifelessly to the ropes, the Professor climbed down to them, and they were surprised to see in his hand the two small pieces of bread they had given him the night before. He had hoarded it up all night, and instead of eating it he said with cheery voice, 'Well, boys, all is up. Divide this among you. It may give you strength enough to swim.' There was not a man among them that would touch it until the Professor first partook of it. It was only a small morsel for each. . . . . He said that he had but one life-preserver on board, and suggested we should draw lots for the man who should leave and lighten the balloon.

While this discussion was on, the boat approached that saved them.

This simple story of Donaldson's true courage, cheerfulness, self-denial, readiness to sacrifice himself for others, is no less than an epic of the noblest heroism that stands an irrefutable answer to the charge later made that Donaldson sacrificed Grimwood.

Three weeks later—to be precise, on the fifteenth of July—Donaldson and his beloved airship, the *P.T. Barnum*, made their last ascent, from Chicago. The balloon was already old—more than a year old—the canvas weakened and in many places rent and patched, the cordage frail. In short, the balloon was in poor condition to stand any extraordinary stress of weather.

His companion on this trip was Mr. Newton S. Grimwood, of *The Chicago Evening Journal*. Donaldson had expected to be able to take two men; and Mr. Maitland, of the *Post & Mail*, was present with the other two in the basket immediately before the hour of starting. At the last moment Donaldson concluded that it was unwise to take more than one, and required lots to be drawn. Maitland tossed a coin, called "Heads," and won; but Mr. Thomas, the press agent, insisted that the usual method of drawing written slips from a hat be followed, and on this second lot-casting Maitland lost his place in the car, but won his life.

The ascent was made about 5 p.m., the prevailing wind carrying them out over Lake Michigan. About 7 p.m., a tug-boat sighted the balloon, then about thirty miles off shore, trailing its basket along the surface of the lake. The tug changed her course to intercept the balloon, but before it was reached, probably through the cutting away of the drag rope and anchor, the balloon bounded into the air, and soon disappeared, and never again was aught of Donaldson or the balloon *Barnum* seen by human eye. A little later a storm of extraordinary fury broke over the lake—a violent electric storm accompanied by heavy rain.

Weeks passed with no news of the voyagers or their ship. A month later the body of Grimwood was found on the shores of Lake Michigan and fully identified.

The precise story of that terrible night will never be written, but knowing the man and his trade, sequence of incident is as plain to me as if told by one of the voyagers. Evidently the balloon sprung a leak early. The last ballast must have been spent before the tug saw her trailing in the lake. Then anchor and drag ropes were sacrificed. This would inevitably give the balloon travelling power for a considerable time,—time of course depending on the measure of the leak of gas,—but ultimately she must again have descended upon the raging waters of the lake, where Grimwood, of untrained strength, soon became exhausted while trying to hold himself secure in the ring, and fell out into the lake.

Thus again relieved of weight, the balloon received a new lease of life, and travelled on probably, to a fatal final descent in some untrodden corner of the northern forest, where no one ever has chanced to stumble across the wreck. For had the balloon made its final descent into the lake, it would have been only after the basket was utterly empty, all the loose cordage cut away, and a type of wreck left that would float for weeks or months and would almost certainly have been found. Indeed, for months afterwards the writer and many others of Donaldson's friends held high hopes of hearing of him returned in safety from some remote distance in the wilds. But this was not to be.

One more incident and I have done.

Six or seven years ago I read in the columns of the *Sun* an article copied from a Chicago paper, evidently written by some close friend of the unfortunate Grimwood, making a bitter attack upon Donaldson for having sacrificed his passenger's life to save his own. The story moved me so much that I wrote an open letter to the Sun over my own signature, in which I sought to refute the charge by recounting the story of Donaldson's noble conduct, and his constant readiness for self-sacrifice in other situations quite as dire.

A few days later, sitting in my office, I was frozen with astonishment when a written card was handed in to me bearing the name "Washington H. Donaldson!" As soon as I could recover myself, the bearer of the card was asked in. He was a man within a year or two of my friend's age at the time of his death, Wash Donaldson's very self in face and figure! He had the same bright, piercing eye, that looked straight into mine; the same lean, square jaws and resolute mouth; the same waving hair, the same low, cool, steady voice—such a resemblance as to dull my senses, and make me wonder and grope to understand how my friend could thus come back to me, still young after so many years.

It was Donaldson's son, a babe in arms at the time his father sailed away to his death!

In a few simple words he told me that he and his family lived in a small village. With infinite grief they had read the article charging his father with unmanly conduct—a grief that was the greater because they possessed no means to refute the charge. Brokenly, with tears of gratitude, he told of their joy in reading my statements in his father's defence, and how he had been impelled to come and try in person to express to me the gratitude he felt he could not write.

Poor though this man may be in this world's goods, in the record of his father's character and deeds he owns a legacy fit to give him place among the Peers of Real Manhood.

Through some mischance I have lost the address of Donaldson's son. Should he happen to read these lines I hope he will communicate with me.

CHAPTER 6

An Aerial Bivouac

In the history of contests since man first began striving against his fellows, seldom has a record performance stood so long unbroken as that of the good airship *Barnum*, made thirty-three years ago. Of her captain and crew of five men, six all told, the writer remains the sole survivor, the only one who may live to see that record broken in this country.

The *Barnum* rose at 4 p.m. July 26, 1874, from New York and made her last landing nine miles north of Saratoga at 6.07 p.m. of the twenty-seventh, thus finishing a voyage of a total elapsed time of twenty-six hours and seven minutes. In the interim she made four landings, the first of no more than ten minutes; the second, twenty; the third, ten; the fourth, thirty-five; and these descents cost an expenditure of gas and ballast which shortened her endurance capacity by at least two or three hours.

Tracing on a map her actual route traversed, gives a total distance of something over four hundred miles, which gave her the record of second place in the history of long-distance ballooning in this country, a record which she still holds.

So far as my knowledge of the art goes, and I have tried to read all of its history, the *Barnum's* voyage of twenty-six hours, seven minutes was then and remained the world's endurance record until 1900; and it still remains, in point of hours up, the longest balloon voyage ever made in the United States.

The longest voyage in point of distance ever made in this country was that of John Wise and La Mountain, in the fifties, from St. Louis, Mo., to Jefferson County, N. Y., a distance credited under the old custom of a little less than twelve hundred miles, while the actual distance under the new rules is between eight hundred and nine hundred miles, the time being nineteen hours. This voyage also remained, I believe, the world's record for distance until 1900, and still remains the American record—and lucky, indeed, will be the aeronaut who beats it.

P. T. Barnum's "Great Roman Hippodrome," now for many years Madison Square Garden, was never more densely crowded than on the afternoon of July 26, 1874. Early in the Spring of that year Mr. Barnum had announced the building of a balloon larger than any theretofore made in this country. His purpose in building it was to attempt to break all previous records for time and distance, and he invited each of five daily city papers of that time to send representatives on the voyage. So when the day set for the ascent arrived, not only was the old Hippodrome packed to the doors, but adjacent streets and squares were solid black with people, as on a *fête* day like the Dewey Parade.

Happily the day was one of brilliant sunshine and clear sky, with scarcely a cloud above the horizon.

The captain of the *Barnum* was Washington. H. Donaldson, by far the most brilliant and daring professional aeronaut of his day, and a clever athlete and gymnast. For several weeks prior to the ascent of the *Barnum*, Donaldson had been making daily short ascents of an hour or two from the Hippodrome in a small balloon—as a feature of the performance. Sometimes he ascended in a basket, at other times with naught but a trapeze swinging beneath the concentrating ring of his balloon himself in tights perched easily upon the bar of the trapeze. And when at a height to suit his fancy—of a thousand feet or more— many a time have I seen him do every difficult feat of trapeze work ever done above the security of a net.

Such was Donaldson, a man utterly fearless, but reckless only when alone, of a steadfast, cool courage and resource when responsible for the safety of others that made him the man out of a million best worth trusting in any emergency where a bold heart and ready wit may avert disaster.

Donaldson's days were never dull.

The day preceding our ascent his balloon was released with insufficient lifting power. As soon as he rose above neighbouring roofs, a very high southeast wind caught him, and, before he had time to throw out ballast, drove his basket against the flagstaff on the Gilsey House with such violence that the staff was broken, and the basket momentarily upset, dumping two ballast bags to the Broadway sidewalk where they narrowly missed several pedestrians.

That he himself was not dashed to death was a miracle. But to him this was no more than a bit unusual incident of the day's work.

The reporters assigned as mates on this skylark in the *Barnum* were Alfred Ford, of the *Graphic*; Edmund Lyons, of the *Sun*; Samuel Mac-Keever, of the *Herald*; W. W. Austin, of the *World* (every one of these good fellows now dead, alas!) and myself, representing the *Tribune*.

Lyons, MacKeever, and myself were novices in ballooning, but the two others had scored their bit of aeronautic experience. Austin had made an ascent a year or two before at San Francisco, was swept out over the bay before he could make a landing, and, through some mishap, dropped into the water midway of the bay and well out toward Golden Gate, where he was rescued by a passing boat. Ford had made several balloon voyages, the most notable in 1873, in the great *Graphic* balloon.

After the voyage of the *Barnum* was first announced and it became known that the *Tribune* would have a pass, everybody on the staff wanted to go. For weeks it was the talk of the office. Even grave graybeards of the editorial rooms were paying court for the preference to Mr. W. F. G. Shanks, that prince of an earlier generation of city editors, who of course controlled the assignment of the pass. But when at length the pass came, the enthusiasm and anxiety for the distinction waned, and it became plain that the piece of paper "Good for One Aerial Trip," etc., must go begging.

At that time I was assistant night city editor, and a special detail to interview the Man in the Moon was not precisely in the line of my normal duties. I was therefore greatly surprised (to put it conservatively) when, the morning before the ascent, Mr. Shanks, in whose family I was then living, routed me out of bed to say:

"See here, Ted, you know Barnum's balloon starts tomorrow on her trial for the record, but what you don't know is that we are in a hole. Before the ticket came everyone wanted to go, from John R. G. Hassard down to the office boy. Now no one will go—all have funked it, and I suppose you will want to follow suit!"

Thus diplomatically put, the hinted assignment was not to be refused without too much personal chagrin.

So it happened that about 3.30 p.m. the next day I arrived at the Hippodrome, loaded down with wraps and a heavy basket nigh bursting with good things to eat and drink, which dear Mrs. Shanks had insisted on providing.

The *Barnum* was already filled with gas, tugging at her leash and swaying restlessly as if eager for the start. And right here, at first sight of the great sphere, I felt more nearly a downright fright than at any stage of the actual voyage; the balloon appeared such a hopelessly frail fabric to support even its own car and equipment. The light cord net enclosing the great gas-bag looked, aloft, where it towered above the roof, little more substantial than a film of lace; and to ascend in that balloon appeared about as safe a proposition as to enmesh a lion in a cobweb.

Already my four mates for the voyage were assembled about the basket, and Donaldson himself was busy with the last details of the equipment. My weighty lunch basket had from my mates even a heartier reception than I received, but their joy over the prospect of delving into its generous depths was short-lived. The load as Donaldson had planned it was all aboard, weight carefully adjusted to what he considered a proper excess lifting power to carry us safely up above any chance of a collision with another flagstaff, as on the day before above the Gilsey House. Thus the basket and all its bounty (save only a small flask of brandy I smuggled into a hip pocket) were given to a passing acrobat.

At 4 p.m. the old Hippodrome rang with applause; a brilliant equestrian act had just been finished. Suddenly the applause ceased and that awful hush fell upon the vast audience which is rarely experienced except in the presence of death or of some impending disaster! We had been seen to enter the basket, and people held their breath.

Released, the balloon bounded seven hundred feet the air, stood stationary for a moment, and then drifted northwest before the prevailing wind.

In this prodigious leap there was naught of the disagreeable sensation one experiences in a rapidly rising elevator. Instead it rather seemed that we were standing motionless, stationary in space, and that the earth itself had gotten loose and was dropping away beneath us to depths unknown. Every cord and rope of the huge fabric was tensely taut, the basket firm and solid beneath our feet. Indeed, the balloon, with nothing more substantial in her construction than cloth and twine, and hempen ropes and willow wands (the latter forming the basket), has always, while floating in mid-air free of the drag rope's tricks, the rigid homogeneity of a rock, a solidity that quickly inspires the most timid with perfect confidence in her security.

Ballast was thrown out by Donaldson,—a little. At Seventh Avenue and Forty-second Street our altitude was 2,000 feet. The great city lay beneath us like an unrolled scroll. White and dusty, the streets looked like innumerable strips of Morse telegraph paper—the people the dots, the vehicles the dashes. Central Park, with its winding waters, was transformed into a superb mantle of dark green velvet splashed with silver, worthy of a royal *fête*. Behind us lay the sea, a vast field of glittering silver. Before us lay a wide expanse of Jersey's hills and dales that from our height appeared a plain, with many a reddish-gray splash upon its verdant stretches that indicated a village or a town.

Above and about us lay an immeasurable space of which we were the only tenants, and over which we began to feel a grand sense of dominion that wrapped us as in royal ermine: if we were not lords of this aerial manor, pray, then, who were? Beneath us, lay—home. Should we ever see it again? This thought I am sure came to all of us. I know it came to me. But the perfect steadiness of the balloon won our confidence, and we soon gave ourselves up to the gratification of our enviable position; and enviable indeed it was. For who has not envied the eagle his power to skim the tree-tops, to hover above Niagara, to circle mountain peaks, to poise himself aloft and survey creation, or to mount into the zenith and gaze at the sun?

Indeed our sense of confidence became such that, while sitting on the edge of the basket to reach and pass Donaldson a rope he asked for, I leaned so far over that the bottle of brandy resting in my hip pocket slipped out and fell into the Hudson.

Oddly, Ford, who was the most experienced balloonist of the party after Donaldson himself, seemed most nervous and timid, but it was naught but an expression of that constitutional trouble (dizziness) so many have when looking down from even the minor height of a step-ladder. In all the long hours he was with us, I do not recall his once standing erect in the basket, and when others of us perched upon the basket's edge, he would beg us to come down. But mind, there was no lack of stark courage in Alfred Ford, sufficiently proved by the fact that he never missed a chance for an ascent.

But safe? Confident? Why, before we were up ten minutes, Lyons and MacKeever were sitting on the edge of the basket, with one hand holding to a stay, tossing out handfuls of small tissue paper circulars bearing "News from the Clouds." Many-coloured, these little circulars as they fell beneath us looked like a flight of giant butter-flies, and we kept on throwing out handfuls of them until our pilot warned us we were wasting so much weight we should soon be out of easy view of the earth! Indeed, the balance of the balloon is so extremely fine that when a single handful of these little tissue circulars was thrown out, increased ascent was shown on the dial of our aneroid barometer!

At 4.30 p.m. we had drifted out over the Hudson at an altitude of 2,500 feet. Here Donaldson descended from the airy perch which he had been occupying since our start on the concentrating ring, when one of us asked how long he expected the cruise to last. He replied that he hoped to be able to sail the *Barnum* at least three or four days.

"But," he added, "I shall certainly be unable, to carry all of you for so long a journey, and shall be compelled to drop you one by one. So you had best draw lots to settle whom I shall drop first, and in what order the rest shall follow."

Sailing then 2,500 feet above the earth, Lyons voiced a thought racing from my own brain for utterance when he blurted out: "What the deuce do you mean by 'drop' us?" Indeed, the question must have been on three other tongues as well, for Donaldson's reply, "Oh, descend to the earth and let you step out then," was greeted by all five of us with a salvo of deep, lusty sighs of relief.

Then we drew lots for the order of our going, MacKeever drawing first Austin second, Lyons third, Ford fourth, and I fifth.

Meantime, beneath us on the river vessels which from our height looked like the toy craft on the lake in Central Park were whistling a shrill salute that, toned down by the distance, was really not unmusical.

Having crossed the Hudson and swept above Weehawken, we found ourselves cruising northwest over the marshes of the Hackensack.

As the heat of the declining sun lessened, our cooling gas contracted and the balloon sank steadily until at 5.10 we were 250 feet above the earth and 100 feet of our great drag rope was trailing on the ground. Within hailing distance of people beneath us, a curious condition was observed. We could hear distinctly all they said, though we could not make them understand a word; our voices had to fill a sphere of air; theirs, with the earth beneath them, only a hemisphere. Thus the modern megaphone is especially useful to aeronauts.

Hereabouts our fun began. Many countrymen thought the balloon running away with us and tried to stop and save us—always by grasping the drag rope, bracing themselves, and trying literally to hold us; when the slack of the rope straightened, they performed somersaults such as our pilot vowed no acrobat could equal. And yet the balance of the balloon is so fine that even a child of ten can pull one down, if only it has strength enough to withstand occasional momentary lifts off the ground. Occasionally one more clever would run and take a quick turn of the rope about a gate or fence—and then spend the rest of the evening gathering the scattered fragments and repairing the damage.

And when there was not fun enough below, Donaldson himself would take a hand and put his steed through some of her fancy paces—as when, approaching a large lake, he told us to hold tightly to the stays, let out gas and dropped us, bang! upon the lake. Running at a speed of twelve or fifteen miles an hour, we hit the water with a tremendous shock, bounded thirty or forty feet into the air, descended again and literally skipped in great leaps along the surface of the water, precisely like a well-thrown "skipping stone." Then out went ballast and up and on we went, no worse for the fun beyond a pretty thorough wetting!

At 6.20 p.m. we landed on the farm of Garrett Harper in Bergen County, twenty-six miles from New York. After drinking our fill of milk at the farmhouse, we rose again and drifted north over Ramapo until, at 7.30, a dead calm came upon us and we made another descent. We then found that we had landed near Bladentown on the farm of Miss Charlotte Thompson, a charming actress of the day whose "Jane Eyre" and "Fanchon" are still pleasant memories to old theatre-goers. Loading our balloon with stones to anchor it, our party paid her a visit and were cordially received. An invitation to join us hazarded by Donaldson, Miss Thompson accepted with delight. I do not know if she is still living, but it she is, she cannot have forgotten her half-hour's cruise in the good airship *Barnum*, wafted silently by a gentle evening breeze, the lovely panorama beneath her half hid, half seen through the purple haze of twilight.

After landing Miss Thompson at 8.18 we ascended for the night, for a night's bivouac among the stars. The moon rose early. We were soon sailing over the Highlands of the Hudson. Off in the east we could see the river, a winding ribbon of silver. We were running low, barely more than 200 feet high. Below us the great drag rope was hissing through meadows, roaring over fences, crashing through tree-tops. And all night long we were continually ascending and descending, sinking into valleys and rising over hills, following closely the contours of the local topography.

During the more equable temperature of night the balloon's height is governed by the drag rope. Leaving a range of hills and floating out over a valley, the weight of the drag pulls the balloon down until the same length of rope is trailing through the valley that had been dragging on the hill. This habit of the balloon produces startling effects. Drifting swiftly toward a rocky precipitous hillside against which it seems inevitable you must dash to your death, suddenly the trailing drag rope reaches the lower slopes and you soar like a bird over the hill, often so low that the bottom of the basket swishes through the tree-tops.

But, while useful in conserving the balloon's energy, the drag rope is a source of constant peril to aeronauts, of terror to people on the earth, and of damage to property. It has a nasty clinging habit, winding round trees or other objects, that may at any moment upset basket and aeronauts. On this trip our drag rope tore sections out of scores of fences, upset many haystacks, injured horses and cattle that tried to run across it, whipped off many a chimney, broke telegraph wires, and seemed to take malicious delight in working some havoc with everything it touched.

At ten o'clock we sighted Cozzen's Hotel, and shortly drifted across the parade ground of West Point, its huge battlemented gray walls making one fancy he was looking down into the inner court of some great mediaeval castle. Then we drifted out over the Hudson toward Cold Spring until, caught by a different current, we were swept along the course of the river.

As we sailed over midstream and two hundred feet above it, with the tall cliffs and mysterious, dark recesses of the Highlands on either hand, the waters turned to a livid gray under the feeble light of the waning moon. No part of our voyage was more impressive, no scene more awe-inspiring. It was a region of such weird lights and gruesome shadows as no fancy could people with aught but gaunt goblins and dread demons, come down to us through generations untold, an unspent legacy of terror, from half-savage, superstitious ancestors.

Suddenly Ford spoke in a low voice: "Boys, I was in nine or ten battles of the Civil War, from Gaines's Mill to Gettysburg, but in none of them was there a scene which impressed me as so terrible as this, no situation that seemed to me so threatening of irresistible perils."

Nearing Fishkill at eleven, a land breeze caught and whisked us off eastward. At midnight we struck the town of Wappinger's Falls— and struck it hard. Our visitation is doubtless remembered there yet. The town was in darkness and asleep. We were running low before a stiff breeze, half our drag rope on the ground. The rope began to roar across roofs and upset chimneys with shrieks and crashes that set the folk within believing the end of the world had come. Instantly the streets were filled with flying white figures and the air with men's curses and women's screams. Three shots were fired beneath us. Two of our fellows said they heard the whistle of the balls, so Donaldson thought it prudent to throw out ballast and rise out of range.

Here the moon left us and we sailed on throughout the remainder of the night in utter darkness and without any extraordinary incident, all but the watch lying idly in the bottom of the basket viewing the stars and wondering what new mischief the drag rope might be planning.

The only duty of the watch was to lighten ship upon too near descent to the earth, and for this purpose a handful of Hippodrome circulars usually proved sufficient. Indeed, only eight pounds of ballast were used from the time we left Miss Thompson till dawn, barring a half-sack spent in getting out of range of the Wappinger's Falls sportsmen, who seemed to want to bag us.

Ford and Austin were assigned as the lookout from 12.00 to 2.00, Lyons and myself from 2.00 to 3.00, and Donaldson and MacKeever from 3.00 to 4.00.

From midnight till 3.00 a.m. Donaldson slept as peaceful as a baby, curled up in the basket with a sandbag for a pillow. The rest of us slept little through the night and talked less, each absorbed in the reflections and speculations inspired by our novel experience.

At the approach of dawn we had the most unique and extraordinary experience ever given to man. The balloon was sailing low in a deep valley. To the east of us the Berkshires rose steeply to summits probably fifteen hundred feet above us. Beneath us a little village lay, snuggled cosily between two small meeting brooks, all dim under the mists of early morning and the shadows of the hills. No flush of dawn yet lit the sky. Donaldson had been consulting his watch, suddenly he rose and called, pointing eastward across the range:

"Watch, boys! Look there!"

He then quickly dumped overboard half the contents of a ballast bag. Flying upward like an arrow, the balloon soon shot up above the mountain-top, when, lo! a miracle. The phenomenon of sunrise was reversed! We our very selves instead had risen on the sun! There he stood, full and round, peeping at us through the trees crowning a distant Berkshire hill, as if startled by our temerity.

Shortly thereafter, when we had descended to our usual level and were running swiftly before a stiff breeze over a rocky hillside, Donaldson yelled:

"Hang on, boys, for your lives!"

The end of the drag rope had gotten a hitch about a large tree limb. Luckily Donaldson had seen it in time to warn us, else we had there finished our careers. We had barely time to seize the stays when the rope tautened with a shock that nearly turned the basket upside down, spilled out our water-bucket and some ballast, left MacKeever and myself hanging in space by our hands, and the other four on the lower side of the basket, scrambling to save themselves. Instantly, of course, the basket righted and dropped back beneath us.

And then began a terrible struggle.

The pressure of the wind bore us down within a hundred feet of the ragged rocks. Groaning under the strain, the rope seemed ready to snap. Like a huge leviathan trapped in a net, the gas-bag writhed, twisted, bulged, shrank, gathered into a ball and sprang fiercely out. The loose folds of canvas sucked up until half the netting stood empty, and then fold after fold darted out and back with all the angry menace of a serpent's tongue and with the ominous crash of musketry.

It seemed the canvas must inevitably burst and we be dashed to death. But Donaldson was cool and smiling, and, taking the only precaution possible, stood with a sheath-knife ready to cut away the drag rope and relieve is of its weight in case our canvas burst.

Happily the struggle was brief. The limb that held us snapped, and the balloon sprang forward in mighty bounds that threw us off our feet and tossed the great drag rope about like a whiplash. But we were free, safe, and our stout vessel soon settled down to the velocity of the wind.

By this time we all were beginning to feel hungry, for we had supped the night before in mid-air from a lunch basket that held more delicacies than substantials. So Donaldson proposed a descent and began looking for a likely place. At last he chose a little village, which upon near approach we learned lay in Columbia County of our own good State.

We called to two farmers to pull us down, no easy task in the rather high wind then blowing. They grasped the rope and braced themselves as had others the night before, and presently were flying through the air in prodigious if ungraceful somersaults. Amazed but unhurt, they again seized the rope and got a turn about a stout board fence, only to see a section or two of the fence fly into the air as if in pursuit of us.

Presently the heat of the rising sun expanded our gas and sent us up again 2,000 feet, making breakfast farther off than ever. Thus, it being clear that we must sacrifice either our stomachs or our gas, Donaldson held open the safety valve until we were once more safely landed on mother earth, but not until after we had received a pretty severe pounding about, for such a high wind blew that the anchor was slow in holding.

This landing was made at 5.24 a.m. on the farm of John W. Coons near the village of Greenport, four miles from Hudson City, and about one hundred and thirty miles from New York.

Here our pilot decided our vessel must be lightened of two men, and thus the lot drawn the night before compelled us to part, regretfully, with MacKeever of the *Herald*, and Austin of the *World*. Ford, however, owing allegiance to an afternoon paper, the *Graphic*, and always bursting with honest journalistic zeal for a "beat," saw an opportunity to win satisfaction greater even than that of keeping on with us. So he, too, left us here, with the result that the *Graphic* published a full story of the voyage up to this point, Saturday afternoon, the twenty-fifth, the *Herald* and the *World* trailed along for second place in their Sunday editions, while *Sun* and *Tribune* readers had to wait till Monday morning for such "News from the Clouds" as Lyons and I had to give them, for wires were not used as freely then as now.

Our departing mates brought us a rare good breakfast from Mr. Coons' generous kitchen—a fourteen-quart tin pail well-nigh filled with good things, among them two currant pies on yellow earthen plates, gigantic in size, pale of crust, though anything but anaemic of contents. Lyons finished nearly the half of one before our reascent, to his sorrow, for scarcely were we off the earth before he developed a colic that seemed to interest him more, right up to the finish of the trip, than the scenery.

Bidding our mates goodbye, we prepared to reascend. Many farmers had been about us holding to our ropes and leaning on the basket, and later we realized we had not taken in sufficient ballast to offset the weight of the three men who had left us.

Released, the balloon sprang upward at a pace that all but took our breath away. Instantly the earth disappeared beneath us. We saw Donaldson pull the safety valve wide open, draw his sheath knife ready to cut the drag rope, standing rigid, with his eyes riveted upon the aneroid barometer. The hand of the barometer was sweeping across the dial at a terrific rate. I glanced at Donaldson and saw him smile. Then I looked back the barometer and saw the hand had stopped—at 10,200 feet! How long we were ascending we did not know. Certain it is that the impressions described were all there was time for, and that when Donaldson turned and spoke we saw his lips move but could hear no sound. Our speed had been such that the pressure of the air upon the tympanum of the ear left us deaf for some minutes. We had made a dash of two miles into cloudland and had accomplished it, we three firmly believed, in little more than a minute.

Presently Donaldson observed the anchor and grapnel had come up badly clogged with sod, and a good heavy tug he and I had of it to pull them in, for Lyons was still much too busy with his currant pie to help us. Nor indeed were the currant pies yet done with us, for at the end of our tug at the anchor rope, I found I had been kneeling very precisely in the middle of pie No. 2, and had contrived to absorb most of it into the knees of my trousers. Thus at the end of the day, come to Saratoga after all shops were closed, I had to run the gauntlet of the porch and office crowd of visitors at the United States Hotel in a condition that only needed moccasins and a war bonnet to make me a tolerable imitation of an Indian.

We remained aloft at an altitude of one or two and one half miles for three hours and a half, stayed there until the silence became intolerable, until the buzz of a fly or the croak of a frog would have been music to our ears. Here was *absolute silence*, the silence of the grave and death, a silence never to be experienced by living man in any terrestrial condition.

Occasionally the misty clouds in which we hung enshrouded parted beneath us and gave us glimpses of distant earth, opened and disclosed landscapes of infinite beauty set in grey nebulous frames. Once we passed above a thunderstorm, saw the lightning play beneath us, felt our whole fabric tremble at its shock—and were glad enough when we had left it well behind. Seen from a great height, the earth looked to be a vast expanse of dark green velvet, sometimes shaded to a deeper hue by cloudlets floating beneath the sun, splashed here with the silver and there with the gold garniture reflected from rippling waters.

Toward noon we descended beneath the region of clouds into the realm of light and life, and found ourselves hovering above the Mountain House of the Catskills. And thereabouts we drifted in crosscurrents until nearly 4.00 p.m., when a heavy southerly gale struck us and swept us rapidly northward past Albany at a pace faster than I have ever travelled on a railway.

We still had ballast enough left to assure ten or twelve hours more travel. But we did not like our course. The prospects were that we would end our voyage in the wilderness two hundred or more miles north of Ottawa. So we rose to 12,500 feet, seeking an easterly or westerly current, but without avail. We could not escape the southerly gale. Prudence, therefore, dictated a landing before nightfall. Landing in the high gale was both difficult and dangerous, and was not accomplished until we were all much bruised and scratched in the oak thicket Donaldson chose for our descent.

Thus the first voyage of the good airship *Barnum* ended at 6.07 p.m. on the farm of E. R. Young, nine miles north of Saratoga.

A year later the *Barnum* rose for the last time—from Chicago— and to this day the fate of the stanch craft and her brave captain remains an unsolved mystery.

CHAPTER 7

The Evolution of a Train Robber

Life was never dull in Grant County, New Mexico, in the early eighties. There was always something doing—usually something the average law-abiding, peace-loving citizen would have been glad enough to dispense with. To say that life then and there was insecure is to describe altogether too feebly a state of society and an environment wherein Death, in one violent form or another, was ever abroad, seldom long idle, always alert for victims.

When the San Carlos Apaches, under Victoria, Ju, or Geronimo, were not out gunning for the whites, the whites were usually out gunning for one another over some trivial difference. Everybody carried a gun and was more or less handy with it. Indeed, it was a downright bad plan to carry one unless you were handy. For with gunning— the game most played, if not precisely the most popular—everyone was supposed to be familiar with the rules and to know how to play; and in a game where every hand is sure to be "called," no one ever suspected another of being out on a sheer "bluff." Thus the coroner invariably declared it a case of suicide where one man drew a gun on another and failed to use it.

This highly explosive state of society was not due to the fact that there were few peaceable men in the country for there were many of them, men of character and education, honest, and as law-abiding as their peculiar environment would permit. Moreover, the percentage of professional "bad men"—and this was a profession then—was comparatively small. It was due rather to the fact that every one, no matter how peaceable his inclinations, was compelled to carry arms habitually for self-defence, for the Apaches were constantly raiding outside the towns, and white outlaws inside. And with any class of men who constantly carry arms, it always falls out that a weapon is the

98

arbiter of even those minor personal differences which in the older and more effete civilization of the East are settled with fists or in a petty court.

The prevailing local contempt for any man who was too timid to "put up a gun fight" when the etiquette of a situation demanded it, was expressed locally in the phrase that one "could take a corncob and a lightning bug and make him run himself to death trying to get away." It is clearly unnecessary to explain why the few men of this sort in the community did not occupy positions of any particular prominence. Their opinions did not seem to carry as much weight as those of other gentlemen who were known to be notably quick to draw and shoot.

I even recall many instances where the pistol entered into the pastimes of the community. One instance will stand telling:

A game of poker (rather a stiff one) had been going on for about a fortnight in the Red Light Saloon. The same group of men, five or six old friends, made up the game every day. All had varying success but one, who lost every day. And, come to think of it, his luck varied too, for some days he lost more than others. While he did not say much about his losings, it was observed that temper was not improving.

This sort of thing went on for thirteen days. The thirteenth day the loser happened to come in a little late, after the game was started. It also happened that on this particular day one of the players had brought in a friend, a stranger in the town, to join the game, When the loser came in, therefore, he was introduced to the stranger and sat down. A hand was dealt him. He started to play it, stopped, rapped on the table attention, and said:

"Boys, I want to make a personal explanation to this yere stranger. Stranger, this yere game is sure a tight wad for a smoothbore. I'm loser in it, an' a heavy one, for exactly thirteen days, and these boys all understand that the first son of a gun I find I can beat, I'm going to take a six-shooter an' make him play with me a week. Now, if you has no objections to my rules, you can draw cards."

Luckily for the stranger, perhaps, the thirteenth was as bad for the loser as its predecessors.

Outside the towns there were only three occupations in Grant County in those years, cattle ranching, mining and fighting Apaches, all of a sort to attract and hold none but the sturdiest types of real manhood, men inured to danger and reckless of it. In the early eighties no faint-heart came to Grant County unless he blundered in—and any such were soon burning the shortest trail out. These men were never better described in a line than when, years ago, at a banquet of California Forty-niners, Joaquin Miller, the poet of the Sierras, speaking of the splendid types the men of forty-nine represented, said:

"The cowards never started, and all the weak died on the road!"

Within the towns, also, there were only three occupations: first, supplying the cowmen and miners whatever they needed, merchandise wet and dry, law mundane and spiritual, for although neither court nor churches were working overtime, they were available for the few who had any use for them; second, gambling, at *monte*, poker, or *faro*; and, third, figuring how to slip through the next twenty-four hours without getting a heavier load of lead in one's system than could be conveniently carried, or how to stay happily half shot and yet avoid coming home on a shutter, unhappily shot, or, having an active enemy on hand, how best to "get" him.

Thus, while plainly the occupations of Grant County folk were somewhat limited in variety, in the matter of interest and excitement their games were wide open and the roof off.

Nor did all the perils to life in Grant County lurk within the burnished grooves of a gun barrel, according to certain local points of view, for always it is the most unusual that most alarms, as when one of my cowboys "allowed he'd go to town for a week," and was back on the ranch the evening of the second day. Asked why he was back so soon, he replied:

"Well, fellers, one o' them big depot water tanks burnt plumb up this mawnin', an' reckonin' whar that'd happen a feller might ketch fire anywhere in them little old town trails, I jes' nachally pulled my freight for camp!"

But a cowboy is the subject of this story—Kit Joy. His genus, and striking types of the genus, have been cleverly described, especially by Lewis and by Adams [1] (someday I hope to meet Andy) that I need say little of it here. Still, one of the cowboy's most notable and most admirable traits has not been emphasized so much as it deserves: I mean his downright reverence and respect for womanhood. No real cowboy ever wilfully insulted any woman, or lost a chance to resent any insult offered by another. Indeed, it was an article of the cowboy creed never broken, and all well knew it. So it happened that when one day a cowboy, in a crowded car of a train held up by bandits, was

---

1. *The Log of a Cowboy* by Andy Adams also published by Leonaur.

appealed to by an Eastern lady in the next seat,—

"Heavens! I have four hundred dollars in my purse which I cannot afford to lose; please, sir, tell me how I can hide it."

Instantly came the answer:

"Shucks! miss, stick it in yer sock; them fellers has nerve enough to hold up a train an' kill any feller that puts up a fight, but nary one o' them has nerve enough to go into a woman's sock after her bank roll!"

Kit Joy was a cowboy working on the X ranch on the Gila. He was a youngster little over twenty. It was said of him that he had left behind him in Texas more or less history not best written in black ink, but whether this was true or not I do not know. Certain it is that he was a reckless dare-devil, always foremost in the little amenities cowboys loved to indulge in when they came to town such as shooting out the lights in saloons and generally "shelling up the settlement,"—which meant taking a friendly shot at about everything that showed up on the streets. Nevertheless, Kit in the main was thoroughly good-natured and amiable.

Early in his career in Silver City it was observed that perhaps his most distinguishing trait was curiosity. Ultimately his curiosity got him into trouble, as it does most people who indulge it. His first display of curiosity in Silver was a very great surprise, even to those who knew him best. It was also a disappointment.

A tenderfoot, newly arrived, appeared on the streets one day in knickerbockers and stockings. Kit was in town and was observed watching the tenderfoot. To the average cowboy a silk top hat was like a red flag to a bull, so much like it in fact that the hat was usually lucky to escape with less than half a dozen holes through it. But here in these knee-breeches and stockings was something much more bizarre and exasperating than a top hat, from a cowboy's point of view. The effect on Kit was therefore closely watched by the bystanders.

No one fancied for a moment that Kit would do less than undertake to teach the tenderfoot "the cowboy's hornpipe," not a particularly graceful but a very quick step, which is danced most artistically when a bystander is shooting at the dancer's toes. Indeed, the ball was expected to open early. To every one's surprise and disappointment, it did not. Instead, Kit dropped in behind the tenderfoot and began to follow him about town—followed him for at least an hour. Everyone thought he was studying up some more unique penalty for the tenderfoot. But they were wrong, all wrong.

As a matter of fact. Kit was so far consumed with curiosity that he forgot everything else, forgot even to be angry. At last, when he could stand it no longer, he walked up to the tenderfoot, detained him gently by the sleeve and asked in a tone of real sympathy and concern: "Say, mistah! 'Fo' God, won't yo' mah let yo' wear long pants?"

Naturally the tenderfoot's indignation was aroused and expressed, but Kit's sympathies for a man condemned to such a juvenile costume were so far stirred that he took no notice of it.

Kit was a typical cowboy, industrious, faithful, uncomplaining, of the good old Southern Texas breed. In the saddle from daylight till dark, riding completely down to the last jump in them two or three horses a day, it never occurred to him even to growl when a stormy night, with thunder and lightning, prolonged his customary three-hour's turn at night guard round the herd to an all-night's vigil. He took it as a matter of course. And his rope and running iron were ever ready, and his weather eye alert for a chance to catch and decorate with the X brand any stray cattle that ventured within his range. This was a peculiar phase of cowboy character. While not himself profiting a penny by these inroads on neighbouring herds, he was never quite so happy as when he had added another maverick to the herd bearing his employer's brand, an increase always obtained at the expense of some of the neighbours.

One night on the Spring round-up, the day's work finished, supper eaten, the night horses caught and saddled, the herd in hand driven into a close circle and bedded down for the night in a little glade in the hills, Kit was standing first relief. The day's drive had been a heavy one, the herd was well grazed and watered in the late afternoon, the night was fine; and so the twelve hundred or fifteen hundred cattle in the herd were lying down quietly, giving no trouble to the night herders. Kit, therefore, was jogging slowly round the herd, softly jingling his spurs and humming some rude love song of the sultry sort cowboys never tire of repeating. The stillness of the night superinduced reflection. With naught to interrupt it, Kit's curiosity ran farther afield than usual.

Recently down at Lordsburg, with the outfit shipping a train load of beeves, he had seen the Overland Express empty its load of passengers for supper, a crowd of well-dressed men and women, the latter brilliant with the bright colours cowboys love and with glittering gems. Tonight he got to thinking about them.

Wherever did they all come from? However did they get so much money? Surely they must come from 'Frisco. No lesser place could possibly turn out such magnificence. Then Kit let his fancy wander off into crude cowboy visions of what 'Frisco might be like, for he had never seen a city.

"What a buster of a town 'Frisco must be!" Kit soliloquized. "Must have more'n a hundred saloons an' more slick gals than the X brand has heifers. What a lot o' fun a feller could have out thar! Only I reckon them gals wouldn't look at him more'n about onct unless he was well fixed for dough. Reckon they don't drink nothin' but wine out thar, nor eat nothin' but oysters. An' wine an' oysters costs money, oodles o' money! That's the worst of it! S'pose it'd take more'n a month's pay to git a feller out thar on the kiars, an' then about three months' pay to git to stay a week. Reckon that's jes' a little too rich for Kit's blood. But, jiminy! Wouldn't I like to have a good, big, fat bank roll an' go thar!"

Here was a crisis suddenly come in Kit's life, although he did not then realize it. It is entirely improbable he had ever before felt the want of money. His monthly pay of thirty-five dollars enabled him to sport a pearl-handled six-shooter and silver-mounted bridle bit and spurs, kept him well clothed, and gave him an occasional spree in town. What more could any reasonable cowboy ask?

But tonight the very elements and all nature were against him. Even a light dash of rain to rouse the sleeping herd, or a hungry cow straying out into the darkness, would have been sufficient to divert and probably save him; but nothing happened. The night continued fine. The herd slept on. And Kit was thus left an easy prey, since covetousness had come to aid curiosity in compassing his ruin.

"A bank roll! A big, fat, full-grown, long-horned, four-year-old roll! *That's* what a feller wants to do 'Frisco right. Nothin' less. But whar's it comin' from, an' when? S'pose I brands a few mavericks an' gits a start on my own? No use, Kit; that's too slow! Time you got a proper roll you'd be so old the skeeters wouldn't even bite you, to say nothin' of a gal a-kissin' of you. 'Pears like you ain't liable to git thar very quick, Kit, 'less you rustles mighty peart somewhar. Talkin' of rustlin', what's the matter with that anyway?"

A cold glitter came in Kit's light blue eyes. The muscles of his lean, square jaws worked nervously. His right hand dropped caressingly on the handle of his pistol.

"That's the proper caper, Kit. Why didn't you think of it before? Rustle, damn you, an', ef you're any good, mebbe so you can git to

'Frisco afore frost comes, or anywhere else you likes. Rustle! By jiminy, I've got it; I'll jes' stand up that thar Overland Express. Them fellers what rides on it's got more'n they've got any sort o' use for. What's the matter with makin' 'em whack up with a feller! 'Course they'll kick, an' thar'll be a whole passle o' marshals an' sheriffs out after you, but what o' that? Reckon Old Blue'll carry you out o' range. He's the longest-winded chunk o' horse meat in these parts. Then you'll have to stay out strictly on the scout fer a few weeks, till they gits tired o' huntin' of you, so you can slip out o' this yere neck o' woods 'thout leavin' a trail.

"An' Lord! but won't it be fun! 'Bout as much fun, I reckon, as doin' 'Frisco. Won't them tenderfeet beller when they hears the guns a-crackin' an' the boys a-yellin'! Le' see; wonder who I'd better take along?"

Scruples? Kit had none. Bred and raised a merry freebooter on the unbranded spoils of the cattle range, it was no long step from stealing a maverick to holding up a train.

With a man of perhaps any other class, a plan to engage in a new business enterprise of so much greater magnitude than any of those he had been accustomed to would have been made the subject of long consideration. Not so with Kit. Cowboy life compels a man to think quickly, and often to act quicker than he finds it convenient to think. The hand skilled to catch the one possible instant when the wide, circling loop of the lariat may be successfully thrown, and the eye and finger trained to accurate snap-shooting, do not well go with a mind likely to be long in reaching a resolution or slow to execute one.

So Kit at once began to cast about for two or three of the right sort of boys to join him. Three were quickly chosen out of his own and a neighbouring outfit. They were Mitch Lee and Taggart, two white cowboys of his own type and temper, and George Cleveland, a negro, known as a desperate fellow, game for anything. It needed no great argument to secure the co-operation of these men. A mere tip of the lark and the loot to be had was enough.

The boys saw their respective bosses. They "allowed they'd lay off for a few days and go to town." So they were paid off, slung their Winchesters on their saddles, mounted their favourite horses, and rode away. They met in Silver City, coming in singly. There they purchased a few provisions. Then they separated and rode singly out of town, to rendezvous at a certain point on the Miembres River.

The point of attack chosen was the little station of Gage (tended by a lone operator), on the Southern Pacific Railway west of Deming, a point then reached by the west-bound express at twilight. The evening of the second day after leaving the Gila, Kit and his three *compadres* rode into Gage. One or two significant passes with a six-shooter hypnotized the station agent into a docile tool. A dim red light glimmered away off in the east. As the minutes passed, it grew and brightened fast. Then a faint, confused murmur came singing over the rails to the ears of the waiting bandits. The light brightened and grew until it looked like a great dull red sun, and then the thunder of the train was heard.

Time for action had come!

The agent was made to signal the engineer to stop. With lever reversed and air brakes on, the train was nearly stopped when the engine reached the station. But seeing the agent surrounded by a group of armed men, the engineer shut off the air and sought to throw his throttle open. His purpose discovered, a quick snapshot from Mitch Lee laid him dead, and, springing into the cab, Mitch soon persuaded the fireman to stop the train.

Instantly a fusillade of pistol shots and a mad chorus of shrill cowboy yells broke out, that terrorized train crew and passengers into docility.

Within fifteen minutes the express car was sacked, the postal car gutted, the passengers were laid under unwilling contribution, and Kit and his pals were riding northward into the night, heavily loaded with loot. Riding at great speed due north, the party soon reached the main travelled road up the Miembres, in whose loose drifting sands they knew their trail could not be picked up. Still forcing the pace, they reached the rough hill-country east of Silver early in the night, *cached* their plunder safely, and a little after midnight were carelessly bucking a *monte* game in a Silver City saloon. The next afternoon they quietly rode out of town and joined their respective outfits, to wait until the excitement should blow over.

Of course the telegraph soon started the hue and cry. Officers from Silver, Deming, and Lordsburg were soon on the ground, led by Harvey Whitehill, the famous old sheriff of Grant County. But of clue there was none. Naturally the station agent had come safely out of his trance, but with that absence of memory of what had happened characteristic of the hypnotized. The trail disappeared in the sands of the Miembres road. Shrewd old Harvey Whitehill was at his wits' end.

Many days passed in fruitless search. At last, riding one day across

"WHITEHILL FOUND A FRAGMENT OF A KANSAS NEWSPAPER"

the plain at some distance from the line of flight north from Gage, Whitehill found a fragment of a Kansas newspaper. As soon as he saw it he remembered that a certain merchant of Silver came from the Kansas town where this paper was published. Hurrying back to Silver, Whitehill saw the merchant, who identified the paper and said that he undoubtedly was its only subscriber in Silver. Asked if he had given a copy to any one, he finally recalled that some time before, about the period of the robbery, he had wrapped in a piece this newspaper some provisions he had sold to a negro named Cleveland and a white man he did not know.

Here was the clue, and Whitehill was quick to follow it. Meeting a negro on the street, he pretended to want to hire a cook. The negro had a job. Well, did he not know someone else? By the way, where was George Cleveland?

"Oh, boss, he done left de Gila dis week an' gone ober to Socorro," was the answer.

Two days later Whitehill found Cleveland in a Socorro restaurant, got the "drop" on him, told him his pals were arrested and had confessed that they were in the robbery, but that he, Cleveland, had killed Engineer Webster. This brought the whole story.

"'Foh God, boss, I nebber killed dat engineer. Mitch Lee done it, an' him an' Taggart an' Kit Joy, dey done lied to you outrageous."

Within a few days, caught singly, in ignorance of Cleveland's arrest, and taken completely by surprise, Joy, Taggart, and Lee were captured on the Gila and jailed, along with Cleveland, at Silver City, held to await the action of the next grand jury.

But strong walls did not a prison make adequate hold these men. Before many weeks passed, an escape was planned and executed. Two other prisoners, one a man wanted in Arizona, and the other a Mexican horse-thief, were allowed to participate in the outbreak.

Taken unawares, their guard was seized and bound with little difficulty. Quickly arming themselves in the jail office, these six desperate men dashed out of the jail and into a neighbouring livery stable, seized horses, mounted, and rode madly out of town, firing at everyone in sight. In Silver in those days no gentleman's trousers fitted comfortably without a pistol stuck in the waistband. Therefore, the flying desperadoes received as hot a fire as they sent. By this fire Cleveland's horse was killed before they got out of town, but one of his pals stopped and picked him up.

Instantly the town was in an uproar of excitement. Everyone knew that the capture of these men meant a fight to the death. As usual in such emergencies, there were more talkers than fighters. Nevertheless, six men were in pursuit as soon as they could saddle and mount. The first to start was the driver of an express wagon, a man named Jackson, who cut his horse loose from the traces, mounted bareback, and flew out of town only a few hundred yards behind the prisoners. Six others, led by Charlie Shannon and La Fer, were not far behind Jackson. The men of this party were greatly surprised to find that a Boston boy of twenty, a tenderfoot lately come to town, who had scarcely ever ridden a horse or fired a rifle, was among their number, well mounted and armed—a man with a line of ancestry worthwhile, and himself a worthy survival of the best of it.

The chase was hot. Jackson was well in advance, engaging the fugitives with his pistol, while the fugitives were returning the fire and throwing up puffs of dust all about Jackson. Behind spurred Shannon and his party.

At length the pursuit gained. Five miles out of Silver, in the Piñon Hills to the northwest, too close pressed to run farther, the fugitives sprang from their horses and ran into a low post oak thicket covering about two acres, where, crouching, they could not be seen. The six pursuers sent back a man to guide the sheriff's party and hasten reinforcements, and began shelling the thicket and surrounding it. A few minutes later Whitehill rode up with seven more men, and the thicket was effectually surrounded. To the surprise of every one, a hot fire poured into the thicket failed to bring a single answering shot. Whitehill was no man to waste ammunition on such chance firing, so he ordered a charge. His little command rode into and through the thicket at full speed, only to find their quarry gone, gone all save one. The Mexican lay dead, shot through the head! Kit's party had dashed through the thicket without stopping, on to another, and their trail was shortly found leading up a rugged *cañon* of the Pinos Altos Range.

Whitehill divided his party. Three men followed up the bottom of the *cañon* on foot, five mounted flankers were thrown out on either side. At last, high up the *cañon*, Kit's party was found at bay, lying in some thick underbrush. It was a desperate position to attack, but the pursuers did not hesitate. Dismounting, they advanced on foot with rifles cocked, but with all the caution of a hunter trailing a wounded grizzly. The negro opened the ball at barely twenty yards' range with a shot that drove a hole through the Boston boy's hat. Dropping at first with surprise, for he had not seen the negro till the instant he rose to fire, the Boston boy returned a quick shot that happened to hit the negro just above the centre of the forehead and rolled him over dead.

Approaching from another direction, Shannon was first to draw Taggart's file. Taggart was lying hidden in the brush; Shannon standing out in the open. Shot after shot they exchanged, until presently a ball struck the earth in front of Taggart's face and filled his eyes full of gravel and sand. Blinded for the time, he called for quarter, and came out of the brush with his hands up and another man with him. Asked for his pistol, Taggart replied:

"Damn you, that's empty, or I'd be shooting yet."

Meantime, Whitehill was engaging Mitch Lee. In a few minutes, shot through and helpless, Lee surrendered.

It was quick, hot work!

All but Kit were now killed or captured. He had been separated from his party, and La Fer was seen trailing him on a neighbouring hillside.

At this juncture the sheriff detailed Shannon to return to town and get a wagon to bring in the dead and wounded, while he started to join La Fer in pursuit of Kit.

An hour later, as Shannon was leaving town with a wagon to return to the scene of the fight, a mob of men, led by a shyster lawyer, joined him and swore they proposed to lynch the prisoners. This was too much for Shannon's sense of frontier proprieties. So, rising in his wagon, he made a brief but effective speech.

"Boys, none of our men are hurt, although it is no fault of our prisoners. A dozen of us have gone out and risked our lives to capture these men. You men have not seen fit, for what motives we will not discuss, to help us. Now, I tell you right here that any who want can come, but the first man to raise a hand against a prisoner I'll kill."

Shannon's return escort was small.

But once more back in the hills of the Pinos Altos, Shannon found a storm raised he could not quell, even if his own sympathies had not drifted with it when he learned its cause. His friend La Fer lay dead, filled full of buckshot by Kit before Whitehill's reinforcements had reached him, while Kit had slipped away through the underbrush, over rocks that left no trail.

La Fer's death maddened his friends. There was little discussion. Only one opinion prevailed. Taggart and Lee must die.

Nothing was known of the prisoner wanted in Arizona, so he was spared.

Taggart and Lee were put in the wagon, the former tightly bound, the latter helpless from his wound. Short rope halters barely five feet long were stripped from the horses, knotted round the prisoners' necks, and fastened to the limb of a juniper tree. Taggart climbed to the high wagon seat, took a header and broke his neck. The wagon was then pulled away and Lee strangled.

With Cleveland, Lee, and Taggart dead, Engineer Webster and La Fer were fairly well avenged. But Kit was still out, known as the leader and the man who shot La Fer, and for days the hills were full of men hunting him. Hiding in the rugged, thickly timbered hills of the Gila, taking needed food at night, at the muzzle of his gun, from some isolated ranch, he was hard to capture.

Had Kit chosen to mount himself and ride out of the country, he might have escaped for good. But this he would not do. Dominated still by the fatal curiosity and covetousness that first possessed him, later mastered him, and then drove him into crime, bound to repossess himself of his hidden treasure and go out to see the world, Kit would not leave the Gila. He was alone, unaided, with no man left his friend, with all men on the alert to capture or to kill him, the unequal contest nevertheless lasted for many weeks.

There was only one man Kit at all trusted, a "nester" (small ranchman) named Racketty Smith. One day, looking out from a leafy thicket in which he lay hid, saw Racketty going along the road. A lonely outcast, craving the sound of a human voice, believing Racketty at least neutral, Kit hailed him and approached. As he drew near, Racketty covered him with his rifle and ordered him to surrender. Surprised, taken entirely unawares, Kit started to jump for cover, when Racketty fired, shattered his right leg and brought him to earth. To spring upon and disarm Kit was the work of an instant.

Kit was sentenced to imprisonment at Santa Fe. A few years ago, having gained three years by good behaviour, Kit was released, after having served fourteen years.

However Kit may still hanker for "a big, fat, four-year-old, long-horned bank roll," and whatever may be his curiosity to "do 'Frisco proper," it is not likely he will make any more history as a train robber, for at heart Kit was always a better "good man" than "bad man."

CHAPTER 8

Circus Day at Mancos

Cowboys were seldom respecters of the feelings of their fellows. Few topics were so sacred or incidents so grave they were not made the subject of the rawest jests. Leading a life of such stirring adventure that few days passed without some more or less serious mishap, reckless of life, unheedful alike of time and eternity, they made the smallest trifles and the biggest tragedies the subjects of chaff and badinage till the next diverting occurrence. But to the Cross Cañon outfit Mat Barlow's love for Netty Nevins was so obviously a downright worship, an all-absorbing, dominating cult, that, in a way, and all unknown to her, she became the nearest thing to a religion the Cross Cañonites ever had.

Eight years before Mat had come among them a green tenderfoot from a South Missouri village, picked up in Durango by Tom McTigh, the foreman, on a glint of the eye and set of the jaw that suggested workable material. Nor was McTigh mistaken. Mat took to range work like a duck to water. Within a year he could rope and tie a mossback with the best, and in scraps with Mancos Jim's Pah-Ute horse raiders had proved himself as careless a dare-devil as the oldest and toughest trigger-twitcher of the lot.

But persuade and cajole as much as they liked, none of the outfit were ever able to induce Mat to pursue his education as a cowboy beyond the details incident to work and frolic on the open range. Old past-masters in the classics of cowboy town deportment, expert light shooters, *monte* players, dance-hall beaux, elbow-crookers, and red-eye riot-starters laboured faithfully with Mat, but, all to no purpose. To town with them he went, but with them in their debauches he never joined; indeed as a rule he even refused to discuss such incidents with them academically. Thus he delicately but plainly made it known to the outfit that he proposed to keep his mind as clean as his conduct.

Such a curiosity as Mat was naturally closely studied. The combined intelligence of the outfit was trained upon him, for some time without result. He was the knottiest puzzle that ever hit Cross Cañon. At first he was suspected of religious scruples and nicknamed "Circuit Rider." But presently it became apparent that he owned ability and will to curse a fighting outlaw bronco till the burning desert air felt chill, and it became plain he feared God as little as man. Mat had joined the outfit in the Autumn, when for several weeks it was on the jump; first gathering and shipping beeves, then branding calves, lastly moving the herd down to its Winter range on the San Juan. Throughout this period Cross Cañon's puzzle remained hopeless; but the very first evening after the outfit went into Winter quarters at the home ranch, the puzzle was solved.

Ranch mails were always small, no matter how infrequent their coming or how large the outfit. The owner's business involved little correspondence, the boys' sentiments inspired less. Few with close home-ties exiled themselves on the range. Many were "on the scout" from the scene of some remote shooting scrape and known by no other than a nickname. For most of them such was the rarity of letters that often have I seen a cowboy turning and studying an unopened envelope for a half-day or more, wondering whoever it was from and guessing whatever its contents could be. Thus it was one of the great sensations of the season for McTigh and his red-sashers, when the ranch cook produced five letters for Circuit Rider, all addressed in the same neat feminine hand, all bearing the same postmark. And when, while the rest were washing for supper, disposing of war sacks, or "making down" blankets, Mat squatted in the chimney corner to read his letters, Lee Skeats impressively whispered to Priest:

"Ben, I jest nachally hope never to cock another gun ef that thar little ol' Circuit hain't got a gal that's stuck to him tighter'n a tick makin' a gotch ear, or that ain't got airy damn thing to do to hum but write letters. Size o' them five he's got must 'a kept her settin' up nights to make 'em ever since Circuit jumped the hum reservation. Did you *ever* hear of a feller gettin' five letters from a gal to wonst?"

"I shore never did," answered Ben; "Circuit must 'a been 'prentice to some big Medicine Man back among his tribe and have a bagful o' hoodoos hid out somewhere. He ain't so damn hijus to look at, but he shore never knocked no gal plum loco that away with his p'rsn'l beauty. Must be some sort o' Injun medicine he works."

"Ca'n't be from his mother," cogitated Lee. "Writin' ain't trembly none—looks like it was writ by a school-marm, an' a lally-cooler at that. Circuit will have to git one o' them pianer-like writin' makers and keep poundin' it on the back till it hollers, ef he allows to lope close up in that gal's writin' class.

"Lord! but won't thar be fun for us all Winter he'pin' him 'tend to his correspondence!

"Let's you an' me slip round and tip off the outfit to shet up till after supper, an' then all be ready with a hot line o' useful hints 'bout his answerin' her."

Ben joyously fell in with Lee's plan. The tips were quickly passed round. But none of the hints were ever given, not a single one. A facer lay ahead of them beside which the mere receipt of the five letters was nothing. To be sure, the letters were the greatest sensation the outfit had enjoyed since they stood off successfully two troops of U. S. Cavalry, come to arrest them for killing twenty marauding Utes. But what soon followed filled them with an astonishment that stilled their mischievous tongues, stirred sentiments long dormant, and ultimately, in a measure, tuned their own heart-strings into chord with the sweet melody ringing over Circuit's own.

Supper was called, and upon it the outfit fell—all but Circuit. They attacked it wolf-fashion according to their habit, bolting the steaming food in a silence absolute but for the crunching of jaws and the shrill hiss of sipped coffee. The meal was half over before Circuit, the last letter finished, tucked his five treasures inside his shirt, stepped over the bench to a vacant place at the table, and hastily swallowed a light meal; in fact he rose while the rest were still busy gorging themselves. And before Lee or the others were ready to launch at Circuit any shafts of their rude wit, his manoeuvres struck them dumb with curiosity.

Having hurried from the table direct to his bunk, Circuit was observed delving in the depths of his war sack, out of which he produced a set of clean under-clothing, complete from shirt to socks, and a razor. Besides these he carefully laid out his best suit of store clothes, and from beneath the "heading" of the bunk he pulled a new pair of boots. All this was done with a rapidity and method that evinced some set purpose which the outfit could not fathom, a purpose become the more puzzling when, five minutes later, Circuit returned from the kitchen bearing the cook's wash-tub and a pail of warm water. The tub he deposited and filled in an obscure corner of the bunkroom, and shortly thereafter was stripped to the buff, laboriously bathing himself. The bath finished, Circuit carefully shaved, combed his hair, and dressed himself in his cleanest and best.

While he was dressing, Bill Ball caught breath enough to whisper to Lee: "By cripes! I've got it. Circuit's got a hunch some feller's tryin' to rope an' hobble his gal, an' he's goin' to ask Tom for his time, fork a cayuse, an' hit a lope for a railroad that'll take him to whatever little ol' humanyville his gal lives at."

"Lope hell," answered Lee; "it's a run he's goin' to hit, with one spur in the shoulder an' th' other in th' flank. Why, th' way he's throwin' that whisker-cutter at his face, he's plumb shore to dewlap and wattle his fool self till you could spot him in airy herd o' humans as fer as you could see him."

But Bill's guess proved wide of the mark.

As soon as Circuit's dressing was finished and he had received assurance from the angular fragment of mirror nailed above the wash-basin that his hair was smoothly combed and a new neckerchief neatly knotted, he produced paper and an envelope from his war sack, seated himself at the end of the long dinner-table, farthest from the fireplace, lighted a fresh candle, spread out his five treasures, carefully sharpened a stub pencil, and duly set its lead end a-soak in his mouth, preparatory to the composition of a letter. The surprise was complete. Such painstaking preparation and elaborate costuming for the mere writing of a letter none present—or absent, for that matter—had ever heard of. But it was all so obviously eloquent of a most tender respect for his correspondent that boisterous voices were hushed, and for at least a quarter of an hour the Cross Cañonites sat covertly watching the puckered brows, drawn mouth, and awkwardly crawling pencil of the writer.

Presently Lee gently nudged Ball and passed a wink to the rest; then all rose and softly tiptoed their way to the kitchen.

Comfortably squatted on his heels before the cook's fireplace, Lee quietly observed: "Fellers, I allow it's up to us to hold a inquest on th' remains o' my idee about stringin' Circuit over that thar gal o' his'n. I moves that th' idee's done died a-bornin', an' that we bury her. All that agrees, say so; any agin it, say so, 'n' then git their guns an' come outside."

There were no dissenting votes. Lee's motion was unanimously carried.

"Lee's plumb right," whispered McTigh; "that kid's got it harder an' worse than airy feller I ever heerd tell of, too hard for us to lite in

114

stringin' him 'bout it. Never had no gal myself; leastways, no good one; been allus like a old buffalo bull whipped out o' th' herd, sorta flockin' by my lonesome, an'—an'—" with a husky catch of the voice, "an' that thar kid 'minds me I must a' been missin' a *hell* of a lot hit 'pears to me I wouldn't have no great trouble gittin' to like."

Then for a time there was silence in the kitchen.

Crouching over his pots, the black cook stared in surprised inquiry at the semicircle of grim bronzed faces, now dimly lit by the flickering embers and then for a moment sharply outlined by the flash of a cigarette deeply inhaled by nervous lips. The situation was tense. In each man emotions long dormant, or perhaps by some never before experienced, were tumultuously surging; surging the more tumultuously for their long dormancy or first recognition. Presently in a low, hoarse voice that scarcely carried round the semicircle, Chillili Jim spoke:

"Fellers, Circuit shore 'minds me pow'ful strong o' my ol' mammy. She was monstrous lovin' to we-uns; an' th' way she scrubbed an' fixed up my ol' pa when he comes home from the break-up o' Terry's Rangers, with his ol' carcass 'bout as full o' rents an' holes as his ragged gray war clothes! Allus have tho't ef I could git to find a gal stuck on me like mammy on pa, I'd drop my rope on her, throw her into th' home ranch pasture, an' nail up th' gate fer keeps."

"'Minds me o' goin' to meetin' when I was a six-year-old," mused Mancos Mitch; "when Circuit's pencil got to smokin' over th' paper an' we-uns got so dedburned still, 'peared to me like I was back in th' little ol' meetin'-house in th' mosquito clearin', on th' banks o' th' Lee in ol' Uvalde County. Th' air got that quar sort o' dead smell 'ligion allus 'pears to give to meetin'-houses, a' I could hear th' ol' pa'son a-tellin' us how it's th' lovinest that allus gits th' longest end o' th' rope o' life. Hits me now that ther ol' sky scout was 'bout right. Feller cain't possibly keep busy *all* th' love in his system, workin' it off on nothing but a pet hoss or gun; thar's allus a hell of a lot you didn't know you had comes oozin' out when a proper piece o' calico lets you next."

"Boys," cut in Bill Ball, the dean of the outfit's shooters-up of town and shooters-out of dance-hall lights; "boys, I allow it 's up to me to 'pologize to Circuit. Ef I wasn't such a damned o'nery kiyote I'd o' caught on befo'. But I hain't been runnin' with th' drags o' th' she herd so long that I can't 'preciate th' feelin's o' a feller that's got a good gal stuck on him, like Circuit. Ef I had one, you-all kin gamble yer *alce* all bets would be off with them painted dance-hall beer jerkers, an' it would be out in th' brush fo' me while th' corks was poppin', gals cussin', red-eye flowin', an' chips rattlin'. That thar little ol' kid has my 'spects, an' ef airy o' th' Blue Mountain outfit tries to string him 'bout not runnin' with them oreide propositions, I'll hand 'em lead till my belt's empty."

Ensued a long silence; at length, by common consent the inquest was adjourned, and the members of the jury returned to the bunk-room, quiet and solemn as men entering a death chamber. There at the table before the guttering candle still sat Circuit, his hair now badly tousled, his upper lip blackened with pencil lead, his brows more deeply puckered, his entire underlip apparently swallowed, the table littered with rudely scrawled sheets.

Slipping softly to their respective bunks, the boys peeled and climbed into their blankets. And there they all lay, wide-awake but silent, for an hour or two, some watching Circuit curiously, some enviously, others staring fixedly into the dying fire until from its dull-glowing embers there rose for some visions of bare-footed, nut-brown, fustian-clad maids, and for others the finer lines of silk and lace draped figures, now long since passed forever out of their lives. Those longest awake were privileged to witness Circuit's final offering at the shrine of his love.

His letter finished, enclosed, addressed, and stamped, he kissed it and laid it aside, apparently all unconscious of the presence of his mates, as he had been since beginning his letter. Then he drew from beneath his shirt something none of them had seen before, a buck-skin bag, out of which he pulled a fat blank memorandum book, *into which he proceeded to copy, in as small a hand as he could write, every line of his sweetheart's letters.* Later they learned that this bag and its contents never left Circuit's body, nestled always over his heart, suspended by a buckskin thong!

Out of the close intimacies cow-camp life promotes, it was not long before the well-nigh overmastering curiosity of the outfit was satisfied. They learned how the "little ol' blue-eyed sorrel top," as Bill Ball had christened her, had vowed to wait faithfully till Circuit could earn and save enough to make them a home, and how Circuit had sworn to look into no woman's eyes till he could again look into hers. Before many months had passed, Circuit's regular weekly letter to Netty—regular when on the ranch—and the ceremonial purification and personal decking that preceded it, had become for the Cross Cañon outfit a public ceremony all studiously observed. None were ever too tired, none too grumpy, to wash, shave, and "slick up" of letter nights, scrupulously as Moslems bathe their feet before approaching the shrine of Mahomet and still as Moslems before their shrine all sat about the bunk-room while Circuit wrote his letter and copied Netty's last. Indeed, more than one well-started wild town orgy was stopped short by one of the boys remarking: "Cut it, you kiyotes! Netty wouldn't like it!"

And thus the months rolled on till they stacked up into years, but the interchange of letters never ceased and the burden of Circuit's buckskin bag grew heavier.

Twice Circuit ventured a financial *coup*, and both times lost—invested his savings in horses, losing one band to Arizona rustlers, and the other to Mancos Jim's Pah-Utes. After the last experience he took no further chances and settled down to the slow but sure plan of hoarding his wages.

Come the Fall of the eighth year of his exile from Netty, Circuit had accumulated two thousand dollars, and it was unanimously voted by the Cross Cañon outfit, gathered in solemn conclave at Circuit's request, that he might venture to return to claim her. And before the conclave was adjourned, Lee Skeats, the chairman, remarked: "Circuit, ef Netty shows airy sign o' balkin' at th' size o' your bank roll, you kin jes' tell her that thar 's a bunch out here in Cross Cañon that's been lovin' her sort o' by proxy, that'll chip into your matrimonial play, plumb double the size o' your stack, jest fo' th' hono' o' meetin' up wi' her an' th' pleasure o' seein' their pardner hitched."

The season's work done and the herd turned loose on its Winter range on the San Juan, the outfit decided to escort Circuit into Mancos and there celebrate his coming nuptials. For them the one hundred and seventy intervening miles of alternating *cañon* and *mesa*, much of the journey over trails deadly dangerous for any creature less sure-footed than a goat, was no more than a pleasant *pasear*. Thus it was barely high noon of the third day when the thirty Cross Cañonites reached their destination.

Deep down in a mighty gorge, nestled beside the stream that gave its name alike to *cañon* and to town, Mancos stewed contentedly in a temperature that would try the strength and temper of any unaccustomed to the climate of southwestern Colorado. Framed in Franciscan-gray sage brush, itself gray as the sage with the dust of pounding hoofs and rushing whirlwinds, at a little distance Mancos looked like an aggregation of dead ash heaps, save where, here and there, dabs of faded paint lent a semblance of patches of dying embers.

While raw, uninviting, and even melancholy in its every aspect, for the scattered denizens of a vast region round about Mancos's principal street was the local Great White Way that furnished all the fun and frolic most of them ever knew. To it flocked miners from their dusky, pine-clad gorges in the north, grangers from the then new farming settlement in the Montezuma Valley, cowboys from Blue Mountain, the Dolores, and the San Juan; Navajos from Chillili, Utes from their reservation—a motley lot burning with untamed elemental passions that called for pleasure "straight."

Joyously descending upon the town at a breakneck lope before a following high wind that completely shrouded them in clouds of dust, it was not until they pulled up before their favourite feed corral that the outfit learned that Mancos was revelling in quite the reddest red-letter day of its existence, the day of its first visitation by a circus—and also its last for many a year thereafter.

In the eighties Mancos was forty miles from the nearest railway, but news of the reckless extravagances of its visiting miners and cowboys tempted Fells Brothers'"Greatest Aggregation on Earth of Ring Artists and Monsters" to visit it. Dusted and costumed outside of town, down the main street of Mancos the circus bravely paraded that morning, its red enamelled paint and gilt, its many-tinted tights and spangles, making a perfect riot of brilliant colours over the prevailing dull gray of valley and town.

Streets, stores, saloons, and dance halls were swarming with the outpouring of the ranches and the mines, men who drank abundantly but in the main a rollicking, good-natured lot.

While the Cross Cañonites were liquoring at the Fashion Bar (Circuit drinking *sarsaparilla*), Lame Johny, the barkeeper, remarked: "You-uns missed it a lot, not seein' the pr'cesh. She were a ring-tailed tooter for fair, with the damnedest biggest noise-makin' band you ever heard, an' th' p'rformers wearin' more pr'tys than I ever allowed was made. An' say, they've got a gal in th' bunch, rider I reckon, that's jest that damned good to look at it *hurts*. Damned ef I kin git her outen my eyes yet. Say, she's shore prittier than airy red wagon in th' show built like a quarter horse, got eyes like a doe, and a sorrel mane she could hide in. She 's sure a *chile con carne* proposition, if I ever see one."

"Huh!" grunted Lee; "may be a good-looker, but I'll gamble she ain't in it with our Sorrel-top; hey, boys? Here 's to *our* Sorrel-top, fellers, an' th' day Circuit prances into Mancos wi' her."

Several who tried to drink and cheer at the same time lost much of their liquor, but none of their enthusiasm. After dinner at Charpiot's, a wretched counterfeit of the splendid old Denver restaurant of that name, the Cross Cañonites joined the throng streaming toward the circus.

For his sobriety designated treasurer of the outfit for the day and night, Circuit marched up to the ticket wagon, passed in a hundred dollar bill and asked for thirty tickets. The tickets and change were promptly handed him. On the first count the change appeared to be correct, but on a recount Circuit found the ticket-seller had cunningly folded one twenty double, so that it appeared as two bills instead of one. Turning immediately to the ticket-seller, Circuit showed the deception and demanded correction.

"Change was right; you can't dope and roll me; gwan!" growled the ticket-agent.

"But it's plumb wrong, an' you can't rob me none, you kiyote," answered Circuit; "hand out another twenty, and do it sudden!"

"Chase yourself to hell, you bow-legged hold-up," threatened the ticket-seller.

When, a moment later, the ticket man plunged out of the door of his wagon wildly yelling for his clan, it was with eyes flooding with blood from a gash in his forehead due to a resentful tap from the barrel of Circuit's gun.

Almost in an instant pandemonium reigned and a massacre was imminent. Stalwart canvasmen rushed to their chief's call till Circuit's bunch were outnumbered three to one by tough trained battlers on many a tented field, armed with hand weapons of all sorts. Victors these men usually were over the town roughs it was customarily theirs to handle; but here before them was a bunch not to be trifled with, a quiet group of thirty bronzed faces, some grinning with the anticipated joy of the combat they loved, some grim as death itself, each affectionately twirling a gleaming gun. One overt act on the part of the circus men, and down they would go like ninepins and they knew it—knew it so well that, within two minutes after they had assembled, all dodged into and lost themselves in the throng of onlookers like rabbits darting into their warrens.

"Mighty pore 'pology for real men, them elephant-busters," disgustedly observed Bill Ball. "Come fellers, le's go in."

"Nix for me," spoke up Circuit; "I'm that hot in the collar over him tryin' to rob me I've got no use for their old show. You-all go in, an' I'll go down to Chapps' and fix my traps to hit the trail for the railroad in the mornin'.'"

On the crest of a jutting bastion of the lofty escarpment that formed the west wall of the *cañon*, the sun lingered for a good-night kiss of the eastern cliffs which it loved to paint every evening with all the brilliant colours of the spectrum; it lingered over loving memories of ancient days when every niche of the Mancos cliffs held its little bronze-hued line of primitive worshippers, old and young, devout, prostrate, fearful of their Red God's nightly absences, suppliant of his return and continued largess; over memories of ceremonials and pastimes barbaric in their elemental violence, but none more primitively savage than the new moon looked down upon an hour later.

Supper over, on motion of Lee Skeats the Cross Cañonites had adjourned to the feed corral and gone into executive session.

Lee called the meeting to order.

"Fellers," he said, "that dod-burned show makes my back tired. A few geezers an' gals flipfloopin' in swings an' a bunch o' dead ones on ol' broad-backed work hosses that calls theirselves riders! Shucks! thar hain't one o' th' lot could sit a real twister long enough to git his seat warm; about th' second jump would have 'em clawin' sand.

"Only thing in their hull circus wo'th lookin' at is that red-maned gal, an' she looks that sweet an' innercent she don't 'pear to rightly belong in that thar bare-legged bunch o' she dido-cutters. They-all must 'a mavericked her recent. Looks like a pr'ty ripe red apple among a lot o' rotten ones.

"Hated like hell to see her thar, specially with next to nothin' on, fer somehow I couldn't help her 'mindin' me o' our Sorrel-top. Reckon ef we busted up their damn show, that gal'd git to stay a while in a decent woman's sort o' clothes. What say, shall we bust her!"

"Fer one, I sits in an' draw cards in your play cheerful," promptly responded Bill Ball; "kind o' hurt me too to see Reddy thar. An' then them animiles hain't gittin' no squar' deal. Never did believe in cagin' animiles more'n men. Ef they need it bad, kill 'em; ef they don't, give 'em a run fo' their money, way ol' Mahster meant 'em to have when He made 'em. Let's all saddle up, ride down thar, tie onto their tents, an' pull 'em down, an' then bust open them cages an' give every dod-blamed animile th' liberty I allows he loves same as humans! An' then, jest to make sure she's a good job, le's whoop all their hosses ove' to th' Dolores an' scatter 'em through th' piñons!"

This motion was unanimously carried, even Circuit cheerfully consenting, from memories of the outrage attempted upon him earlier in the day. Ten minutes later the outfit charged down upon the circus at top speed, arriving among the first comers for the evening performance. Flaming oil torches lit the scene, making it bright almost as day.

By united action, thirty lariats were quickly looped round guy ropes and snubbed to saddle horns, and then, incited by simultaneous spur digs and yells, thirty fractious broncos bounded away from the tent, fetching it down in sheets and ribbons, ropes popping like pistols, the rent canvas shrieking like a creature in pain, startled animals threshing about their cages and crying their alarm. Cowboys were never slow at anything they undertook. In three minutes more the side shows were tentless, the dwarfs trying to swarm up the giant's sturdy legs to safety or to hide among the adipose wrinkles of the fat lady, and the outfit tackled the cages.

In another three minutes the elephant, with a sociable shot through his off ear to make sure he should not tarry, was thundering down Mancos's main street, trumpeting at every jump, followed by the lion, the great tuft of hair at the end of his tail converted, by a happy thought of Lee Skeats, into a brightly blazing torch that, so long as the fuel lasted, lighted the shortest cut to freedom for his escaping mates—for the lion hit as close a bee-line as possible trying to outrun his own tail. For the outfit, it was the lark of their lives. Crashing pistol shots and ringing yells bore practical testimony to their joy. But they were not to have it entirely their own way.

Just as they were all balled up before the rhinoceros, staggered a bit by his great bulk and threatening horn, out upon them charged a body of canvasmen, all the manager could contrive to rally, for a desperate effort to stop the damage and avenge the outrage. In their lead ran the ticket seller, armed with a pistol and keen for evening up things with the man who had hit him, dashing straight for Circuit. Circuit did not see him, but Lee did; and thus in the very instant Circuit staggered and dropped to the crack of his pistol, down beside Circuit pitched the ticket man with a ball through his head. Then for two minutes, perhaps, a hell of fierce hand-to-hand battle raged, cowboy skulls crunching beneath fierce blows, circus men falling like autumn leaves before the cowboys' fire. And so the fight might have lasted till all were down but for a startling diversion.

Suddenly, just as Circuit had struggled to his feet, out from among the wrecked wagons sprang a dainty figure in tulle and tights, masses of hair red as the blood of the battlers streaming in waves behind her,

"Out sprang a dainty figure in tulle and tights, and fired at the nearest of the common enemy"

and fired at the nearest of the common enemy, which happened to be poor Circuit. Swaying for a moment with the shock of the wound, down to the ground he settled like an empty sack, falling across the legs of the ticket-seller.

Startled and shocked, it seemed, by the consequences of her deed, the woman approached and for a moment gazed down, horror-stricken, into Circuit's face. Then suddenly, with a shriek of agony, she dropped beside him, drew his head into her lap, wiped the gathering foam from his lips, fondled and kissed him. Ripping his shirt open at the neck to find his wound, she uncovered Circuit's buckskin bag and memorandum book, showing through its centre the track of a bullet that had finally spent itself in fracturing a rib over Circuit's heart, the ticket-seller's shot, that would have killed him instantly but for the shielding bulk Netty's treasured letters interposed. Moved, perhaps, by some subtle instinctive suspicion of its contents, she glanced within the book, started to remove it from Circuit's neck, and then gently laid it back above the heart it so long had lain next and so lately had shielded.

Meantime about this little group gathered such of the Cross Cañonites as were still upon their legs, while, glad of the diversion, their enemies hurriedly withdrew; round about the outfit stood, their fingers still clutching smoking guns, but pale and sobered.

Circuit lay with eyes closed, feebly gasping for breath, and just as the girl's nervous fingers further rent his shirt and exposed the mortal wound through the right lung made by her own tiny pistol, Circuit half rose on one elbow and whispered: "Boys, write—write Netty I was tryin' to git to her."

And then he fell back and lay still.

For five minutes, perhaps, the girl crouched silent over the body, gazing wide-eyed into the dead face, stunned, every faculty para-lyzed.

Presently Lee softly spoke:

"Sis, if, as I allows, you're Netty, you shore did Mat a good turn killin' him 'fore he saw you. Would 'a hurt him pow'ful to see you in this bunch; hurts us 'bout enough, I reckon."

Roused from contemplation of her deed, the girl rose to her knees, still clinging to Circuit's stiffening fingers, and sobbingly murmured, in a voice so low the awed group had to bend to hear her:

"Yes, I'm Netty, and every day while I live I shall thank God Mat never knew. This is my husband lying dead beneath Mat. They made me do it—my family—nagged me to marry Tom, then a rich horse-breeder of our county, till home was such a hell I couldn't stand it. It was four long years ago, and never since have I had the heart to own to Mat the truth. His letters were my greatest joy, and they breathed a love I little have deserved.

"Reckon that's dead right, Netty," broke in Bill Ball; "hain't a bit shore myself airy critter that ever stood up in petticoats deserved a love big as Circuit's. Excuse *us*, please."

And at a sign from Bill, six bent and gently lifted the body and bore it away into the town.

★★★★★★

In the twilight of an Autumn day that happened to be the twenty-second anniversary of Circuit's death, two grizzled old ranchmen, ambling slowly out of Mancos along the Dolores trail, rode softly up to a corner of the burying ground and stopped. There within, hard by, a woman, bent and gnarled and gray as the sage-brush about her, was tenderly decking a grave with *piñon* wreaths.

"Hope to never cock another gun, Bill Ball, ef she ain't thar ag'in!"

"She shore is, Lee," answered Bill; "provin' we-all mislaid no bets reconsiderin', an' stakin' Sorrel-top to a little ranch and brand."

Thus, happily, does time sweeten the bitterest memories.

CHAPTER 9

Across the Border

Yes, there he was, just ahead of me on the platform of the Union Depot in Kansas City, my partner, James Terry Gardiner, who had wired me to meet him there a few weeks after I had closed the sale of our Deadman Ranch, in November, 1882. While his back was turned to me, there was no mistaking the lean but sturdy figure and alert step.

From the vigorous slap of cordiality I gave him on his shoulder, he winced and shrank, crying: "Oh, please don't, old man. Been sleeping in Mexican northers for a fortnight, and it's got my shoulder muscles tied in rheumatic knots. Don Nemecio Garcia started me off from Lampasos with the assurance that my ambulance was generously provisioned and provided with his own camp-bed, but when night of the first day's journey came, I found the food limited to *tortillas, chorisos*, and coffee, and the bed a sheepskin—no more. Stupid of an old campaigner not to investigate his equipment before starting, was it not?"

"Worse than that, I should say—sheer madness," I answered. "How did it happen?"

"Well, you see, Don Nemecio is the *alcalde*, of his city, and he showered me with such grandiloquent Spanish phrases of concern for my comfort that I fancied he had outfitted me in extraordinary luxury.

"But that's over now, thank goodness. And now to business.

"In the north of the State of Coahuila, one hundred miles west of the Rio Grande border, lies the little town called Villa de Musquiz. To the north and west of it for two hundred miles stretches the great plain the natives call *El Desierto*, known on the map as *Bolson de Mapimi*, the resort of none but bandits, smuggler Lipans, and Mescaleros. Into it the natives never venture, and little of it is known except the scant information brought back by the scouting cavalry details.

"Just south of the town lie the Cedral Coal Mines I have been examining—but that is neither here nor there. What I want to know is, are you game for a new ranch deal?"

When I nodded an affirmative, he continued:

"Well, immediately north of the town lies a tract of 250,000 acres in the fork of the Rio Sabinas and the Rio Alamo, which is the greatest ranch bargain I ever saw. Heavily grassed, abundantly watered by its two boundary streams, the valleys thickly timbered with cottonwood, the plains dotted with mesquite and live oak, in a perfect climate, it is an ideal breeding range. And it can be bought, for what, do you think? Fifty thousand Mexican dollars (29,000 gold) for a quarter of a million acres! Go bag it, and together we'll stock it.

"Of course you'll run some rather heavy risks—else the place would not be going so cheap—but no more than you have been taking the last five years in the Sioux country. A little bunch of Lipans are constantly on the warpath, Mescalero raiding parties drop in occasionally, and the bandits seem to need a good many *prestamos*; but all that you have been up against. Better take a pretty strong party, for the authorities thought it necessary to give me a cavalry escort from Lampasos to Musquiz and back. And, by the way, pick up a boy named George E. Thornton, Socorro, N. M., on your way south. While only a youngster, he is one of the best all-round frontiersmen I ever saw, and speaks Spanish tolerably. Had him with me in the Gallup country."

Details were settled at breakfast, and there Gardiner resumed his journey eastward, while I took the next train for Denver. A fortnight later found me in Socorro, plodding through its sandy streets to an adobe house in the suburbs where Thornton lodged.

As I neared the door a big black dog sprang fiercely out at me to the full length of his chain, and directly thereafter the door framed an extraordinary figure. Then barely twenty-one, and downy still of lip, Thornton's gray eyes were as cold and calculating, the lines of his face as severe and even hard, his movements as deliberate and expressive of perfect self-mastery as those of any veteran of half a dozen wars. Six feet two in height, straight as a white pine, ideally coupled for great strength without sacrifice of activity, he looked altogether one of the most capable and safe men one could wish for in a scrap; and so, later, he well proved himself.

He greeted me in carefully correct English; and while quiet, reserved, and cold of speech as of manner, the tones in which he assured

126

me any friend of Mr. Gardiner was welcome, conveyed faint traces of cordiality that roused some hope that he might prove a more agreeable campmate than his dour mien promised. We were not long coming to terms; indeed the moment I outlined the trip contemplated, and its possible hazards, it became plain he was keen to come on any terms. To my surprise, he proposed bringing his dog, Curly. I objected that so heavy a dog would be likely to play out on our forced marches, and, anyway, would be no mortal use to us. His reply was characteristic:

"Curly goes if I go, sir; but any time you can tell me you find him a nuisance, I'll shoot him myself. I've had him four years, had him out all through Victoria's raid of the Gila, and he's a safer night guard than any ten men you can string around camp: nothing can approach he won't nail or tell you of. With Curly, a night-camp surprise is impossible."

Whatever cross Curly represented was a mystery. Two-thirds the height and weight of a mastiff, he had the broad narrow pointed muzzle of a bear, and a shaggy reddish-black coat that further heightened his resemblance to a cinnamon, with great gray eyes precisely the colour of his master's, and as fierce. Whichever character was formed on that of the other I never learned—the man's on the dog's, or the dog's on the man's. Certain it is that not even the luckiest chance could have brought together man and beast so nearly identical in all their traits. Both were honest, almost to a fault. Neither possessed any vice I ever could discover. Each was wholly happy only when in battle, the more desperate the encounter the happier they. Neither ever actually forced a quarrel, or failed to get in the way of one when there was the least colour of an attempt to fasten one on them. And yet both were always considerate of any weaker than themselves, and quick to go to their defence. Many a time have I seen old Curly seize and throttle a big dog he caught rending a little one—as I have seen George leap to the aid of the defenceless. Each weighed carefully his kind, and found most wanting in something requisite to the winning of his confidence; and such as they did admit to familiar intimacy, man or beast, were the salt of their kind.

On the train, south-bound for San Antonio, I learned something of Thornton's history. The son of a judge of Peoria, Ill., he had until fifteen the advantage of the schools of his city. Then, possessed with a longing for a life of adventure in the West, he ran away from home, worked in various places at various tasks, until, at sixteen (in 1887) he had made his way to Socorro. Arrived there, he attached himself to a small party of prospectors going out into the Black Range, into a region then wild and hostile as Boone found Kentucky. And there for the last five years he had dwelt, ranging through the Datils and the Mogallons, prospecting whenever the frequently raiding Apaches left him and his mates time for work. Indeed, it was Thornton who discovered and first opened the Gallup coal field, and he held it until Victoria ran him out. During this time he was in eight desperate fights—the only man to escape from one of them; but out of them he came unscathed, and trained to a finish in every trick of Apache warfare.

At San Antonio we were met by Sam Cress, who for the last four years had been foreman of my Deadman Ranch. Cress was born on Powell River, Virginia, but had come to Texas as a mere lad and joined a cow outfit. He had really grown up in the Cross Timbers of the Palo Pinto, where, in those years, any who survived were past masters not only of the weird ways and long hours and outlaw broncos, but also of the cunning strategy of the Kiowas and Comanches who in that time were raiding ranches and settlements every "light of the moon." Cress was then twenty-five—just my age—and one of the rare type of men who actually hate and dread a fight, but where necessary, go into it with a jest and come out of it with a laugh, as jolly a camp-mate and as steady a stayer as I ever knew. Charlie Crawford, a half-breed Mexican, taken on for his fluency in Spanish, completed our outfit. Two mornings later the Mexican National Express dropped us at the Lampasos depot about daylight, from which we made our way over a mile of dusty road winding through mesquite thickets to the Hotel Diligencia, on the main *plaza*.

A norther was blowing that chilled us to the marrow, and of course, according to usual Mexican custom, not a room in the hotel was heated. The best the little Italian proprietor could do for us was a pan of charcoal that warmed nothing beyond our finger tips. As soon as the sun rose, we squatted along the east wall of the hotel and there shivered until Providence or his own necessity brought past us a peon driving a burro loaded with mesquite roots. We bought this wood and dumped it in the central *patio* of the hotel and there lighted a campfire that made us tolerably comfortable until breakfast.

Ignorant then of Mexico and its customs, I had fancied that when a proper hour arrived for a call on the *alcalde*, Don Nemecio Garcia, I should have a chance to warm myself properly and had charitably asked my three mates to accompany me on the visit. But when at ten o'clock Don Nemecio received us in his office, we found him tramping up and down the room, wrapped in the warm folds of an ample cloak; his neck and face swathed in mufflers to the eyes, arctics on his feet, and no stove or fireplace in the room. As leading merchant of the town, he soon supplied us with provisions and various articles, and with four saddle and three pack horses for our journey.

The next day, while my men were busy arranging our camp outfit, I took train for Monterey to get a letter from General Treviño, commanding the Department of Coahuila, to the *comandante* of the garrison at Musquiz. On this short forenoon's journey I had my first taste of the disordered state of the country.

About ten o'clock our train stopped at the depot of Villaldama, where I observed six *guardias aduaneras* (customs guards) removing the packs from a dozen mules, and transferring them to the baggage car. Just as this work was nearing completion, a band of fourteen *contradistas* dashed up out of the surrounding chaparral, dropped off their horses, and opened at thirty yards a deadly fire on the guards. With others in the smoker, next behind the baggage car, I had a fine view of the battle, but a part of the time we were directly in the line of fire, for four of our car windows were smashed by bullets, and many bullets were buried in the car body. Such encounters between guards and smugglers in Mexico were always a fight to the death, for under the law the guards received one-half the value of their captures, while of course the smugglers stood to win or lose all.

As soon as fire opened, the guards jumped for the best cover available, and put up the best fight they could. But the odds were hopelessly against them. In five minutes it was all over. Three of the guards lay dead, one was crippled, and the other two were in flight. To be sure two of the smugglers were bowled over, dead, and two badly wounded, but the remaining ten were not long in repossessing themselves of their goods; and when our train pulled out, the baggage car riddled with bullets till it looked like a sieve, the ten were hurriedly repacking their mules for flight west to the Sierras. Later I learned that early that morning the guards had caught the *conducta* with only two men in charge, who had shrewdly skipped and scattered to gather the party that arrived just in time to save their plunder.

Mexican import duties in those days were so enormous that very many of the best people then living along the border engaged regularly in smuggling, as the most profitable enterprise offering. American hams, I remember, were then sixty cents a pound, and everything else in proportion. Even in the city of Monterey, stores that displayed on their open shelves little but native products, had warehouses where you could buy (at three times their value in the States) almost any American or European goods you wanted.

Well recommended to General Treviño from kinsmen of his wife, who was a daughter of General Ord of our army, he gave me a letter to Captain Abran de la Garza, commanding at Musquiz, directing him to furnish me any cavalry escort or supplies I might ask for, and the following day we started north from Lampasos on our one-hundred-mile march to Musquiz.

The first two days of the journey, for fully sixty miles, we travelled across the lands of Don Patricio Milmo, who thirty years earlier had arrived in Monterey, a bare-handed Irish lad, as Patrick Miles. Through thrift, cunning trading, and a diplomatic marriage into one of the most powerful families of the city, he had oreid his name and gilded the prospects of his progeny, for he had become the richest merchant of Monterey and the largest landholder of the state.

On this march north Curly's value was well demonstrated. The first two nights I divided our little party into four watches, so that one man should always be awake, and on the *qui vive*. But it took us no more than these two nights to discover that Curly was a better guard than all of us put together. Throughout the noon and early evening camp he slept, but as soon as we were in our blankets he was on the alert, and nothing could move near the camp that he did not tell us of it in low growls, delivered at the ear of one or another of the sleepers. However, nothing happened on the journey up, save at the camp just north of Progreso, where some of the villagers tried slip up on our horses toward midnight, and Curly's growls kept them off. Their trails about our camp were plain in the morning. The evening of the third day we reached Musquiz, one of the oldest towns of the northern border, nestled at the foot of a tall sierra amid wide fields of sugar cane, irrigated by the clear, sweet waters of the Sabinas.

At eight o'clock the next morning I called on Captain Abran de la Garza, the *comandante*, to present my letter from General Treviño.

Like the monarch of all he surveyed, he received me in his bed-chamber. As soon as I entered, it became apparent the Captain was a sportsman as well as a soldier.

The room was perhaps thirty by twenty feet in size. Midway of the north wall stood a rude writing table on which were a few official papers. Ranged about the room were a dozen or more rawhide-seated chairs, each standing stiffly at "attention" against the wall scrupulously equidistant order. Glaring at me in crude lettering from a broad rafter facing the door was the grimly patriotic sentiment, "*Libertad o Muerte*." (Liberty or Death!) In the southwest corner of the room stood a low and narrow cot, beneath whose thin serape covering a tall, gaunt cadaverous frame was plainly outlined. From the headpost of the cot dangled a sword and two pistols. *And to every bed, table, stand, and chair was hobbled a gamecock*—a rarely high-bred lot by their looks, that joined in saluting my entrance with a volley of questioning crows! It was, I fancy, altogether the most startling reception visitor ever had.

In a momentary pause in the crowing, there issued from a throat riven and deep-seamed from frequent floodings with fiery torrents of mescal, and out of lungs perpetually surcharged with cigarette smoke, a hoarse croaking, but friendly toned, "*Buenos dias, señor. Sirvase tomar un asiento. Aqui tiene vd su casa!*" and peering more closely into the dusky corner, I beheld a great face, lean to emaciation, dominated by a magnificent Roman nose with two great dark eyes sunk so deep on either side of its base they must forever remain strangers to one another. The nose supported a splendid breadth of high forehead, which was crowned with a shock of coal-black hair, while the jaws were bearded to the eyes. It was the face of an ascetic Crusader, sensualised in a measure by years of isolated frontier service and its attendant vices and degeneration, but still a face full of the noble melancholy of a Quixote.

Propping himself on a great bony knot of an elbow, the Captain made polite inquiry respecting my journey, and then asked in what could he serve me. But when I had explained that I wanted to meet the owner of the Santa Rosa Ranch, and contemplated going out to see it, it was only to learn, to my great disappointment, that it had been sold the week previous to two Scotchmen. Fancy! in a country visited by foreigners, as a rule, not so often as once a year.

Nor was I consoled when, noting my obvious chagrin, the Captain sought to lighten the blow by saying: "But, my dear sir, this is indeed evidence God is guarding you. That ranch has been a legacy of contention and feud for generations. Besides, what good could you get of it? Its nearest line to the town is six miles distant, and no life or property would be safe there a fortnight. Far the best cattle ranch in this section, a fourth of it irrigable, and as fine sugar-cane land as one could find, do you fancy it would be tenantless as when God first made it if safe for occupancy? Why, my dear sir, within the last six months Juan

Gaian's Lipans have killed no less than seventy of our townsmen, some in their fields, some in the very suburbs of the town, while Mescaleros are raiding a little lower down the river, and Nicanor Rascon is apt to sweep down any day with his *bandidos* and plunder strong boxes and stores. It is with shame I admit it, for I, Don Abran, am responsible for the peace and safety of this district. But, *mil demonios!* what can I do with one troop of cavalry against bandits ruthless as savages, and savages cunning as bandits?

"Oh! but if I only had horses! Those devils take remounts when they like from the *remudas* of *rancheros*, but I, *carajo!* I am always limited to my troop allotment.

"Burn a hundred candles to the Virgin, *amigo mio*, as a thank offering for your deliverance, and wait and see what happens to the Scotchmen; and while waiting, it will be my great pleasure to show you some of the grandest cock-fighting you ever saw. Look at them! Beauties, are they not? Purest blood in all Mexico! Kept me poor four years getting them together! But now! Ah! now, it will not be long till they win me ranches and *remoudas!*

"Ah! me. Time was not so very long ago when Abran de la Garza was called the most dashing *jefe de tropa* in the service, when *señoritas* fell to him as alamo leaves shower down to autumn winds; when pride consumed him, and ambition for a Division was burning in his brain. But now this demon of a frontier has scorched and driven him till naught remains to him but the chance of an occasional fruitless skirmish, his thirst for mescal, his greed for *aguilas*, and his cocks to win them! But, *señor*, bet no money against them, for it would grieve me to win from a stranger introduced by my General."

Then, with a grave nod of friendly warning, he turned an affectionate gaze upon his pets. Meantime, as if conscious of his pride in them, the cocks were boastfully crowing *paeans* to their own victories, past and to come, in shrill and ill-timed but uninterrupted concert, bronze wings flapping, crimson crests truculently tossing insolent challenge for all comers.

With the one plan of my trip completely smashed, I felt too much upset to continue the interview, and excused myself. But after a forenoon spent alone beside the broad and swift current the Sabinas was pouring past me, gazing at the dim blue mountain-crests in the west that I had learned marked its source, the irresistible call to penetrate the unknown impressed and then possessed me so completely that, at our midday breakfast, I announced to the Captain I had decided to follow the river to its head, and pass thence into the desert for a thirty-days' circle to the north and west.

"But, *valga nu Dios*, man," he objected, "I have no force I can spare for sufficient time to give you adequate escort for such a journey. It would be madness to undertake it with less than fifty men. I am responsible to my general for your safety, and cannot sanction it. Beyond the Alamo Cañon the only waters are in isolated springs in the plains and in natural rainfall tanks along the mountain crests, known to none except the Indians and Tomas Alvarez, an old half-breed Kickapoo long attached to my command as scout, who ranged that country years ago with his tribe, and who guides my troop on such short scouts as we have been able to make beyond the Alamo, and—"

"Pardon," I ventured to interrupt, "that will do nicely; give me Alvarez and one good trustworthy soldier, and we'll make the circle without trouble."

"Six of you! Why, you'd never get twenty miles out of town in that direction. I can't permit it."

"Pardon again, Don Abran," I broke in, "but we have for years been accustomed to move in small parties through country that held a hundred times more hostiles than you have here, and you can trust us to take care of ourselves. Go we shall in any event, without your men if you withhold them."

"Well, well, *hijo mio*," he responded, "if you are bound to go, we will see. Only I shall write my general that I have sought to restrain you."

To us the prevailing local fears seemed absurd. Admittedly there were only sixteen of the Lipans then left, men, women, and children, their chief, Juan Galan, the son by a Lipan squaw, of the father of Garza Galan, then the leading merchant of the town, and later a distinguished governor of his State. Originally a powerful tribe occupying both banks of the lower Rio Grande to the south of the Comanches, in their wars with Texans and Mexicans the Lipans had dwindled until only this handful remained. Three years earlier the entire band had been captured after a desperate fight, and removed by the Mexican authorities to a small reservation five hundred miles southwest of Musquiz.

But at the end of two years, as soon as the guard over them relaxed, indomitable as Dull Knife and his Cheyennes in their desperate fight (in 1879) to regain their northern highland home, Juan Galan and his pathetically small following jumped their reservation and dodged and fought their way back to the Musquiz Mountains; and there for the last ten months, constantly harassed and harassing, they had been fighting for the right to die among the hills they loved. To the natives they were bloodthirsty wolves, beasts to be exterminated; to an impartial onlooker they were a heroic band courting death in a splendid last fight for fatherland. Their bold deeds would fill a book. Even in this town of fifteen hundred people guarded by a troop of cavalry, no one ventured out at night except from the most pressing necessity; and of the seventy killed by them since their return, nearly a third were macheted in the streets of Musquiz during Juan Galan's night raids on the town.

The most effective work against them was done by a band of about a hundred Seminole-negro half-breeds, to whom the Government had made a grant of four square leagues twenty-five miles west of Musquiz, on the Nacimiento. Come originally out of the Indian territory in the United States, where the Seminoles had cross-bred with their negro slaves, this same band a few years earlier had been most efficient scouts for our own troops at Fort Clark, and other border garrisons, and it was this record that led the Mexican Government to seek and lodge them on the Nacimiento, as a buffer against the Lipans.

That night arrangements for our trip were concluded: the captain consented to furnish me old Tomas Alvarez and a young soldier named Manuel, but only on condition that he himself should escort us, with fifty men of his troop, one day's march up the river, which would carry us beyond the recent range of the Lipans. So early the next morning we marched out westward, passing the last house a half-mile outside the centre of the town, along a dim, little-travelled trail that followed the river to the Seminole village on the Nacimiento. The day's journey was without incident, other than our amusement at what seemed to us the captain's overzealous caution in keeping scouts out ahead and to right and left of the column, and in posting sentries about our night camp.

The following morning, a Sunday, after much good advice, the kindly captain bade us a reluctant farewell, and led his troops down-river toward home, while our little party of six headed westward up-river. Near noon we sighted the Seminole village, and shortly entered it, a close cluster of low *jacals* built of poles and mud. Odd it looked, as we entered, a deserted village, no living thing in sight but a few dogs. Thus our surprise was all the greater when, nearing the farther edge of the village, our ears were greeted with the familiar strains of "Jesus, Lover of My Soul," issuing from a large *jacal* which we soon learned was the Seminole church. Fancy it! the last thing one could have dreamed of! An honest old Methodist hymn sung in English by several score devout worshippers in the heart of Mexico, on the very dead line between savagery and civilization, and at that, sung by a people all savage on one side of their ancestry and semi-savage on the other.

Before the singing of the hymn was finished, startled by the barking of their dogs, out of the low doorway sprang half a dozen men, strapping big fellows,—one, the chief, bent half double with age,—all heavily armed. The moment they saw we were Americans we were most cordially received, and even urged to stop a few days with them, and give them news of the Texas border. But for this we had no time; and after a short visit—for which the congregation adjourned service—we filled our canteens, let our horses drink their fill at the great Nacimiento spring that burst forth a veritable young river from beneath a low bluff beside the town, and struck out westward for Alamo Cañon. Our afternoon march gave us little concern, for our route lay across rolling, lightly timbered uplands that offered little opportunity for ambush. That night we made a "dry camp" on the divide, preferring to approach the Alamo in daylight.

Having struck camp before dawn the next morning, by noon we saw ahead of us a great gorge dividing the mountain we were approaching—great in its height, but of a scant fifty yards in breadth, perpendicular of sides, a narrow line of brush and timber creeping down along its bottom, but stopping just short of the open plains. Scouting was useless. If there were any Indians about, we certainly had been seen, and they lay in ambush for us in a place of their own choosing. We must have water, and to get it must enter the *cañon*. So straight into the timber that filled the mouth of the gorge we rode at a run, riding a few paces apart to avoid the possible potting of our little bunch, and a hundred yards within the outer fringe of timber we reached the water our animals so badly needed.

And right there, all about the "sink" of the Alamo, where the last drops of the stream sank into the thirsty sands, the bottom was covered thick with fresh moccasin tracks, and in a little opening in the bush near to the sink smouldered the embers of that morning's camp-fire of a band of Lipans. Apparently we were in for it and seriously debated a retreat. Our position could not be worse. Tomas told us that the trail of the Lipans led straight up the valley, and for eight miles the *cañon* was never more than three hundred yards wide, and often no more than fifty, with almost perpendicular walls rising on either side two hundred or more feet in height, so nearly perpendicular that we would for the entire distance be in range from the bordering cliff crests, while any enemy there ambushed would be so safely covered they could follow our route and pick us off at their leisure.

To be sure, the brush along the stream afforded some shelter, but no real protection. However, out now nearly fifty miles from Musquiz and well into the country we had come to see, we pushed ahead. Cress, Thornton, and Manuel prowling afoot through the brush a hundred yards in advance, Crawford, Tomas and myself bringing up the rear with the horses. And so we advanced for nearly half a mile when the Lipan trail turned east, toward Musquiz, up a crevice in the cliff a goat would have no easy time ascending. Thus we were led to argue that the Lipans had left their camp before discovering our approach, and by this time were probably miles away to the east.

Mounting, therefore, we made the beat pace our pack animals could stand up through the eight miles of the narrows, riding well apart from each other, the only safeguard we could take, all craning our necks for view of the cliff crests ahead of us. But no living thing showed save a few deer and coyotes, and two mountain lions that, alarmed by our clattering pace, slipped past us back down the gorge. When at last we reached the end of the narrows and the *cañon* broadened to a width of several hundred yards, all but fifty or seventy-five yards of the belt of timber lining the stream along the south wall being comparatively level grassy bunch land, nearly devoid of cover, we congratulated ourselves that we had not been scared into a retreat.

Keen to put as much distance as we could between us and the Lipans, we travelled on up the *cañon* at a sharp trot, keeping well to its middle, until about 5 p.m., when we reached a point where it widened into a broad bay, nearly seven hundred yards from crest to crest, with a dense thicket of mesquite trees near its centre that made fine shelter and an excellent point of defence for a night camp. The stream hugged the east wall of the *cañon*, where it had carved out a tortuous bed perhaps one hundred and fifty yards wide, and so deep below the bench we occupied that only the tops of tall cottonwoods were visible from the thicket.

While the rest of us were busy unsaddling and unpacking, Thornton slung all our canteens over his shoulder, and started for the stream. But no sooner had he disappeared below the edge of the bench, a scant two hundred yards from our camp, before a rapid rifle fire opened which, while we knew it must proceed from his direction, echoed back from one cliff wall to the other until it appeared like an attack on our position from all sides, while the echoes multiplied to the volume of cannon fire at the sound of each shot. Indeed, never have I heard such thunderous, crashing, ear-splitting gun-detonations except on one other occasion, when aboard the British battle ship *Invincible* and in her six-inch gun battery while a salute was being fired.

Frightened by the fire, one of our pack horses stampeded down the *cañon*. Sending Manuel in pursuit, and leaving Tomas at the camp, Crawford, Cress, and I ran for the break of bench-land, to reach and aid Thornton. Nearing it, all three dropped flat, and crawled to its edge, just in time to see George make a neat snap shot at a Lipan midway of a flying leap over a log, and drop him dead. Old George was standing quietly on the lower slope of the bench just above the timber, while the shots from eight or ten Lipan rifles were raining all about him! The Lipans lay in the timber only one hundred to one hundred and fifty yards away, and it was a miracle they did not get him.

Instantly Cress and Crawford slipped back out of range, made a detour that brought them to the bench edge within fifty yards of the Lipans' position, and opened on them a cross fire, while I lay above George and shelled away at the smoke of their discharge, for not one showed a head after George potted the jumper. Five minutes after Cress and Crawford opened on them, the Lipan fire ceased entirely. For an hour we scouted along the bank trying to locate them, but apparently they had withdrawn.

Then, while the others covered us, George and I slipped through the bush to investigate his kill, and found a great gaunt old warrior at least sixty years old, wrinkled of face as if he might be a hundred, but sound of teeth and coal-black of hair as a youth, his face and body scarred in nearly a score of places from bullet and machete wounds,—the sign manual writ indelibly on his war-worn frame by many a doughty enemy. We carried him to the bench crest, Crawford fetched a spade and we dug a grave and buried him with his weapons laid upon his breast, as his own people would have buried him, and then we fired across his grave the final salute he obviously so well had earned.

More than he would have done for us? Yes, I dare say. But then our points of view were different. Throughout his long life a terror to all whites he doubtless had been; upon us he was stealthily slipping, ruthless as a tiger; but then he and his tribesmen and lands had so long been prey to the greed of white invaders of his domain that it is hard to blame him for fighting, according to the traditions of his race, to the death.

Lying in camp within the thicket that night, naturally without a fire, Thornton made it plain that his voluntary start for water was providentially timed. He told us that, while descending the slope to the timber, he saw the head of a little column of Indians, stealing up the valley through the brush, saw them before they saw him; but just as he saw them, he slipped on some pebbles and nearly fell, making a noise that attracted their attention. Instantly they slid into cover, and opened fire on him.

Asked by me why he himself had not sought cover, George answered, "No show to get one except by keeping out in the open on the high ground, and I *wanted one!*"

It was plain the Lipans had sighted us when too late to lay an ambush for us in the narrows, had made a short cut through the hills and dropped down into the stream bed with the plan to attack us at our night camp. Evidently they had not expected us to camp so early, and were jogging easily along through the brush, for once off their guard. But for George's chance start for the stream, nothing but faithful old Curly's perpetual watchfulness could have saved us from a bad mix-up that night. Already it had been so well proved that we could safely trust Curly to guard us against surprise, we slept soundly through the night, without disturbance of any sort.

The next forenoon's march to the head waters of the Alamo was an anxious one, and was made with the utmost caution, for we were sure the Lipans would be lying in wait for us; but no sign of them did we again see for three weeks.

Leaving the Alamo, we made a great circle through the desert, swinging first north toward the Sierra Mojada, then south, and ultimately eastward toward Monclova. The trip proved to be one of great hardship and danger, but only from scarcity of water; for while at isolated springs we found recent camps of one sort of desert prowler or another, we neither met nor saw any. Finally, late one night of the fourth week, we reached a little spring called Zacate, out in the open plain only about thirty miles south of Musquiz. But between us and only five miles south of the town stretched a tall range through which Tomas knew of only two passes practicable for horsemen; one, to the west, via the Alamo, the route we had come, would involve a journey of eighty miles, while by the other, an old Indian and smugglers' trail crossing the summit directly south of Musquiz, we could make the town in thirty-two miles. The latter route Tomas strongly opposed as too dangerous. Twelve miles from where we lay it entered the range, and for fifteen miles followed terrible rough *cañons* wherein, every step of the way, we should be right in the heart of the recent range of the Lipans, and where every turn offered chance of a perfect ambush. But with our horses exhausted, worn to more shadows from long marches through country affording scant feed, with not one left that could much more than raise a trot, we finally decided to chance the shorter route. That night we supped on cold antelope meat and biscuits, to avoid building a fire, and rolled up in our blankets, but not to rest long undisturbed.

Shortly after midnight Curly roused us with low growls. Though the moon was full, the night was so clouded one could hardly see the length of a gun-barrel. Curly's warnings continuing, George and Tomas rolled out of their blankets and crawled out among and about the horses, and lay near them an hour or more, till Curly's growls finally ceased. Then we called them in and all lay down, and finished the night in peace. Early the next morning, however, a short circle discovered the trail of three Indians who had crept near to the horses and reconnoitred our position. Their back trail led due northeast, the direction we had to follow; and when we had ridden out half a mile from the Ojo Zacate, we found where their trail joined that of the main band. The "sign" showed they had been south toward Monclova on a successful horse-stealing raid, for it was plain they had passed us in the night with a bunch of at least twenty horses, heading toward a point of the range only five or six miles west of where we should be compelled to enter it.

We were in about as bad a hole as could be conceived. Plainly the Indians knew of our presence in the vicinity. It was equally certain their scouts would be watching our every move throughout the day, and there was not one chance in a thousand of our crossing the range without attack from some ambush of such vantage as to leave small ground for hope that we could survive it. All but Cress and Thornton urged me to turn back, although we were all nearly afoot, and had no food left except two or three pounds of flour, and a little meat. After very short deliberation I decided to go ahead. The Lipans knew precisely where we were, and if they wanted us they could (in the event of a retreat) easily run us down and surround us and hold us off food and water until we were starved out sufficiently to charge their position and be shot down. Better far put up a bold bluff and take chances of cutting through them.

So on we plodded slowly toward the hills, all of us walking most of the way to save our horses all we could. At 2 p.m. we cut the old trail Tomas was heading us toward, and shortly thereafter entered the mouth of a frightfully rough *cañon*, its bottom and slopes thickly covered with *nopal*, *sotol*, and *mesquite*, and, later, higher up, with pines, junipers, oaks, and spruces, with here and there groups of great boulders that would easily conceal a regiment. Two or three miles in, the gorge deepened until tall mountain slopes were rising steeply on either side of us, and narrowed until we had to pick our way over the rough boulders of the dry stream-bed.

Our advance was slow, for it had to be made with the utmost caution. Thornton, Cress, and Tomas scouted afoot, one in the bottom of the gorge, and one half-way up each of its side walls, while Manuel and Crawford followed two hundred yards behind them, also afoot, driving the saddle and pack horses; and I trailed two hundred yards behind the horses, watching for any sign of an attempted surprise from the rear. Thus scattered, we gave them no chance to bowl over several of us at the first fire from any ambush they might have arranged.

From the windings of the *cañon* we were out of sight of each other much of the time; personally, I recall that afternoon as one of the most lonely and uncomfortable I ever passed. I slipped watchfully along, stopping often to listen, eyes sweeping the hillsides and the gulch below me, searching every tree and boulder, with no sound but the soughing of the wind through the tree-tops, and an occasional soft clatter of shingle beneath the slipping hoofs of my unshod horse.

But throughout the afternoon the only sign of man or beast that I saw was a lot of *sotol* plants recently uprooted, and their roots eaten by bears.

Shortly after dark we reached the only permanent water in the *cañon*, a clear, cold, sweet spring, bursting out from beneath a rock, only to sink immediately into the arid sands of the dry stream-bed. Immediately below the spring and midway of the gorge bottom stood an island-like uplift, twenty yards in length by ten in width, covered with brush, leaving on either side a narrow, rocky channel, and from either side of these two channels the *cañon* walls, heavily timbered, rose very steeply. Just above these narrows, the gorge widened into seven or eight acres of level, park-like, well-grassed bench-land, and into this little park we turned our horses loose for the night, for they were too worn to stray.

Having made eight or ten miles up the *cañon* during the afternoon march, we were now within a mile of the summit, and no more than seven miles from Musquiz. Indeed we should have tried to reach the town that night had not Tomas told us the next three miles of the trail were so steep and rough he could not undertake to fetch us over it unless we abandoned our animals, saddles, and packs.

We turned into our blankets early, after a cold supper, for we did not care to chance a fire. Cress and I slept together in the channel to the west of the island; Manuel and Tomas to the east of it quite out of our sight; Thornton and Crawford ten paces north, in sight of both ourselves and the Mexicans. A little moonlight filtered down through the trees, but not enough to enable us to see any distance.

Scarcely were we asleep, it seemed to me, before Curly awakened Cress and myself, growling immediately at our heads. Rising in our blankets, guns in hand, and listening intently, we could hear on the hillside above us what sounded like the movements of a bear. Whatever it might be, it was approaching. Not a word had been spoken, and Curly's growls were so low we had no idea any of the others had been roused. So we sat on the alert for perhaps fifteen minutes, when the sounds above us began receding, and we lay down again. But just as we were passing back into dreamland, Curly again startled us with a sharper, fiercer note that meant trouble at hand.

As we rose to a sitting posture, in the dim moonlight we could plainly see a dark crouching figure twenty yards below, which advanced a step or two, stopped as if to listen, and again advanced and stopped. What it was we could not make out. At first I thought it must be a bear, but presently I felt sure I caught the glimmer of a gun barrel, and nudged Cress with my elbow. We were in the act of raising our rifles to down it, whatever it might be, when Thornton sang out, "Hold on, boys; that's old Tomas!" And, indeed, so it proved. All had been awakened at the first alarm, and Thornton had seen Tomas roll from his blankets into the bottom of the east channel, and crawl away on the scout for the cause of Curly's uneasiness that so nearly had cost him his life. He had been so intent for movement on the hillsides he had not noticed us watching him.

The next morning we were moving by dawn, Tomas, Cress, and myself in the lead, the others trailing along one hundred or two hundred yards behind us. For half a mile the gorge widened, as most mountain gorges do near their heads, into beautiful grassy slopes rising steeply before us, thickly timbered with post oak. Then, issuing from the timber, we saw it was a blind *cañon* we were in, a *cul de sac*, with no pass through the crest of the range.

Before us rose a very nearly perpendicular wall for probably six hundred feet, up which the old trail zigzagged, climbing from ledge to ledge, so steep that when, later, we were fetching our horses up it, one of the pack horses lost its balance and fell fifty feet, crippling it so badly we had to kill it. The cliff face, about three hundred yards in width, and flanked to right and left by the walls of the *cañon*, was entirely bare of trees, but thickly strewn with boulders. From an enemy on the top of the two flanking walls, climbers up the cliff face could get no shelter whatever. Thus it was important that our advance should reach the summit as quickly as possible. So, up the three of us scrambled, about thirty yards apart, disregarding the trail.

When we were nearly half-way up, and just as we had paused to catch our breath, several rifle shots rang out in quick succession, which, from some peculiar echo of the *cañon*, sounded as if they had been fired beneath us. Upon turning, we could see nothing of our three mates or the horses—they were hidden from our view by the timber. Fancying they were attacked from the rear, I was about to call a return to their relief, when I saw Thornton run to the near edge of the timber, drop on one knee behind a tree, and open fire on the cliff-crest directly above our heads.

Whirling and looking up, I was just in time to see eight or ten men bob up on the crest and take quick snap shots at the three of us in the lead, and then duck to cover. We were so nearly straight under them, however, that they overshot us, although they were barely one hundred yards from us. Dropping behind boulders we peppered back at the flashes of their rifles, which was all we three in the lead thereafter saw of them; for after the first volley most of them lay close and directed their fire at the men in the edge of the timber, but occasionally a rifle was tipped over the edge of a boulder and fired at random in our direction. And all the time they were yelling at us, "*Que vienen, puercos! Que vienen!*" (Come on, pigs! Come on!)

I was puzzled. Both Cress and I thought they were Mexicans, but Tomas insisted they were Lipans. And sure enough it was the Lipans all spoke Spanish and dressed like Mexican peons. Whoever they might be, we could not stay where we were. By the firing and voices there were at least a dozen of them, and obviously it was only a matter of moments before they would occupy the two flanking walls and have us openly exposed.

It was a bad dilemma. Retreat was impossible, down a gorge commanded at short range from both sides. If we took shelter in it, they could starve us out; if we attempted to descend it, they could easily pick us off; if any of us escaped back to the plain it would only be to incur greater exposure if they pursued, or probably to perish of hunger before we could reach any settlements. Thus the situation called for no reflection—it was charge and dislodge them, or die.

Yelling to the boys below to close up on us, we three settled down to the maintenance of the hottest fire we could deliver at the rifle flashes above us, to cover their advance. Luckily there were many boulders scattered along the grassy treeless slope they had to advance across to reach the foot of the cliff. Thus by darting from one boulder to another they had tolerable cover and were able to reach us with no worse casualties than a comparatively slight flesh wound through Manuel's side and the shooting away of Thornton's belt buckle.

Then we started the charge, led really by Thornton, who, active as a goat, would have raced straight into the downpour of lead if I had not continually restrained him. Three would scramble up fifteen or twenty feet, and then drop behind boulders, while the other three kept up a heavy fire on the summit; and then the rear rank would advance to a line with their position, while they shelled the enemy. All the time a rain of bullets was splashing on the rocks all about us, but luckily for us they did not expose themselves enough to deliver an accurate fire.

After we had made five or six such rushes, and were about halfway up, we could hear the voices of what sounded like the larger part of the band receding. Supposing they were swinging for the two side walls to flank us we doubled our speed and presently dropped beneath the shelter of a wall of rock about four feet high, from behind which our enemy had been firing.

Two or three minutes earlier their fire had ceased, and what to make of it we did not know. We found that an exposure of our hats on our gun-muzzles drew no fire; yet, driven by sheer desperation, and expecting that every man of us would get shot full of holes, we simultaneously sprang over the rock, and dropped flat on the summit—amid utter silence, about the most happily surprised lot of men in all Mexico! The enemy had decamped. But where? And with what purpose? And why had they not flanked us!

Careful scouting soon showed they had retired in a body down the trail we must follow to reach Musquiz, as for nearly three miles the descent was as rough and difficult as the ascent had been.

Leaving Cress, who was ill, and Manuel, who was weak from loss of blood, to hold the summit, the rest of us descended to fetch up our horses, and a hard hour's job we had of it, for we packed on our backs the load of the dead pack horse and those of his mates the last half of the ascent, rather than risk losing another animal.

Upon our return we found Manuel gloating over three trophies—a hat shot through the side by a ball that had evidently "creased" the wearer's head, an old Spanish spur and a gun scabbard—which he seemed to find salve for the burning wound in his side.

Beneath us to the north lay Musquiz, in plain sight, a scant six miles distance. In the clear dry air of the hills, it looked so near that a good running jump might land one in the *plaza*, and yet none of us expected we all should enter it again. The odds were against it, for below us lay three miles of hill trail any step down which might land us in a worse ambush than the last and we never imagined the enemy would fail to engage us again. But the descent had to be made, and down it we started, Cress and Manuel bringing up the rear with the horses, the rest of us scouting ahead, dodging from rock to tree, advancing slowly, expecting a volley, but receiving none.

For a mile the band followed the trail, and we followed their fresh tracks; then they left the trail and turned west through the timber. However, we never abated our watchfulness until well out of the hills and near the outskirts of the town, which we reached shortly after noon. There, breakfasting generously if not comfortably with Don Abran and his gamecocks, I got news that made me less regretful of my failure to obtain the Santa Rosa Ranch: one of its two Scotch purchasers had been killed two days before my return, in attempting to repel a raid on his camp by Nicanor Rascon!

With Cress too ill to travel, the next morning I left Crawford to care for him, bade farewell to good old Don Abran, and started for Lampasos with Thornton and Curly.

We nooned at Santa Cruz, a big sheep ranch midway between Musquiz and Progreso, leaving there about two o'clock. An hour later, we heard behind us a clatter of racing hoofs, and presently were overtaken by a hatless Mexican, riding bareback at top speed, who told us that shortly after our departure the Lipans had raided Santa Cruz, and that of its twelve inhabitants, men, women and children, he was the only survivor. Thus were the Lipans still levying heavy toll for their wrongs!

Toward evening we entered Progreso a village reputed among the natives to be a nest of thieves and assassins. While Thornton was away buying meat and I was rearranging our pack, six of the ugliest-looking Mexicans I ever saw strolled across the plaza, evidently to size up our outfit. Apparently it was to their liking, for when, twenty minutes later, we were riding into the ford of the Rio Salado just south of the town, the six, all heavily armed, loped past us, and when they emerged from the ford openly and impudently divided, three taking to the brush on one side of the road, and three on the other, riding forward and flanking the trail we had to follow. From then till dark their hats were almost constantly visible, two or three hundred yards ahead of us. Our horses being so jaded, we were sure they were not the prize sought, and it remained certain they were after our saddles and arms.

Riding quietly on behind them until it was too dark to see our move or follow the trail, we slipped off to the westward of the road, and camped in a deep depression in the plain, where we thought we could venture a small fire to cook our supper. But the fire proved a blunder. Before the water was fairly boiling in the coffee pot, Curly signalled trouble, and we jumped out of the fire-light and dropped flat in the bush just as the six fired a volley into the camp, one of the shots hitting the fire and filling our frying-pan with cinders and ashes. For an hour or more they sneaked about the camp, constantly firing into it, while we lay close without returning a single shot, content they would not dare try to rush us while uncertain of our position. And so it proved, for at length Curly's warnings ceased, and we knew they had withdrawn.

Waiting till midnight, we saddled and packed and made a wide detour to the west, striking the road again perhaps four miles nearer Lampasos, which we reached safely late in the next afternoon; our grand old camp-guard, Curly, in better condition than either of us.

★★★★★★

Curiously, seven months later, in August, 1883, while on another ranch-hunting trip in Mexico, this time along the eastern slope of the Sierra Madre in northern Chihuahua at least five hundred miles distant from Musquiz, I learned the solution of our puzzle as to whether our last fight in Coahuila was with Lipans or Mexicans. The manager of the Corralitos Ranch, which I was then engaged in examining, was Adolph Munzenberger. The previous Winter he had lived in Musquiz, as Superintendent of the Cedral Coal Mines. While there, however, I

"THE SIX, ALL HEAVILY ARMED, LOPED PAST US"

had not met him or his family.

One evening at dinner, Mrs. Munzenberger asked me, "Have you ever, perchance, been in Coahuila?"

"Yes," I answered, "I spent several weeks in the State last Winter."

"And how did you like it?" she asked.

"Well, I must say I found rather too many thrills there for comfort," I replied. And when I mentioned affair on the *sierra* south of Musquiz, she broke in with:

"Indeed! And you are the crazy gringo Don Abran tried to stop from going into the desert! We heard of it; in fact, it was the talk of the town, and no one expected you would ever get back. And by the way, it was a contraband *conducta* owned by friends of ours who attacked you back of the town! Droll, is it not?"

"Perhaps—now," I doubtfully answered.

"Yes," Mrs. Munzenberger continued, "they were on their way to Monclova. The night before the attack, the wife of the owner (one of the leading merchants of the town) took me to their camp in the brush near town to see their goods; and a lovely lot of American things they had."

"But why did they attack us?" I queried.

"Well, you see, it was this way," she explained. "The smugglers broke camp long before dawn, and started south over the same trail by which you were approaching; they wanted to get over the summit before the Lipans or guards were likely to be stirring, for it was a point at which *conductas* were often attacked. But shortly after sunrise, and just as they advance guard reached the summit, they discovered your party ascending, and, mistaking your uniformed soldiers for *guardias*, the leader lined a dozen of his men along the ridge, and opened on you, while his *mayordomo* rushed the pack mules of the *conducta* back down the trail they had come. Early in the fight they discovered you wore a party of *gringos*, and not guards, and decamped as soon as their *conducta* had time to reach a point where they could leave the rail.

"Had their goods not been at stake, they would have wiped you out, if they could, for the leader's brother got shot in the head of which he died the same day. Indeed, when the two men you left behind started to leave the country, he had planned to follow and kill them, but luckily Don Abran heard of it, and restrained him."

And this explained the mystery why they had not flanked us!

★★★★★★

Brave to downright rashness, George Thornton lasted only about

"WE LAY CLOSE WITHOUT RETURNING A SINGLE SHOT"

two years longer.

The Winter of 1883-84 he spent with me on my Pecos Ranch. Early in the Spring he came to me and said:

"Old man, if you want to do me a favour, get me an appointment as Deputy United States Marshal in the Indian Territory. I'm going to quit you, anyway. My guns are getting rusty. It's too slow for me here."

"Why, George," I replied, "if you are bound to die why don't you blow your brains out yourself?"—for at the time few new marshals in the Indian Territory survived the first year of their appointment.

"Never mind about me," he answered; "I'll take care of George. Anyway, I'd rather get leaded there than rust here."

So I got him the appointment.

A few months later, when the Territory was thrown open to settlement, Thornton homesteaded one hundred and sixty acres of land which early became a town site, and now is the business centre of the city of Guthrie. Had he lived and retained possession of his homestead, it would have made him a millionaire. But greedy speculators soon started a contest of his title.

While this contest was at its height, one day Thornton learned some Indians living a few miles from the town were selling whiskey, contrary to Federal law. As he was mounting for the raid, having intended to go alone, a man he scarcely knew offered to accompany him, and Thornton finally deputized him.

The story of his end was told by the Indians themselves, who later were captured by a large force of marshals, and tried for his murder. They said that just at dusk they saw two horsemen approaching. Presently they recognized Marshal Thornton and at once opened fire on him, eight of them, from behind the little grove of cottonwoods in which they were camped. Immediately Thornton shifted his bridle to his teeth, and charged them straight, firing with his two ".41" Colts. The moment he charged, his companion dodged into a clump of timber, where they saw him dismount. On came Thornton straight into their fire shooting with deadly accuracy, killing two of their number, and wounding another before he fell.

Presently, at the flash of a rifle from the brush where his companion had dismounted, Thornton pitched from his horse dead. They had done their best to kill him, they frankly swore, but it was his own deputy's shot that laid him low.

All the collateral circumstantial evidence so fully corroborated this that the Indians were acquitted. The shot that killed him hit him in the back of the head and was of a calibre different from that of the Indians' guns; and his deputy never returned to Guthrie.

That it was a murder prearranged by some of the greedy contestants for his land, was further proved by the fact that every scrap of his private papers was found to have disappeared, and, through their loss, his family lost the homestead.

Curly's end is another story. Happily he was spared to me some years.

CHAPTER 10

The Three-Legged Doe and the Blind Buck

We had just pulled the canoe out of the water and turned it over after a wet day in the bush across Giant's Lake, and were drying ourselves before the camp-fire, when Con taught a lesson and perpetrated a confidence. His keen, shrewd eyes twinkling, and a broad smile shortening his long, lean face till its great Roman nose and pointed chin were hobnobbing sociably together, the best hunter and guide on the Gatineau sat pouring boiling water through the barrel and into the innermost holy of holies of the intricate lock mechanism of his .303 Winchester—*to dry it out and prevent rusting* from the wetting it had received in the bush.

"Sure! youse never heerd of it before?" he asked in surprise. "Dryin' a gun with hot water 's safest way to keep her from rustin'; carries out all th' old water hangin' round her insides 'n' makes her so damned hot Mr. Rust don't even have time to throw up a lean-to 'n' get to eatin' of her 'fore the new water's all gone; 'n' Mr. Rust can't get to eat none 'thout water, no more'n a deer can stay out of a salt lick, or Erne Moore can keep away from the *habitaw* gals, or Tit Moody can get his own consent to stop his tongue waggin' off tales 'bout how women winks down t' Tupper Lake—when *he's* rowin' 'em."

"Shouldn't think such a little water as you have used would make the gun hot enough to dry it out," I suggested.

"Hot! Won't make her hot! Why, she's hotter now 'n' billy Buell got last October when that loony *habitaw* cook o' ourn made up all our marmalade and currant jelly into pies that looked 'n' bit 'n' tasted like wagon dope wropt in tough brown paper; hot! 's hot this minute 's Elise Lièvre's woman got last Spring when she heerd o' him a-sittin'

151

up t' a Otter Lake squaw. Why, say! youse couldn't no more keep a gun from rustin' in this wet bush 'thout hot water than Warry Hilliams can kill anything goin' faster than three-legged deer.

"Rust! Youse might 'a well try to catch a *habitaw* goin' to a weddin' 'thout more ribbons on his bridle 'n' harness than his gal has on her gown 's hunt for rust in a hot-watered gun!"

Catching a hint of a yarn, I asked if there were many three-legged deer in the bush.

"W'an't but one ever, far 's I know," he replied. "'N' almighty lucky it was for Warry that one come a-limpin' along his way, for it give him th' only chance he'll probably ever have to say he got to shoot a deer.

"Warry? Why he's jest the best ever happened—'t least the best ever happened 'round this end o' the bush. Lives down to——; better not tell you right where he lives, for I stirred up th' letters in his name, so 'f any of his friends heerd you tell th' story they won't know it's on *him*; fer he's jest that good I'd rather hurt anybody, 'cept my woman or bird, than hurt him.

"Warry! Why, with a rod 'n' line 'n' reel, whether it's with flies, spoons, or minnows, castin' or trollin', or spearin' or nettin', Warry's th' *ex*pertest fish-catcher that ever waded the rapids or paddled th' lakes o' this old Province o' Quebec. But it's gettin' a *leetle* hard for Warry late years—fish 's come to know him so well that after he's made a few casts 'n' hooked one or two that's got away, they know his tricks so well they just passes the word 'round, 'n' it's 'pike' for th' pike, 'beat it' for th' bass, 'trot' for th' trout, 'n' 'skip' for the salmon, until now, after th' first day or two, 'bout all Warry can get in reach of 's mud turtles.

"'N'd that's what comes o' knowin' too much and gettin' too *damned* smart—nobody or nothin' left to play with! Warry? Why, say, if he'd only knowed it thirty or forty years ago, Warry had th' chance to live 'n die with th' *re*pute o' bein' th' greatest sport specialist that ever busted through the Quebec bush—if he'd only jest kept to fishin'. But the hell o' it is, Warry's always had a fool idee in his head he can hunt, 'n' he can't, can't sort o' begin to hunt! 'N' darned if I could ever quite figure out why, 'n' him so smart, 'nless because he goes poundin' through the bush like a bunch o' shantymen to their choppin', with his head stuck in his stummick, studyin' some new trick to play on a trout, makin' so much noise th' deer must nigh laugh theirselves to death at *him* a-packin' o' a gun.

"Hunt? Warry? Does he hunt? Sure, every year for th' last thirty years to my knowledge—only that's all; he jest hunts, never kills nothin'. Leastways he never did till three year ago, 'n' I ought t' know, for I always guides for him. Why, I mind one time he was stayin' over on the Kagama, he got so hungry for meat he up 'n' chunks 'n' kills 'n' cooks 'n' eats a porcupine, th' p'rmiscous shootin' o' which is forbid by Quebec law, 'cause they're so slow a feller can run 'em down 'n' get 'em with a stick or stone, 'n' don't need t' starve just 'cause he's got no gun.

"Three years ago he'd been up for the fly fishin' in late June 'n' trollin' for gray trout in September, 'n then here he comes again th' last week in October t' hunt. 'N' she was the same old story: nothing doing!

"I could set him on th' best runways, 'n' Erne 'n' me could dog th' bush till our tongues hung out 'n' we could hardly open our mouths 'thout barkin'; could run deer past him till it must 'a looked—if he'd had a loose look about him—like a Gracefield *habitaw* weddin' pr'cession, 'n' thar he'd set with his eyes fast on th' end o' his gun, I guess, a-waitin' for a sign of a *bite* 'fore he'd jerk her up to try 'n' get somethin'. 'N' the queerest part was, he seemed to enjoy it just 's much 's if he'd brought down a three-hundred-pound buck to drag the wind out o' Erne 'n' me at th' end o' a tump-line. Most fellers 'd got mad 'n' cussed their luck. But not him—kindest, sweetest-tempered man I ever knew. Guess he knowed we'd done our best 'n' had some kind o' secret inside information that he hadn't.

"O' course, sometimes Warry'd get his gun on, but by that time th' deer had quit th' runway 'n' was in th' lake up to their bellies pullin' lily pads, or curled up in th' long grass o' a swale fast asleep.

"But all fellers has a day sometime, if they lives long enough— though some o' them seems t' have t' get t' live a almighty long time t' get t' see it. At last Warry's came.

"Erne 'n' me been doggin' a swamp where th' deadfall tangle was so thick we was so nigh stripped o' clothes we couldn't 'a gone t' camp if there'd been any women about. Drivin' toward where a runway crossed a neck 'tween two lakes, a neck so narrow two pike could scarce pass each other on it, there we'd sot Warry 't th' end o' th' neck. Jest 'fore we got t' him we heard a shot, 'n' I remarked t' Erne, 'Guess th' old man thinks he's got a *bite*.' 'N' then we broke through a thick bunch o' spruce; 'n' we both nigh fell dead to see old Warry sawin' at th' throat o' a doe, tryin' to 'pear 's natural 's if he'd never done nothin' else but kill 'n' dress deer. Mebbe Erne 'n' me wan't pleased none th' old man had made a kill!

"Erne was ahead; 'n' just as Warry rose up from th' throat-cuttin', Erne dropped into th' weeds 'n' rolled 'n' 'round holdin' o' his stummick, laughin' fit t' kill his fool self, till I thought he'd gone crazy. Then my eye lit on th' fore quarters o' th' doe, 'n' I guess I throwed more twists laughin' than Erne did—*for that there doe was shy a leg*, hadn't but three legs; nigh fore leg gone midway 'tween knee and dewclaw, shot off 'n' healed up Godo'mi'ty knows when.

"Warry? He didn't seem t' care none, too darned glad t' get anythin' shape o' a deer."

That same evening one of us asked Con if he had ever run across any other mutilated game, recovered of old wounds.

"Sure!" he answered, "'specially once when I was almighty glad to git it, 'n' a whole lot gladder still that nobody was 'round t' see 'n' know 'n' tell just what I got 'n' how I got it. She 's been a secret these five year; stuck t' her tighter 'n' Erne Moore holds th' gals down t' Pickanock dances, 'n' that 's closer 'n' a burl on a birch. Fact is, I never told nobody 'fore now; 'n' I wouldn't be tellin' it t' youse now, only just 'fore we come up here I got a letter from one o' th' two brothers we blindfolded, sayin' his brother was dead an' he goin' t' Californy t' live, 'n' wa'n't comin' into th' bush no more.

"If that feller got hold o' her, my brother 'n' me 'd have t' go t' Australia or th' Cape, for him that's still livin' 's just about 's mean a feller 's Warry's a good one; an' any little *re*pute we've built up 's guides 'n' hunters, he'd put in th' rest o' his life tryin' t' smash 's flat 's that fool *habitaw* cook got when Larry Adams sot on him for cookin' pa'tridges as soup. He'd just par'lyze her till we couldn't even get a job goin' t' hunt 'n' fetch th' cows out o' a ten acre pasture. 'N' th' worst o' 't is I don't know that I'd blame him so almighty much for doin' it, for there was sure somethin' comin' t' us for foolin' them I don't believe we got yet.

"Th' two o' them came up from across th' line—ain't goin' t' tell you what place they come from or even th' State—in late October, for th' two weeks dog-runnin' season; youse know there is only two weeks th' Quebec law lets us run hounds, 'thout a heavy fine. Never 'd seen either o' them before, but friends o' theirs we'd been guidin' for gave brother 'n' me a big recommend, 'n' they wrote up ahead 'n' hired us t' put up th' teams t' haul them 'n' their traps in, 'n' then guide 'em.

"Soon 's they showed up on th' depot platform at Gracefield, I knowed brother 'n' me was up agin it hard. Train must 'a been a half-hour late gettin' to Maniwaki for th' time she lost unloadin' them two fellers' *necessities* for a two-weeks' deer hunt: 'bout a dozen gun cases, 'n' fishin' tackle 'nough for ten men, 'n' trunks 'n' boxes that took three teams t' haul 'em out t' th' Bertrand farm. Fact is, them boxes held enough ca'tridges t' lick out another Kiel rebellion 'n' leave over 'nough t' run all th' deer 'tween Thirty-one Mile Lake 'n' the Lievre plumb north into James's Bay, for if there's anythin' your average sportin' deer-hunters can be counted on for sure's death 'n' taxes, it's t' begin throwin' lead, at th' rate o' about ten pound apiece a day, the minute they gets into th' bush, at rocks "n' trees 'n' loons 'n' chipmucks—never killin' nothin' but their chance o' seein' a deer.

"'N' these bloomin' beauties o' our'n was no exception. Th' lead they wasted on th' two-mile portage from th' Government road t' th' lake would equip all the Injuns on the Desert Reservation for a winter's hunt.

"Why, when Tom 'n' me got hold o' th' box they'd been takin' ca'tridges from t' heave her into the boat, she was so light, compared t' th' others we'd been handlin', we landed her plumb over th' boat in th' water; 'n' damned if she didn't nigh float. She was the only thing they had light 'nough t' even try t' float ('cept their own shootin',) which sure wasn't heavy 'nough t' sink none, 'n' could 'a fell out o' a canoe 'n' been picked up a week later bumpin' 'round with th' other worthless drift.

"Took us a whole day to run their stuff over t' th' camp, 'n' it only a mile across th' lake from th' landin'; 'n' when night come we was 's near dead beat 's if we'd been portagin' a man's load apiece on a tump-line—'n' that's a tub o' pork 'n' a sack 'o flour weighin' two hundred and seventy five pounds—over every portage 'tween Pointe a Gatineau 'n' th' Baskatong.

"O' course th' gettin' them fellers over theirselves was a easy diversion, they was that t' home 'bout a canoe! Youse may not believe it, but after tryin' a half-hour 'n' findin' we couldn't even get them into a canoe at th' landin' 'thout upsettin' or knockin' th' bottom outen her, we had t' help them into a thirty-foot 'pointer' made t' carry a crew o' eight shantymen 'n' their supplies on the spring drives, 'n' then had t' pull our damnedest t' get them across th' lake 'fore they upset her, jumpin' 'round 't shoot at somethin' they couldn't hit!

"'N' eat! Well, they ate a few! We was only out for two weeks, 'n' when we loaded th' teams 'peared t' me like we had 'nough feed for six months, but after th' first meal 't looked t' me we'd be down

155

t' eatin' what we could kill inside o' a week. Looked like no human's stummick could hold all they put in their faces, 'n' brother, he said he thought their legs 'n' arms must be holler.

"'N' sleep! When 't come t' wakin' of 'em up th' next mornin' they was like a pair o' bears that 'd holed up for th' winter, 'n' it nigh took violence t' get 'em out at all. We started in runnin' th' hounds, "'n' brother 'n' me had the best on th' Gatineau—Frank 'n' Loud, 'n' old Blue, 'n' Spot—dogs that can scent a deer trail 's far 's Erne Moore can smell supper cookin', 'n' that 's far from home 's Le Blanc farm his father used to own, over Kagama way, 'bout eight miles from Pickanock, where he lives. We run th' dogs for four days, 'n' it was discouragin', most discouragin'. Country was full o' deer when we was last out, three weeks before, 'n' th' dogs voiced 'n' seemed t' run plenty right down to 'n' past where we'd sot th' two on th' runways; but they swore they never see nothin', said th' hounds been runnin' on old scent, sign made the night before.

"Then brother 'n' me took t' doggin' too, makin' six dogs, 'n' givin' us a chance t' see anythin' that jumped up in th' bush. Still nothin' came past 'em, they said, though we saw many a deer jump up out o' th' swamps 'n' go white flaggin' theirselves down th' runways toward the two 'hunters.'

"We just couldn't understand it 'n' made up our minds t' try 'n' find out why they never got t' see none.

"So the sixth day I placed one o' them myself on a runway half as wide 'n' beat most 's hard 's th' Government road, full o' fresh sign, picked a place where a big pine stump stood plumb in th' middle o' th' runway, 'n' sot him behind it where he had a open view thirty yards up th' runway th' direction we'd be doggin' from.

"Then I let on t' break through th' bush t' th' swamp we was goin' t' dog, but 'stead o' that I only went a little piece 'n' left brother to start th' hounds at a time we'd arranged ahead, while I lay quiet behind a bunch o' balsam 'thin fifty yards o' my hunter. After 'bout twenty minutes, the time I was supposed t' need t' get t' th' place t' start th' hounds, I heard old Frank give tongue—must 'a struck a fresh trail th' minute he was turned loose. Then it wa'n't long 'till th' other three began t' sing, runnin' 'n' singin' a chorus that's jest th' sweetest music on earth t' my ears.

"Talk about your war 'n' patriotic songs, your 'Rule Britannias' 'n' 'Maple Leaves,' your church hymns 'n' love songs, 'n' fancy French op'ras like they have down t' Ottawa that Warry Hilliams took me to wonst! Why, say, do youse think any o' them is in it with a hound chorus, th' deep bass o' th' old hounds 'n' th' shrill tenor o' th' young ones—risin' 'n' swellin' 'n' ringin' through th' bush till every idle echo loafin' in th' coves o' th' ridges wakes up 'n' joins in her best, 'n' you'd think all th' hounds in this old Province was runnin' 'n' chorusin' 'tween the Bubs 'n' Mud Bay; 'n' then th' chorus dyin' down softer 'n' softer till she's low 'n' sweet 'n' sorta holy-soundin', like your own woman's voice chantin' t' your youngest—say, do youse think there's any music in th' world 's good 's th' hounds make runnin'?

"Well, I sot there behind th' balsams till th' dogs was drawin' near, 'n' then I slips softly through th' bush t' where I'd left Mr. Hunter; 'n' how do youse s'pose I found him, 'n' it no more'n half past seven in th' mornin'? Youse never 'd guess in a thousand year. I'll jest tumpline th' whole bunch o' youse 't one load from th' landin 't' th' Bertrand farm if that feller wa'n't settin' with his back t' th' stump, facin' up th' runway, his rifle 'tween his knees 'n' his fool head lopped over on one shoulder, *dead asleep*! No wonder they never see nothin', was it?

"First I thought I'd wake him. Then I heard a deer comin' jumpin' down th' runway, 'n' knowin' 'for I could get him wide awake 'nough t' cock 'n' sight his gun th' deer 'd be on us, I slipped up behind th' stump 'n' laid my rifle 'cross its top, th' muzzle not over a foot above his noddin' head. I was no more'n ready 'fore here come—a buck? No, I guess not, 'cause they was jest crazy for some good buck heads; no, jest a doe, but a good big one. Here she come boundin' along, her head half turned listening t' th' dogs, 'n' never seein' *him*, he sot so still. When she got 'thin 'bout fifty feet I fired 'n' dropped her—'n' then hell popped th' other side o' th' stump! Guess he thought he was jumped by Injuns. Slung his gun one way 'n' split th' bush runnin' th' other, leapin' deadfalls 'n' crashin' through tangles so fast I had t' run him 'bout fifty acres t' get t' cotch 'n' stop him.

"That feller was with us jest about ten days longer, but he never got time t' tell us jest what he thought was follerin' him or what was goin' t' happen if he got cotched. Likely 's not he'd been runnin' yet if I hadn't collared him.

"O' course they was glad at last t' get some venison—leastways youse'd think so t' see them stuffin' theirselves with it—but they never let up a minute round camp roastin' brother 'n' me for not runnin' them a buck; swore that we hadn't run 'em any was proved by my gettin' nothin' but th' doe.

"Finally, they up 'n' wants a still-hunt! Them still-hunt, that we could scarce get along the broadest runway 'thout makin' noises a deer'd hear half a mile! Still-hunt! Still-hunt, after we'd been runnin' the hounds for a week and they'd shot off 'bout a thousand rounds o' ca'tridges round camp 'n' comin' back from doggin', till there wa'n't a deer within eight miles o' th' lake that wa'n't upon his hind legs listenin' where th' next bunch o' trouble was comin' from. But still-hunt it was for our'n, 'n' at it we went for th' next two days. Don't believe we'd even 'a started, though, if we hadn't known two days at th' most 'd cure them o' still-huntin'. Gettin' out 'fore sun-up, with every log in th' *brules* frosted slippery 's ice 'n' every bunch o' brush a pitfall, climbin' 'n' slidin' jumpin' 'n' balancin', any 'n' every kind o' leg motion 'cept plain honest walkin', was several sizes too big a order for them. So th' second mornin' out settled their still-huntin'.

"Then they wanted brother 'n' me t' still-hunt—while they laid round camp, I guess, 'n' boozed, th' way they smelled 'n' talked nights when we got in.

"'N' still-hunt we did, plumb faithful, 'n' hard 's ever in our lives when we was in bad need o' th' meat, for several days; 'n' would youse believe it? We never got a single shot. Sometimes we saw a white flag for a second hangin' on top o' a bunch o' berry bushes—that was all; most o' th' deer scared out o' th' country, 'n' th' rest wilder 'n' Erne gets when another feller dances with his best gal.

"Well, we just had t' give up 'n' own upbeat. 'N' Goda'mi'ty! but didn't them two cheap imitation hunters tell us what they thought o' us pr'fessionals—said 'bout everything anybody could think of, 'cept cuss us. 'N' there was no doubt in our minds they wanted to do that. If they'd been plumb strangers, 'stead o' friends o' one o' our parties, it's more'n likely brother 'n' me'd wore out a pair o' saplings over their fool heads, 'n' paddled off 'n left them t' tump-line theirselves out o' th' bush. But I told brother 't was only a day or two more, 'n' we'd chew our own cheeks 'stead o' their ears.

"The last day we had in camp they asked us t' make one more try with th' hounds. We took th' two ridges north o' th' shanty deer-lick 'n' drove west, with them on a runway sure to get a deer if there was any left t' start runnin'. Scarcely ten minutes after we loosed th' hounds I heard them stopped 'n' bayin', over on th' slope o' th' ridge brother was on, bayin' in a way made me just dead sure they had a bear.

"Now a bear-kill, right then t' go home 'n' lie about, tellin' how they fit with it, would 'a suited our sham hunters better 'n' a whole passle o' antlers; so I busted through th' bush fast as I could, fallin' 'n' rippin' my clothes nigh off—only t' find our hounds snappin' 'n' bayin' round a mighty big buck, that when I first sighted him, seemed to be jest standin' still watchin' th' hounds. Never saw a deer act that way before, 'n' him not wounded, 'n' nobody'd shot. Jest couldn't figure 't out at all. But I was so keen t' get them fellers a bunch o' horns I didn't stop t' study long what p'rsonal private reasons that buck had for stoppin' 'n' facin' th' hounds.

"I was in the act o' throwin' my .303 t' my face, when brother hollered not t' shoot, 'n' t' come over t' him. 'N' by cripes! while I was crossin' over t' brother, what in th' name o' all th' old hunters that ever drawed a sight do youse think I noted about that buck? Darned if that buck wa'n't *blind*—stone blind—blind 's a bat!

"Poor old warrior! He'd stand with his head on one side listenin' t' th' hounds till he had one located close up, 'n' then he'd rear 'n' plunge at th' hound; 'n' if there happened t' be a tree or dead timber in his way, he'd smash into it, sometimes knockin' himself a'most stiff. But when all was clear th' hounds stood no show agin him, blind as he was. Old Loud 'n' Frank, that naturally put up a better fight than th' young dogs, he tore up with his front hoofs so bad they like t' died.

"Run th' buck knowed he couldn't, 'n' there he stood at bay t' fight to a finish 'n' sell out dear 's he could. If it hadn't been a real kindness t' kill him, I'd never 'a shot that brave old buck, 'n' left our hunters t' buy any horns they *had* t' have down t' Ottawa. But he was already pore 'n' thin 's deer come out in March, 'n' if we let him go 'd be sure t' starve or be ate by th' wolves. So I put a .303 behind his shoulder, 'n' brother 'n' me ran up 'n' chunked th' dogs off.

"'N' what do youse think we found had blinded that buck? Been lately in a terrible fight with another buck. His head 'n' neck 'n' shoulders was covered with half-healed wounds where he'd been gashed 'n' tore by th' other's horns 'n' hoofs; 'n' somehow in the fight both his eyes 'd got put out! Guess when he lost his eyes th' other buck must a' been 'bout dead himself, or it 'd 'a killed him 'fore quittin'.

"Then it hit brother 'n' me all of a heap that we'd be up agin it jest a leetle bit too hard t' stand if we hauled a blind buck into camp; fellers 'd swear that t' get t' kill a buck at all brother 'n' me had t' range th' bush till we struck a blind one; 'n' then they'd probably want us t' go out 'n' see if we couldn't find some sick or crippled 'nough so we could get to shoot 'em.

"Brother was for leavin' him 'n' sayin' nothin'; but th' old feller had a grand pair o' horns it seemed a pity t' lose, 'n' so I just drove a .303

sideways through his eyes; 'n' when we got t' camp we 'counted for th' two shots in him by tellin' them he was circlin' back past us 'n' we both fired t' wonst.

"'N' by cripes! t' this day nobody but youse knows that Con Tee-ples dogged 'n' still-hunted th' bush for two weeks for horns 'thout killin' nothin' but a blind buck."

CHAPTER 11

The Lemon County Hunt

One crisp winter morning a party of us left New York to spend the week end at the Lemon County Hunt Club. It was there I first met Sol, the dean of Lemon County hunters and for eight seasons the winner, against all comers, of the famous annual Lemon County Steeple Chase. At the hurdles, whether in the great public set events or in private contests, Sol was never beaten, while in the drag hunts it was seldom indeed he was not close up on the hounds from "throw-in" to "worry."

To the Club Mews he had come under the tragic name of Avenger, but such was the marvellous equine wisdom he displayed that at the finish of his third hunt in Lemon County, he was rechristened Solomon by his new owner—soon shortened to Sol for tighter fit among sulphurous hunt expletives. At that night's dinner Sol and his deeds were the chief topic of conversation and also its principal toast. And why not, when no hunting stable in the world holds a horse in all respects his equal? Why not toast a horse now twenty-six years old who has missed no run of the Lemon County hounds for the last eight years, never for a single hunting-day off his feed or legs? Why not toast a horse that takes ordinary timber in his stride and eats up the stiffest stone walls for eight full hunting seasons without a single fall? Why not toast a horse with the prescience and generalship of a Napoleon, a horse who drives straight at all obstacles in a fair field, but who never imperils his rider's head beneath over-hanging boughs; who foresees and evades the "blind ditches" and other perils lurking behind hedges and walls and who lands as steady and safe on ice as he takes off out of muck? Why not toast this venerable but still indomitable King of Hunters?

The next morning it was my privilege to meet him. In midwinter,

161

he of course was not in condition. Descriptions of his weird physique, and jests over his grotesquely large and ill-shaped head, made by half a dozen voluble huntsmen over post-prandial bottles, I thought had prepared me against surprise. Certainly they had described such a horse as I had never seen.

But having come to the door of his box, I was astounded to see slouching lazily in a corner with eyes closed, the nigh hip dropped low, a horse that at first glance appeared to be Don Quixote's Rosinante reincarnate, a gigantic "crow-bait" with a head as long and coarse as an eighteen-hand mule's, an under lip pendulous as a camel's dropping ears nearly long enough to brush flies off his nostrils, with such an ingrowing concavity of under jaw and convexity of face as would have enabled his head to supply the third of a nine-foot circle, a face curved as a scimitar and nearly as sharp. Both in shape and dimensions it was the grossest possible caricature of a Roman-nosed equine head the maddest fancy could conceive.

Slapped lightly on the quarter, Sol was instantly transformed.

Eyes out of which shone wisdom preternatural in a horse, opened and looked down upon us with the calm questioning reproach one might expect from a rude awakening of the Sphinx; then the tall ears straightened and the great bulk rose to the full majesty of its seventeen hands; and while slats, hip bones, and shoulder blades were distressingly prominent, a glance got the full story of Sol's wonderful deeds and matchless record for safe, sure work.

With massive, low-sloping shoulders, tremendous quarters, exceptionally short of cannon bone and long from hock to stifle as a greyhound; with a breadth of chest and a depth of barrel beneath the withers that indicated most unusual lung capacity, behind the throat-latch Sol showed, in extraordinary perfection, all the best points of a thoroughbred hunter that make for speed, jumping ability, and endurance.

And as he so stood, a flea-bitten, speckled white in colour, he looked like a section out of the main snowy range of the Rocky Mountains: the two wide-set ears representing the Spanish Peaks; his sloping neck their northern declivity; his high withers, sharply outlined vertebrae, and towering quarters the serrated range crest; his banged tail a glacier reaching down toward its moraine!

Sol needed exercise, and that afternoon I was permitted the privilege of riding him. Mounted from a chair and settled in the saddle, I felt as if I must surely be bestriding St. Patrick's Cathedral. But at a shake of the reins the parallel ceased. His pasterns were supple as an Arab four-year-old's, his muscles steel springs.

Myself quite as gray as Sol and, relatively, of about the same age, as lives of men and horses go, we early fell into a mutual sympathy that soon ripened into a fast friendship. At Christmas I returned to the club to spend holiday week, in fact sought the invitation to be with Sol. Every day we went out together, Sol and I, morning and afternoon. Bright, warm, open winter days, so soon as the spin he loved was finished, I slid off him, slipped the bit from his mouth (leaving head-stall hanging about his neck), and left him free to nibble the juicy green grasses of some woodland glade and, between nibble times, to spin me yarns of his experiences. For the subtle sympathy that existed between us—sprung of our trust in one another and sublimated in the heat of our mutual affection had sharpened our perceptions until intellectual inter-communication became possible to us. I know Sol understood all I told him, and I don't think I misunderstood much he told me. So here is his tale, as nearly as I can recall it.

"Ye know I'm Irish, and proud of it. It's there they knew best how to make and condition an able hunter. No pamperin', softenin' idleness in box stalls or fat pastures, or light road-joggin', goes in Ireland between huntin' seasons. It's muscle and wind we need at our trade in Ireland, and neither can be more than half diviloped in the few weeks' light conditionin' work that all English and most American cross-country riders give their hunters. Steady gruellin' work is what it takes to toughen sinews and expand lungs, and it's the Irish huntsman that knows it. So between seasons we drag the ploughs and pull the wains, toil at the rudest farm tasks, and thus are kept in condition on a day's notice to make the run or take the jump of our lives.

"Humiliatin'? Hardly, when we find it gives us strength and staying power to lead the best the shires can send against us: they've neither power nor stomach to take Irish stone and timber.

"'It's a royal line of blood, his,' I've often heard Sir Patrick say; 'a clean strain of the best for a hundred years, by records of me own family. His head? There was never a freak in the line till he came; and where the divil and by what misbegotten luck he came by it is the mystery of Roscommon. And it's by that same token we call him Avenger, for no sneerin' stranger ever hunted with him that didn't get the divil's own peltin' with clods off his handy Irish heels.'

"And the head groom had it from the butler and passed it on to me that the old Master of the Roscommon Hounds was ever swearin' over his third bottle, of hunt nights, when I was no more than a five-year-old and the youngsters would be fleerin' at Sir Pat over the shape of me head:

"'Faith, an' it's Avenger's head ye don't like, lads, is it? By the powers o' the holy Virgin but it's me pity ye have that none of ye can show the likes in your stables. By the gray mare that broke King Charlie's neck, it's the head of him holds brains enough to distinguish ten average hunters, brains no ordinary brain pan could hold; an' it's a brain-box shape of a shot sock makin' the disfigurin' hump below his eyes. It's a four-legged gineral is Avenger, with the cunnin' foresight of a Bonaparte and the cool judgment of a Wellington.'

"Ah! but they were happy days on the old sod, buckin' timber, flyin' over brooks, stretchin' over stone or lightin' light as bird atop of walls too broad to carry and springin' on, with a good light-handed man up that knew his work and left ye free to do yours! And a sad night it was for me when Sir Pat, stripped by years of gambling of all he owned but the clothes he stood in and me, staked and lost me to a hunt visitor from Quebec!

"I was a youngster then, only a nine-year-old, but I'll niver forget the two weeks' run from Queenstown to Quebec whereon hunting tables were reversed and I became the rider and the ship me mount, across country the roughest hunter ever lived through: niver a moment of easy flat goin', but an endless series of gigantic leaps that nigh jouted me teeth loose, churned me insides till they wouldn't even hold dry feed, and gave me more of a taste than I liked of what I had been givin' Roscommon huntsmen over lane side wall jumps—a rise and a jolt, a rise and a jolt, till it was wonderin' I was the ears were not shaken from me head.

"Humiliation? It was there at Quebec I got it! In old Roscommon usually it was lords and ladies rode me of hunt days, men and women bred to the game as I meself was.

"But at Quebec, the best—and I had the best—were beefy members of their dinkey colonial Government or fussy, timid barristers I had to carry on me mouth. Seldom it was I carried a good pair of hands and a cool head in me nine years' runnin' with the Quebec and Montreal hounds. And lucky the same was for me, for it forced me to take the bit in me teeth, rely on meself, and regard me rider no more than if he were a sack of flour: I jist had it to do to save me own legs and me rider's neck, for to run by their reinin' and pullin' would have brought us a cropper at about two out of every three obstacles. Faith, and I believe it's an honest leaper's luck I've always had with me, anyway, for me Quebec work was jist what I needed to train me for an honourable finish with the Lemon County Yankees.

"One Autumn night years ago, when I was eighteen, a clever young Yankee visitor from New York appeared at our club. For two days I watched his work on other mounts, and liked it. He was good as any two-legged product of the old sod itself, a handsome youngster a bit heavier than Sir Pat, a reckless, deep drinkin', hard swearin', straight ridin' sort, but with a head and hands ye knew in a minute ye could trust, by name Jack Lounsend. The third hunt after his arrival, it was me delight to carry him, and for the first time in years to allow me rider his will of me. And you can bet your stud and gear, I gave him the best I had, for the sheer love of him, and him so near the likes of me dear Sir Pat.

"Nor was me work to go unvalued, for, to me great delight, he bought me and brought me to the States—straight away to Lemon County—along with two of me huntmates he fancied. And a sweet country I found this same Lemon County, with timber and stone nigh as stiff, and sod as sound as old Roscommon's own.

"But troubles lay ahead of me I'd not foreseen. Instead of goin' into Jack's private string, as I'd hoped, the early record I made for close finishes and safe, sure work made me wanted by the chief patron of the hunt, a New York multi-railroad-aire with a well diviloped habit of gettin' everything he goes after. So, while I venture to believe Jack hated to part with me, the patron got me.

"And a good man up the patron himself proved, one I'd always be proud enough to carry; but, as Jack used to say, the hell of it was the Lemon County Hunt numbered more bunglin' duffers than straight riders, the sort a youngster or a hot-head would be sure to kill.

"So when, as often happened, the patron was busy with faster runs and a hotter 'worry' than our hunt afforded, it frequently fell to me lot to carry the half-broke of all ages, seldom a one bridle wise to our game, as sure to pull me at the take-off of a leap as to give me me head on a run through heavy mud, the sort no horse could carry and finish dacently with except by takin' the bit in his teeth and himself makin' the runnin'. And even so, it was a tough task fightin' their rotten heavy hands and loose seat! But, by the glory of old Roscommon, never once have I been down in me eight years with the Lemons!

"Once, to be sure, on me first run, by the way, I slashed into one of your brutal wire fences, the first I'd ever seen—looked a filmy thing you could smash right through—caught a shoe in it, and nigh wrenched a shoulder blade in two. Sure, I never lost me feet, but it laid me up a few days; and you can gamble any odds you like no wire has ever caught me since; and, more, that I now hold record as the only horse in the county that takes wire as readily as timber, where it's necessary—though sure it is I'll dodge for timber every time where I won't lose too much in place.

"Down they come to Lemon County, a lot of those New York beauties, men and women, togged out so properly you'd think they'd spent their whole lives in the huntin' field; but at the first obstacle you'd see their faces go white as their stocks, and then all over you they'd ride from tail to ears, their arms sawin' at your mouth fit to rip your under jaw off, like they thought it was a backin' contest they were entered for. And sure back to the rear it soon was for them, back till the hounds were mere glintin' specks flyin' across a distant hill-crest, the riders' red coats noddin' poppies; back till only faint echoes reached them of the swellin', quaverin' chorus of the madly racin' pack; back for all but him or her whom old Sol had his will of,—for rider never lived could hold me to the wrong jump or throw me from my stride, nor was fence ever built I'd not find a place to leap without layin' a toe on it.

"Once the hounds give voice, it's the divil himself couldn't hold me, whether it's the short, sharp war-cry of the Irish or the sweet, deep bell-notes of these Yankee hounds that to me ever seem chantin' a mournful dirge for the quarry. Sure, it's the faster Irish hounds that make the grandest runnin', but it's the deep-throated mellow chorus of a Yankee pack I love best to hear.

"*Nouveaux riches*, whatever kind of bounders that spells, is what Bob Berry calls the lot of mouth-sawers New York sends us; and whenever the patron is out or Jack has his way, it's niver one of them I'm disgraced with.

"Sometimes it's me good old Jack up; sometimes hard swearin', straight goin' Bob; sometimes little Raven, as true a pair of hands and light and tight a seat as hunter ever had; sometimes Lory Ling, as reckless as the old Roscommon sire of him I used to carry when I was a five-year-old, with a ring in his swears, a stab in his heels, and a cut in his crop that can lift a dead-beat one over as tall gates as the best and freshest can take; sometimes it's Priest, that with the language of him and the hell-at-a-split pace he'll hold a tired one to but ill desarves the holy name he wears; and sometimes—my happiest times—it's a daughter of the patron up, with hands like velvet and the nerve and seat of a veteran.

"Horse or human, it's blood that tells, every time, me word for that. Be they old or young, you can niver mistake it. Can't stop anything with good blood in it—gallops straight, takes timber in its stride, and finishes smartly every time. Know it may not, but it balks at nothing, sets its teeth and drives ahead till it learns.

"And perhaps that wasn't driven well home on me last Fall!"

"Out to us came a little woman, a scant ninety-pounder I should say, so frail she wouldn't look safe in a drag, and a good bit away on the off side of middle age; but the mouth of her had a set that showed she'd never run off the bit in her life, and her eye—my eye! but she had an eye, did that woman. And it was hell-bent to hunt she was, bound to follow the bounds, though all she knew of a saddle came of five-mile-an-hour jogs along town park bridle paths, and all her hands looked fit for was holdin' a spaniel.

"Well, it was Lory and Priest took her on, turn about, usually me that carried her, and it was break her slender little neck I thought the divils would in spite of me. Took her at everything and spared her nowhere, bowled her along across meadow and furrow, over water, timber, and walls, like she was a lusty five-year-old, and all the time a guyin' her in a way to take the heart out of anything but a thorough-bred. 'Don't mind the fence!' Lory would sing out, 'if you get a fall, just throw your legs in the air and keep kickin' to show you're not dead; we never want to stop for any but the dead on this hunt.' And smash on my quarters would come her crop, and on we'd go!

"Again, when we'd be nearin' a fence across which two were scramblin' up from croppers, Lory would brace her with: 'Don't git scared at that smoke across the fence; it's nothin' but the boys that couldn't get over burnin' up their chance of salvation!' And into me slats her little heel would sock the steel, and high over the timber I'd lift her for sheer joy of the nerve of her!

"But it was not always me that had her. One day I saw a cold-blood give her a fall you'd think would smash the tiny little thing into bran; landed so low on a ditch bank he couldn't gather, and up over his head she flew and on till I thought she was for takin' the next wall by her lonesome. And when finally she hit the ground it was to so near bury herself among soft furrows that it looked for a second as if she'd taken earth like any other wily old fox tired of the runnin'.

"But tired? She? Not on your bran mash! Up she springs like a yearlin' and asks Lory is her hat on straight—which it was, straight up and down over her nigh ear. 'Oh, damn your hat,' answers Lory; 'give us your foot for a mount if you're not rattled. Why, next year you'll be showin' your friends holes in the ground on this hunt course you've dug with your own head!' And up it was for her and away again on old cold-blood. Faith, but those cold-bloods make it a shame they're ever called hunters. Fall the best must, one day or another; but while the thoroughbred goes down fightin', strugglin' for his feet and ginerally either winnin' out or givin' his rider time to fall free if down he must go, the cold-blood falls loose and flabby as an empty sack, and he and his rider hit the ground like the divil had kicked them off Durham Terrace. Ah, but it was the heart of a true thoroughbred had Mrs. Bruner, and whether up on cold or hot blood, along she'd drive at anything those two hare-brained dare-devils would point her at, spur diggin', crop splashin'!

"Nor is all our fun of hunt days. Between times the lads are always larkin' and puttin' up games on each other out of the stock of divilment that won't keep till the next run, each never quite so happy as when he can git the best of a mate on a trade or a wager.

"One day little Raven and I galloped over to Lory's place.

"'Whatever mischief are you and His Wisdom up to?' sings out Lory to Raven, the minute we stopped at his porch.

"'Nary a mischief,' answers Raven; 'want some help of you.'

"'Give it a name,' says Lory.

"'Easy,' says Raven; 'the master's got a new fad—crazy to mount the hunt on white horses. I've old Sol here, and Jack has a pair of handy white ones for the two whips, but where to get a white mount for Jack stumps us. Jogged over to see if you could help us out.'

"Lory was lollin' in an easy-chair, lookin' out west across his spring lot. Directly I saw a twinkle in his eye, and followin' the line of his glance, there slouchin' in a fence corner I saw Lory's old white workmare, Molly. Sometimes Molly pulled the buggy and the little Lings, but usually it was a plough or a mower for hers. I'd heard Lory say she was eighteen years old and that once she was gray, but now she's white as a first snow-fall.

"'How would old gray Molly do, Raven?' presently asks Lory.

"'Do? Has she ever hunted?' asks Raven.

"'Divil a hunt of anything but a chance for a rest,' says Lory; 'never had a saddle on, as far as I know, but she has the quarters and low sloping shoulders of a born jumper, and it's you must admit it. Let's have a look at her.'

"So out across the spring lot the three of us went, to the corner where Molly was dozin'. And true for Lory it was, the old lady had fine points; when lightly slapped with Raven's crop she showed spirit and a good bit of action.

"'She's sure got a good strain in her,' says Raven; 'where did you get her, Lory?'

"'Had her twelve years,' says Lory; 'brought her on from my Wyoming ranch; she and a skullful of experience and a heartful of disappointment made up about all two bad winters left of my ranch investments. The freight on her made her look more like a back-set than an asset, but she was a link of the old life I couldn't leave.'

"'Well, give her a try out,' laughs Raven, 'and if she'll run a bit and jump, we may have some fun passin' her up to Jack.'

"So Lory takes her to the stable, has her saddled and mounts, and I hope never to have another rub-down if she didn't gallop on like she'd never done anything else—stiff in the pasterns and hittin' the ground fit to bust herself wide open, but poundin' along a fair pace. Then we went into a narrow lane and I gave her a lead over some low bars, and here came game old Molly stretchin' over after me like fences and her were old stable-mates.

"'Well, I *will* be damned,' says Raven; 'she's a hoary wonder. Give her a week of handlin' and trim her up, and it'll be Jack for mother at a stiff price; he's so bent on his fad, he'll take a chance on her age.'

"And then it was clinkin' glasses and roarin' laughter in the house with them, while I began tippin' Molly a few useful points at the game as soon as the groom left us in adjoinin' stalls.

"Four days later Lory brought Molly over to the hunt-club mews, and if I'd not been on to their mischievous plot, I'll be fired if I'd known her. It was a cunnin' one, was Lory, and he'd banged her tail, hogged her mane, clipped her pasterns, polished her hoofs, groomed, fed up, and conditioned her, and (I do believe) polished her yellow old fangs, till she looked as fit a filly as you'd want to see.

"And soon after, when Molly was unsaddled and stalled, into an empty box alongside of me slips Lory with Tom, the best whip and seat of our hunt, and says Lory: 'You never seem to mind riskin' your neck, Tom.'

"'Thank ye kindly, sir,' says Tom; 'hall in the day's work.'

"'Well, if you'll give the old gray mare a week's practice at wall and timber, gettin' out early when none but the sun and the pair of you are yet up, I'll give you the little rifle you lovin'ly handled at my place the other day. But mind, it's your neck she may break at the first wall, for I've niver taken her over anything much higher than a pig sty.'

"'Right-o, sir,' says Tom; 'an' there's any jump in the old girl, I'll git it out of 'er.'

"The next Saturday afternoon, the biggest meet of the season, up rides that divil of a Lory on Molly, him in a brand-new suit of ridin' togs and her heavy-curbed and martingaled like she was a wild four-year-old, the pair lookin' so fine I scarce knew the man or Raven the mare.

"'Hi, there, Lory!' says Raven; 'wherever did you get the corkin' white un?'

"'Sh-h-h! you damn fool,' says Lory.

"'The hell you say!' whispers Raven, reins aside, chucklin' low to the two of us, and with a knee-press which I knew meant, 'Sol, jist you watch 'em!'

"And we were no more than turned about when up rides the master, Jack, both ears pointin' Molly, and says:

"'Good-looker you have there, Lory. New purchase?

"'No, indeed,' says Lory; 'old hunter I've had some years; brought her on from the West; just up off grass and not quite prime yet; guess she'll finish, though.

"Think of it—the nerve of the divil—and him knowin' she was more likely to finish at the first fence than ever to reach the check. For the day's course was a full ten-mile run, and a check was laid half-way for a blow or a change of mounts.

"Presently the hounds opened at the 'throw-in,' an Irish pack it takes near a steeplechase pace to stay with, and we were off on as stiff a course as even Lemon County can show. And a holy miracle was Lory's ridin' that day. For nigh four miles he held tight behind two duffers who, while up on top-notchers, pulled their mounts so heavily that they took a top rail off nearly every fence they rose to and swerved for low wall-gaps, till he'd got Molly's nerves up a bit. Then, takin' a chance on the last mile, Lory threw crop and spur into her and raced straight ahead, liftin' her over wall and timber to try the best, until close up on Jack. Just then Jack turned and watched them, just as they were approachin' a heavy four-foot jump, a broad stone wall and ditch. Sure, I thought it was all up with Lory, but at it he hurled her, and I'll be curbed if she didn't take it as cleverly as I could.

"Old Molly finished third at the check, but at the expense of a pair of badly torn and bleedin' knees, got scrapin' over stone and wood, which that rascal of a Lory hid by swervin' to a white clay bank and plasterin' her wounds with the clay, and then she was led away by his groom.

"Joggin' back from the 'worry' that evenin', Jack lay tight in Lory's flank till Lory had consented, apparently with great reluctance, to sell him Molly for five hundred dollars.

"The very next week, Jack, Raven, and the two whips turned out on white hunters, Jack of course upon Molly and happy over the successful workin' out of his fad. But good old Jack's happiness was short-lived, for after the 'throw-in' he was not seen again of the hunt that day, The first fence Molly negotiated in fine style, but at the second she came a terrible cropper that badly jolted Jack and knocked every last ounce of heart out of her, cowed her so completely that she'd be in that same meadow yet if there'd not been a pair of bars to lead her through, and divil a man was ever found could make her try another jump.

"Great was the quiet fun of Lory and Raven, though Lory's lasted little longer than Jack's joy of his white mount. Of course Jack was too game to let on he knew he'd been done, but not too busy to sharpen a rowel for Lory.

"And the rankest wonder it was Lory niver saw it till Jack had him raked from flank to shoulder—just stood and took it without a blink, like a donkey takes a lash.

"Within a week of Molly's downfall Lory was out on me one day, when up rides Jack and says:

"'There's a splendid hunter in me stable I want ye to have, Lory. Got more than I can keep, and your stable must be a bit shy since you parted with the white mare. He's the bay seventeen-hander in the Irish lot. Stands me over a thousand, but you can have him at your own price; don't want the hardest, straightest rider of the hunt shy of fit meat and bone to carry him.'

"Belikes it was the blarney caught him, but anyway Lory buried his muzzle in Jack's pail till he could see nothin' but what Jack said it held, and took the bay at six hundred dollars just on a casual lookover.

"It was a good action, a grand jumpin' form, and rare pace the bay showed on a short try-out that afternoon, so much so I overheard Lory tellin' himself, when he was after dismounting just outside me box: 'Gad! but ain't old Jack easy money!'

"But when Lory and the bay showed up at the next day's meet, I noticed the bay's ears layin' back or workin' in a way to tell any but a blind one it was dirty mischief he was plannin'. Nor was he long playin' it. For about a third of the run the bay raced like a steeple-chaser tight on the heels of the hounds, leadin' even the master, for Lory could no more hold him than his own glee at the grand way they were takin' gates and walls. But suddenly that bay divil's-spawn swerves from the course, dashes up and stops bang broadside against a barn; and there, with ears laid back tight to his head and muzzle half upturned, for four mortal hours the bay held Lory's off leg jammed so tight against the barn that, rowel and crop-cut hard as he might, the only thing Lory was able to free was such a flow of language, it was a holy wonder Providence didn't fire the barn and burn up the pair of them.

"And as Jack passed them I heard the divil sing out: 'Ha! Ha! Lory! it was the gray mare wanted to jump but couldn't, and it's the bay can jump but won't! It's an "oh hell!" for you and a "ha! ha!" for me this time!'

"Which, while they're still fast friends, was the last word ever passed between them on the subject of the funker and the balker."

CHAPTER 12

El Tigre

"A cat may look at a king, but the son of a village lawyer may not venture to bare his heart to the daughter of the Duque de la Torrevieja. And yet a man of our blood was ennobled early in the wars with the Moors, while the Duke's forebears were still simple men-at-arms, knighted under a name that in itself carries the ring of the heroic deeds that earned it."

The speaker, Mauro de la Lucha-sangre (literally "Mauro of the Bloody Battle"), stood one June morning of 1874 beneath the shade of a gnarled olive-tree on the banks of the Guadaira River, rebelliously stamping a heel into the soft turf. Son of the foremost lawyer of his native town of Utrera, educated in Sevilla at the best university of his province, already at twenty-four himself a fully accredited *licenciado*, Mauro's future held actually brilliant prospects for a man of the station into which he was born. And yet, most envied of his classmates though he was, to Mauro himself the future loomed black, forbidding, cheerless.

Mauro's father, by legacy from his father, was the attorney and counsellor of the Duque de la Torrevieja; and so might Mauro have been for the next duke had there not cropped out in him the daring, the love of adventure, the pride, and the confidence that had lifted the first Lucha-sangre above his fellows. It was a case of breeding back— away back over and past generations of fawning commoners to the times when Lucha-sangre swords were splitting Moorish *casques* and winning guerdons.

Nor in spirit alone was Mauro bred back. He was deep of chest, broad of shoulder, lithe and graceful. His massive neck upbore a head of Augustan beauty, lighted by eyes that alternately blazed with the pride and resolution of a *Cid* and softened with the musings of a

Manrique. Mauro was a Lucha-sangre of the twelfth century, reincarnate.

Little is it to be wondered at that, as the lad was often his father's message-bearer to the duke, he found favour in the eyes of the duke's only daughter, Sofia; and still less is it to be wondered at that he early became her thrall. Of nights at the university he was ever dreaming of her; up out of his text-books her lovely face was ever rising before him in class.

Of a rare type was Sofia in Andalusia, where nearly all are dark, for she was a true *rubia*, blue of eye, fair of skin, and with hair of the wondrously changing tints of a cooling iron ingot.

And now here was Mauro, just back from Sevilla, almost within arms'-reach of his divinity, and yet not free to seek her. And as the rippling current of the Quadaira crimsoned and then reddened and darkened till it seemed to him like a great ruddy tress of Sofia's waving hair, Mauro sprang to his feet and fiercely whispered: "*Mil demonios!* but she shall at least know, and then I'll kiss the old *padre*, and his musty office goodbye and go try my hand at some man's task!"

Opportunity came earlier than he had dared hope. The very next morning the elder Lucha-sangre sent Mauro to the castle with some papers for the duke's approval and signature. Still at breakfast, the duke received him in the great banquet-hall of the castle, the walls covered with portraits of Torreviejas gone before, several of the earlier generations so dim and gray with age they looked mere spectres of the limner's art.

While the duke was reading the papers, Mauro stood with eyes riveted to the newest portrait of them all, that of Sofia's mother—Sofia's very self matured—herself a native of a northern province wherein to this day red hair and blue eyes are a frequent, almost a prevailing type, that tell the story of early Gothic invasions. So absorbed in the picture, so completely possessed by it was Mauro, that when the duke turned and spoke to him, he did not hear.

And so he stood for some moments while the duke sat contemplating the fine lines of his face and the splendid pose of his figure; his eyes lightened with admiration, his head nodding approval.

Then gently touching Mauro's arm, the duke queried: "And so you admire the duchess, young man?"

With a start Mauro answered, after a dazed stare at the duke: "A thousand pardons, Excellency! But yes, sir; who in all the world could fail to admire her?"

"OF A RARE TYPE WAS SOFIA IN ANDALUSIA"

"Yes, yes," replied the duke; "God never made but one other quite her equal, and her He made in her own very image—Sofia; *que Dios la aguarda!*"

Mauro gravely bowed, received the papers from the duke, and withdrew.

Turning to his secretary, the duke sighed deeply and murmured: "*Dios mio!* if only I had a son of my own blood like that boy! What a pity he should be tied down to paltry pettifoggery!"

Meantime Mauro, striding disconsolate past an angle of the narrow garden of the inner courtyard, was detained by a soft voice issuing from the seclusion of a bench beneath the drooping boughs of an ancient fig tree: "*Buenos dias, Don Mauro. Bueno es verte revuelto.*"

"*Buenos dias, Condesa;* and it is indeed good to me to be back, good to hear thy voice—the first real happiness I have known since my ears last welcomed its sweet tones. Good to be back! ah! Condesa Sofia, for me it is to live again."

"But, Don Mauro—"

"A thousand pardons, *Condesa,* but thy *duenna* may join thee at any moment, and my heart has long guarded a message for thee it can no longer hold and stay whole,—a message thou mayest well resent for its gross presumption, and yet a message I would here and now deliver if I knew I must die for it the next minute.

"From childhood hast thus possessed me. Never a night for the last ten years have I lain down without a prayer to the Virgin for thy safety and happiness; never a day but I have so lived that my conduct shall be worthy of thee. Though I am the son of thy father's *licenciado*, thou well knowest the blood of a long line of proud warriors burns in my veins. Hope that thou mightst ever even deign to listen to me I have never ventured to cherish—"

"But Don Mauro—"

"Again a thousand pardons, *Condesa,* but I must tell thee thou art the light of my soul. Without thee all the world is a valley of bitterness; with thee its most arid desert would be an Eden. The birds are ever chanting to me thy name. Every pool reflects thy sweet face. Every breeze wafts me the fragrance of thy dear presence. Every thunderous roll of the Almighty's war-drums calls me to attempt some great heroic deed in thine honour, some deed that shall prove to thee the lawyer's son, in heart and soul if not in present station, is not unworthy to tell to thee his love. And—"

"But, Mauro, Mauro m—*mio!*" And with a sob she arose and actually fled through the shrubbery.

Two days later the betrothal of the Countess Sofia to the Count Leon, the eldest son and heir to the Duke de Oviedo, was announced by her father. And that, indeed, was what she had tried but lacked the heart to tell him—that, wherever her heart might lie, her father had already promised her hand!

It was a bitter night for Mauro, that of the announcement, and a sad one for his father. Their conference lasted till near morning. The son pleaded he must have a life of action and hazard; his country at peace, he would train for the bull ring.

"Why not the opera, my son?" the thrifty father replied. "Thou hast a grand tenor voice; indeed the bishop has asked that thou wilt lead the choir of the cathedral. With such a voice thou wouldst have action, see the world, gain riches, while all the time playing the parts, fighting the battles of some great historic character."

"But no, father," answered Mauro; "such be no more than sham fights. Not only must I wear a sword as did the early Lucha-sangres, but I must hear it ring and ring against that of a worthy foe, feel it steal within the cover of his guard, see the good blade drip red in fair battle. True, there be no Moors or French to fight, but what soldier on reddened field ever took greater odds than a lone *espada* takes every time he challenges a fierce Utrera bull? And I swear to thee, *padre mio*, whatever my calling, I shall ever be heedful of and cherish the motto that Lucha-sangre swords have always borne: '*No me sacas sin razon; no me metes sin honour.*'" (Do not draw me without good cause; do not sheath me without honour!)

The less strong-minded of the two, the father yielded, and even furnished funds sufficient for a year's private tutoring by Frascuelo, then the greatest *matador* in all Spain.

Thus the first time Mauro ever appeared before a public assembly was a chief *espada* of a *cuadrilla* of his own, at Valladolid. An apt pupil from the start, bent upon reaching the highest rank, of extraordinary strength and activity, utterly fearless but cool headed, a natural general, at the close of his first *corrida* he was acclaimed the certain successor of the great Frascuelo himself, and at the same time christened *El Tigre* (the Tiger) for the feline swiftness of his movements and the ferocity of his attacks.

The next eight years were for *El Tigre* fruitful of fame and riches but utterly arid and barren of even the most casual feminine attachment. Well educated, clever, with the manners of a courtier, and with physical beauty and personal charm few men equalled, he was invited by the nobility often, received as an equal by the men and literally courted by the women. But the attentions of women were all to no purpose. For *El Tigre* only one woman existed—Sofia, now the Duchess de Oviedo—though he had never again set eyes on her from the hour of their parting beneath the fig tree.

Owners of large Mexican sugar estates in the valley of Cuautla, the duke and Sofia divided their time between Paris and Mexico. Their marriage was far from happy. Before their union, busy tongues had brought Count Leon rumours of her admiration for Mauro, rousing suspicions that were not long crystallizing into certainty that, while she was a faithful, honest wife, he could never win of her the affection he gave and craved. Obviously proud of her, always devoted and kind, he received from her respect and consideration in return, which indeed was all she had to give, for the loss of Mauro remained to her an ever-gnawing grief.

Oddly enough, fate decreed that the destiny of Mauro and Sofia should be worked out far afield from their burning Utreran plains, high up on the cool plateau of Central Mexico.

For several years most generous offers had been made *El Tigre* to bring his *cuadrilla* to Mexico, but, surfeited with fame and rolling in riches, he had declined them. At last, however, in 188—, an offer was made him which he felt forced to accept—six thousand dollars a performance for ten *corridas*, to be given on successive Sundays in the Plaza Bucareli in the City of Mexico, all expenses of himself and his *cuadrilla* to be paid by the management. And so, late in April of that year *El Tigre* arrived in Mexico with his *cuadrilla* and (as stipulated in his contract) sixty great Utreran bulls, for the bulls of Utrera are famed in *toreador* history and song as the fiercest, most desperate fighters *espada* ever confronted.

At the first performance *El Tigre* took the Mexican public by storm. No such execution, daring, and grace had ever been seen in either Bucareli or Colon. *El Tigre* was the toast in every club and *cafe* of the city. Every shop window displayed his portrait. All the journals sung his praises. Maids and matrons sighed for him. Youth and age envied him. *El Tigre's* coffers were well-nigh bursting and his cups of joy overflowing, all but the one none but Sofia could fill.

Where she was at the time *El Tigre* had no idea. And yet, wholly unsuspected by him, not only were she and the duke in Mexico, but both had attended all his performances at Bucareli, up to the last, inconspicuous behind parties of friends they entertained in their box.

Whether it was the duke caught the pallor of Sofia's face in moments of peril for Mauro, or the light of pride and admiration in her eyes during his moments of triumph, sure it is the smouldering fires of the duke's jealousy were rekindled, and he was prompted to plan a test of her bearing, when free of the restraint of his presence. On the morning of the last performance he announced that he must spend the afternoon with his attorneys, and must leave Sofia free to make her own arrangements for attendance at the last *corrida*.

And glad enough was she of the chance. The boxes were far too high above, and distant from, the arena. For days she had coveted any of the seats along the lower rows of open benches, close down to the six-foot barrier between the ring and the auditorium, close down where she could catch every shifting expression of Mauro's mobile face, and—where he could scarcely fail to see and recognize her. The thought of seeking in any way to meet or speak to him never entered her clean mind, but she had been more nearly a saint than a woman if she had been able to deny herself such an opportunity to convey to him, in one long burning glance, a knowledge of the endurance of the love her frightened "Mauro *mio*" had plainly confessed the night of their parting beneath the fig tree. So it naturally followed that the duke was barely out of the house before Sofia rushed away a messenger to reserve a section of the lower benches immediately beneath the box of the *Presidente*, directly in front of which Mauro must come, at the head of his *cuadrilla*, to salute the *Presidente*.

The city was thronged with visitors come to see *El Tigre*. Hotels and clubs were overflowing with them. And thousands of poor peons had for months stinted themselves, often even gone hungry, to save enough *tlacos* to buy admission to the spectacle, to them the greatest and most magnificent it could ever be their good fortune to witness. The day was perfect, as indeed are most June days in Mexico. For two hours before the performance the principal thoroughfares leading to the Plaza Bucareli were packed solid with a moving throne all dressed *en fete*.

In no country in the world may one see such great picturesqueness, variety, and brilliancy of colour in the costumes of the masses as then still prevailed in Mexico. Largely of more or less pure Indian blood, come of a race Cortez found habited in feather tunics and head-dresses brilliant as the plumage of parrots, great lovers of flowers, three and a half centuries of contact with civilization had not served to deprive them of any of their fondness for bright colours. Thus with the horsemen in the graceful *traje de chorro*—sombreros and tight fitting soft leather jackets and trousers loaded with gold or silver ornaments, the footmen swaggering in *serapes* of every colour of the rainbow, the women wrapped in more delicately tinted *rebosas* and crowned with flowers, the winding streets looked like strips of flower garden ambulant.

Bucareli seated twenty thousand, and when all standing-room had been filled and the gates closed, thousands of late comers were shut out.

The level, sanded ring, the theatre of action, was surrounded by a six-foot solid-planked barrier. Behind and above the barrier rose the benches of the auditorium, the "bleachers" of the populace; they rose to a height of perhaps forty or fifty feet, while above the uppermost line of benches were the private boxes of the *elite*. Within the ring were five heavily planked nooks of refuge, set close to the barrier, behind which a hard pressed *toreador* might find safety from a charging bull. These refuges were little used, however, except by the underlings, the *capadores*, or by capsized *picadores*; *espadas* and *banderilleros* disdained them. On the west of the ring was the box of the *Presidente* of the *corrida* (in this instance, the Governor of the Federal District); on the east the main gate of the ring through which the *cuadrilla* entered; on the north the gate of the bull pen.

At a bugle call from the *Presidente's* box, the main gate swung wide and the *cuadrilla* entered, a band of lithe, slender, clean-shaven men, in slippers, white stockings, knee breeches, and jackets of silk ornamented with silver, each wearing the little queue and black rosette attached thereto that from time immemorial Andalusian *toreadores* have sported.

El Tigre headed the squad, followed by two junior *matadores*, three *banderilleros*, three *capadores*, and two mounted *picadores*, while at the rear of the column came two teams of little, half-wild, prancing, dancing Spanish mules, one team black, the other white, each composed of three mules harnessed abreast as for a chariot race, but dragging behind them nothing but a heavy double tree, to which the dead of the day's fight might be attached and dragged out of the arena.

Each of the footmen was wrapped in a large black cloak passed over the left shoulder and beneath the right, the loose end of the cloak draped gracefully over the left shoulder, the right arm swinging free. The *picadores* were mounted (as usual) on old crow baits of horses, mere bags of skin and bones, so poor and thin that neither could even raise a trot; a broad leather blindfold fastened to their head-stalls. Each rider was seated in a saddle high of cantle and ancient of form as those Knights Templar jousted in. The breast of each horse was guarded by a great side of sole leather falling nearly to the knees, while the right leg of each rider was incased in such a stiff and heavy leather leg-guard as to render him afoot almost helpless; and he was further guarded by still another side of sole leather swung from the saddle horn and covering his left leg and much of his horse's barrel. On the right stirrup of each *picador* rested the butt of his lance, a stout eight-foot shaft tipped with a sharp steel prod, barely long enough to catch and hold in the bull's hide.

As the *cuadrilla* entered, a regimental band played *El Hymno Nacional*, the National Anthem, while the vast audience roared and shrieked a welcome to the gladiators.

Marching to the time of the music in long tragic strides, heads proudly erect, right arms swinging and shoulders slightly swaying in the challenging swagger which *toreadores affect*, the *cuadrilla* crossed the arena and halted, close to the barrier, in front of the *Presidente's* box, bared their heads, gracefully saluted the *Presidente*, and received the key to the bull pen and his permission to begin the fight. And as *El Tigre's* eyes fell from the salute to the *Presidente* they rested upon Sofia, doubtless from some subtle telepathic message, for it was a veritable hill of faces he confronted. There she sat on the second bench-row above the top of the barrier, matured and fuller of figure but radiant as at their Utreran parting; there she sat, her gloved hands tightly clenched, her lips trembling, her great blue eyes pouring into his messages of a love so deep and pure that it needed all his self-command to keep from leaping the barrier and falling at her feet.

For a moment he stood transfixed, staggered, almost overcome with surprise and delight again to see her, thrilled with the joy of her message, blazing with revolt at the painful consciousness that she was and must remain another's. His emotions well-nigh stopped the beating of his heart. And so he stood gazing into Sofia's eyes until, self-possession recovered, he gravely bowed, turned, and waved his men to their posts.

Instantly all was action, swift action. Cloaks were tossed to attendants, each footman received a red cape, the two *picadores* took position one on either side of the bull pen gate, the band struck up a tune, the gate was opened and a great Utreran bull bounded into the arena, maddened with the pain of a short *banderilla*, with long streaming ribbons, stuck in his neck as he entered, by an attendant perched above the gate.

His equal had never been seen in a Mexican bull ring. While typical of his Utreran brothers, all princes of bovine fighting stock, this coal-black monster was by the spectators voted their King. Relatively light of quarters and shallow of flank and barrel, he was unusually high and humped of withers, broad and deep of chest and heavy of shoulders—indeed a well-nigh perfect four-legged type of a finely trained two-legged athlete, with a pair of peculiarly straight-upstanding horns that were long and almost as sharp as rapiers. Evidently by his build, he was of a strong strain of East Indian Brahminic blood. For his great weight, his activity was phenomenal—his leaps like a panther's, his turns as quick.

Dazed for an instant by the crash of the music and the brilliant banks of colour about him, he stood angrily lashing his tail and pawing up the sand in clouds—"digging a grave," as Texas cowboys used to call it—his eyes blazing and head tossing, but only for a moment. Then he charged the nearest *picador*, literally leaped so high at him that head and cruel horns crossed above the horse's neck, his own great chest striking the horse just behind the shoulder with such force that man and mount hit the ground stunned and helpless.

Barely were they down when he was upon them and with a single twitch of his mighty neck, had ripped open the horse's barrel and half amputated one of the rider's legs. Then, diverted by the *capadores*, he whirled upon the second *picador* and in another ten seconds had left his horse dead and the rider badly trampled. Next the *banderilleros* tackled him, but such was his speed and ferocity that all three funked the work, and not one of them fastened his flag in the black shoulders.

When the bull had entered the ring, *El Tigre* left the arena—a most unusual proceeding. Now he returned, clad in snow-white from head to foot, a white cap covering head and hair, his face heavily powdered. He slipped in behind and unseen by the bull to the centre of the arena, and there stood erect, with arms folded, motionless as a graven image.

Presently the bull turned, saw *El Tigre*, and charged him straight. *El Tigre* was not even facing him, for the bull was approaching from his left. But there he stood without the twitch of a muscle or the flicker of an eye lid, still as a figure of stone.

A great sob arose from the audience, and all gave him up for lost, when, at the last instant before the bull must have struck, it turned and passed him. Once more the bull so charged and passed. Whether because it mistook him for the ghost of a man or recognized in him a spirit mightier than its own, only the bull knew.

Before the audience had well caught its breath, *El Tigre*, wearing again his usual costume, was striding again to the middle of the arena, carrying a light chair, in which presently he seated himself, facing the bull, a show *banderilla*, no more than six inches long, held in his teeth. And so he awaited the charge until the bull was within actual arm's-reach, when with a swift rise from the chair and a turn of his body quick as that of a fencer's supple wrist, he bent and stuck the teeth-held *banderilla* in the bull's shoulder as he swept past.

Now was the time for the kill.

El Tigre received his sword, *muleta*, and cape. The *muleta* is a straight two-foot stick over which the cape is draped, and, held in the *matador's* left hand, usually is extended well to the right of his body. Thus in an ordinary fight the bull is actually charging the blood-red cape, and not the *matador*. But, with Sofia an onlooker, determined to make this the fight of his life, *El Tigre* tossed aside the *muleta*, wrapped the crimson cape about his body, and stood alone awaiting the bull's charge, his malleable sword-blade bent slightly downward, sufficiently to give a true thrust behind the shoulder, a down-curve into heart or lungs.

With a bull of such extraordinary activity the act was almost suicidal, but *El Tigre* smilingly took the chance. By toreador etiquette, the *matador* must receive and dodge the first two charges; not until the third may he strike. On the first charge *El Tigre* stood like a rock until the bull had almost reached him, and then lightly leaped diagonally across his lowered neck. The second charge, come an instant after the first, before most men could even turn, he dodged. The third he swiftly side-stepped, thrust true, and dropped the great Utreran midway of a leap aimed at his elusive enemy.

It was a deed magnificent, epic, and the plaza rung with plaudits while hats, fans, and even purses and jewels showered into the arena— all of which, by *toreador* etiquette, were tossed back across the barrier to their owners.

Then the teams entered and quickly dragged the dead from the arena; the ugly, dangerously slippery red patches were fresh sanded, and the second bull was admitted. Thus, with more or less like incident, three more bulls were fought and killed.

183

The fifth and last, however, proved a disgrace to his race. Bluff he did, but fight he would not; the noise and crowd unnerved him. At last, frenzied with fear and seeking escape, he made a mighty leap to mount the barrier directly in front of the box of the *Presidente*. And mount it he did, and down it crashed beneath his weight, leaving the bull for a moment half down and tangled in the wreckage, struggling to regain his feet.

Directly in front of the bull, not six feet beyond the sharp points of his deadly horns, sat Sofia. Indeed none about her had risen; all sat as if frozen in their places. And just as well they might have been, for escape into or through the dense mass of spectators about them was utterly impossible. Whatever horror came they must await, helpless.

But at the bull's very start for the barrier, *El Tigre*, realized Sofia's peril and instantly sprang empty-handed in pursuit; for it was early in this the last *corrida* and he did not have his sword,

Leaping the wreckage, *El Tigre* landed directly in front of the bull, happily at the instant it regained its feet, where, with his right hand seizing the bull by the nose—his thumb and two fore-fingers thrust well within its nostrils—and with his left hand grabbing the right horn, with a mighty heave he uplifted the bull's muzzle and bore down upon its horn until he threw it with a crash upon its side that left it momentarily helpless.

But, himself slipping in the loose wreckage, down also *El Tigre* fell, the bull's sharp right horn impaling his left thigh and pinning him to the ground.

Before the bull could rise, the men of the *cuadrilla* had it safely bound and *El Tigre* released. *El Tigre*, however, did not know it. With the shock and pain of his wound he had fainted.

When at length he regained consciousness, it was to find his head pillowed in Sofia's lap, her soft fingers caressing his brow, her tearful eyes looking into his, and to hear her whisper: "Mauro *mio!*"

Just at this moment the Duke de Oviedo approached, no one knew whence.

White with jealousy but steady and cool, he quietly remarked:

"*Madame*, I ought to kill you both, but that my rank precludes. Lucha-sangre, in yourself, as son of a notary and hired *toreador* and purveyor of spectacles, you are unworthy of my sword; nevertheless blood once noble is in your veins. And so as noble it suits me now to count you. As soon as you are recovered of your wound I will send you my second."

"Most happy, duke," answered Mauro; "mine shall be ready to meet him."

★★★★★★

One evening a week later, while the Duke de Oviedo and two Mexican army officers were having drinks at the bar of the Cafe Concordia, General Delmonte, a Cuban long resident in New York and a distinguished veteran of three wars, entered with two American friends. Delmonte was describing to his friends *El Tigre's* last fight, lauding his prowess, extolling his noble presence and high character. Infuriated by the ardent praise of his enemy, the Duke grossly insulted General Delmonte—and was very promptly slapped in the face.

They fought at daylight the next morning, beneath an arch of the ancient aqueduct, just outside the city. Encountering in Delmonte one of the best swordsmen of his time, early in the combat the Duke received a mortal wound. And as he there lay gasping out his life, he murmured a phrase that, at the moment, greatly puzzled his seconds:

"*Gana El Tigre.*" (The Tiger Wins!)

CHAPTER 13

Bunkered

It seems it must have been somewhere about the year 4000 B. C. that we lost sight of the tall peaks of the architectural topography of Manhattan Island, and yet the log of the *Black Prince* makes it no more than twenty days. Not that our day-to-day time has been dragging, for it has done nothing of the sort.

All my life long I have dreamed of indulging in the joy of a really long voyage, and now at last I've got it. New York to Cape Town, South Africa, 6,900 miles, thirty days' straight-away run, and thence another twenty-four days' sail to Mombasa, on a 7,000-ton cargo boat, deliberate and stately rather than fast of pace, but otherwise as trim, well groomed, and well found as a liner, with an official mess that numbers as fine a set of fellows as ever trod a bridge. The captain, when not busy hunting up a stray planet to check his latitude, puts in his spare time hunting kindly things to do for his two passengers—for there are only two of us, the doctor and myself. The doctor signed on the ship's articles as surgeon, I as purser.

Fancy it! Thirty days' clear respite from the daily papers, the telephone, the subway crowds, and the constant wear and tear on one's muscular system reaching for change, large and small! Thirty days free of the daily struggle either for place on the ladder of ambition or for the privilege to stay on earth and stand about and watch the others mount, that saps metropolitan nerves and squeezes the humanities out of metropolitan life until its hearts are arid and barren and cruel as those of the cavemen! Thirty days' repose, practically alone amid one of nature's greatest solitudes, awed by her silences, uplifted by the majesty of her mighty forces, with naught to do but humble oneself before the consciousness of his own littleness and unfitness, and study how to right the wrongs he has done.

Indeed a voyage like this makes it certain one will come actually to know one's own self so intimately that, unless well convinced that he will esteem and enjoy the acquaintance, he had best stay at home. Of my personal experience in this particular I beg to be excused from writing.

Lonesome out here? Far from it. Behind, to be sure, are those so near and dear, one would gladly give all the remaining years allotted him for one blessed half-hour with them. Otherwise, time literally flies aboard the *Black Prince*; the days slip by at puzzling speed. Roughly speaking, I should say the meals consume about half one's waking hours, for we are fed five times a day, and fed so well one cannot get his own consent to dodge any of them.

Indeed I've only one complaint to make of this ship; she is a "water-wagon" in a double sense, which makes it awkward for a man who never could drink comfortably alone. With every man of the mess a teetotaller, one is now and then possessed with a consuming desire for communion with some dear soul of thirsty memory who can be trusted to take his "straight." Of course I don't mean to imply that this mess cannot be trusted, for you can rely on it implicitly every time— to take tea; you can trust it with any mortal or material thing, except your pet brew of tea, if you have one, which, luckily, I haven't.

Indeed, for the thirsty man Nature herself in these latitudes is discouraging, for the Big Dipper stays persistently upside down, dry!— perhaps out of sympathy with the teetotal principles of this ship. And most of the way down here there has been such a high sea running that the only dry places I have noticed have been the upper bridge and my throat. The fact is, about everything aboard this ship is distressingly suggestive to a faithful knight of the tankard: he is surrounded with "ports" that won't flow and giant "funnels" that might easily carry spirits enough to wet the whistles of an army division (but don't), until he is tempted in sheer desperation to take a pull at the "main brace."

All of which, assisted by the advent of a covey of flying fishes and a (Sunday) "school" of porpoises, is responsible for the following, which is adventured with profuse apologies to Mr. Kipling:

ON THE ROAD TO MOMBASA

Take me north of the Equator
Where'er gleams the polar star,
Where "The Dipper" ne'er is empty

And Orion is not far,
Where the eagle at them gazes
And up toward them thrusts the pine—
Anywhere strong men drink spirits
On the right side of "the line."

On the road to Mombas-a,
Drawing nearer toward Cathay,
Where the north star now is under,
'Neath the Southern Cross's ray.

Take me off this water wagon
Where the Captain's ribbon's blue,
Where the Doctor, yclept Barthwaite,
And each man-jack of the crew
Never get a drop of poteen,
Never know the cheer of beer—
Anywhere a thirsty man may
Wet his whistle without fear.

On the road to Mombas-a,
With the Black Prince, day by day
Rolling her tall taffrail under,
'Neath a sky o'ercast and gray.

Take me back to good old Proctor's
Where a man may quench his thirst,
Where a purser with a shilling
Needn't feel he is accursed
By an ironclad owners' ship rule
That her officers shouldn't drink—
Anywhere the ringing glasses
Merrily clink! clink!

On the road to Mombas-a,
Where the only drink is "tay,"
Where a thirst that is a wonder
Burns the throat from day to day.

Take me somewhere close to Rector's
Where a man can get a crab,
Where the blondined waves are tossing
And every eye-glance is a stab,
Where there's froufrou of the jupon
And there's popping of the cork

Anywhere the men and women
Snap their fingers at the stork.

On the road to Mombas-a,
Where e'en mermaids never play,
Where to come would be a blunder
Hunting hot birds and Roger.

But lonesome out here? Never—with the sympathetic North Atlantic winds ever ready to roar you a grim dirge in your moments of melancholy contemplation of the inverted Dipper, with the gentle tropical breezes softly singing through the rigging notes of soothing cadence, with the lethal ocean billows ever leaping up the sides of the ship, foaming with the joy of what they would do to you if they once got you in their embrace!

Lonesome? With the coming and the going of each day's sun gilding cloud-crests, silvering waves, setting you matchless scenes in colour effect, some ravishing in their gorgeous splendour, some soft and tender of tone as the light in the eyes of the woman you worship, scenes beside which the most brilliant stage settings which metropolitans flock like sheep to see are pathetically paltry counterfeits.

Lonesome? With a mighty, joyously bounding charger like the *Black Prince* beneath your feet if not between your knees, gayly taking the tallest billows in his stride, whose ever steady pulse-beat bespeaks a soundness of wind and limb you can trust to land you well at the finish!

Lonesome? Where privileged to descend into the very vitals of your charger and sit throughout the midnight watch, an awed listener to the throbs of the mighty heart that vitalizes his every function, while each vigorously thrusting piston, each smug, palm-rubbing eccentric, each somnolently nodding lever, drives deeper into your lay brain an overwhelming sense of pride in such of your kind as have had the genius to conceive, and such others as have had the skill and patience to perfect, the conversion of inert masses of crude metal into the magnificently powerful and obviously sentient entity that is bearing you!

Lonesome? Skirting the coastline of Africa, a country whose potentates, from the Ptolemies to Tom Ryan, have never failed to make world history worth thinking about!

Lonesome? Bearing up toward that sea-made manacle of fallen majesty, St. Helena, absorbed in memories of Bonaparte's magnificent dreams of world-wide dominion, and of his pathetic end on one of its smallest and most isolated patches!

Lonesome? With a chum at your elbow so close a student of the manly game of war that he can glibly reel off for you every important manoeuvre of all the great battles of history, from those of Alexander the Great down to Tommy Burns's latest!

And now and then the elements themselves sit in and take a hand in our game, sometimes a hand we could very well do without—as twice lately.

The first instance happened early last week. Tuesday tropical weather hit us and drove us into *pajamas*—a cloudless sky, blazing sun, high humidity, while we ploughed our way across long, slow-rolling, unrippled swells that looked so much like a vast, gently heaving sea of petroleum that, had John D. Standardoil been with us he would have suffered a probably fatal attack of heart disease if prevented from stopping right there and planning a pipe line.

Throughout the day close about the ship clouds of flying fish skimmed the sea, and great schools of porpoises leaped from it and raced us, as if, even to them, their native element had become hateful, or as if they sensed something ominous and fearsome abroad from which they sought shelter in our company. One slender little opal-hued diaphanous-winged bird-fish came aboard, and before he was picked up had the happy life grilled out of him on our scorching iron deck, hot almost as boiler plates. Poor little chap! he found with us anything but sanctuary; but perhaps he lived long enough to signal the fact to his mates, for no others boarded us.

And yet for one other opal-hued winged wanderer we have been sanctuary; for when we were about one hundred and fifty miles out of New York a highly bred carrier pigeon, bearing on his leg a metal tag marked "32," hovered about us for a time, finally alighted on our rail, and then fluttered to the deck when offered a pan of water—and drank and drank until it seemed best to stop him. By kindness and ingenuity of Chief Engineer Tucker he now occupies a tin house with a wonderful mansard roof, from which he issues every afternoon for an aerial constitutional, giving us a fright occasionally with a flight over far a-sea, but always returning safely enough to his new diggings.

That Tuesday morning the sun rose fiery red out of the steaming Guinea jungles to the east of us, across its lower half two narrow black bars sinister. It looked as if it had blood in its eye, while the still, heavy, brooding air felt to be ominous of evil, harbouring devilment of some sort. All the mess were cross-grained, silent, or irritable, raw-edged for the first time, for a better lot of fellows one could not ask to ship with. Nor throughout the day did weather conditions or tempers improve. All day long the sky was heavily overcast with dense, low-hanging, dark gray clouds, which, while wholly obscuring the sun, seemed to focus its rays upon us like a vast burning-glass; wherefore it was expedient for the two *pajama*-clad passengers to keep well within the shelter of the bridge-deck awning. Toward sunset, a dense black wall of cloud settled upon the western horizon, aft of us.

But suddenly, just at the moment the sun must have been descending below the horizon to the south of it, the black wall of cloud slowly parted, and the opening so made widened until it became an enormous oval, reaching from horizon half-way to zenith, framing a scene of astounding beauty and grandeur. Range after range of cloud crests that looked like mountain folds rose one above another, with the appearance of vast intervening space between, some of the ranges a most delicate blue or pink, some opalescent, some gloriously gilded, while behind the farthest and tallest range, at what seemed an inconceivably remote distance, but in a perspective entirely harmonious with the foreground, appeared the sky itself, a soft luminous straw-yellow in colour, flecked thickly over with tiny snow-white cloudlets. It was like a glimpse into another and more beautiful world than ours—the actual celestial world.

But, whether or not ominous of our future, we were permitted no more than a brief glimpse of it, for presently the pall of black cloud fell like a vast drop curtain and shut it from our sight. Then night came down upon us, black, starless, forbidding, although in the absence of any fall of the barometer nothing more than a downpour of rain was expected.

But shortly after I had gone to sleep, at two o'clock suddenly something in the nature of a tropical tornado flew up and struck us hard. I was awakened by a tremendous crash on the bridge-deck above my cabin, a heeling over of the ship that nearly dumped me out of my berth, and what seemed like a solid spout of water pouring in through my open weather porthole, with the wind howling a devil's death-song through the rigging and an uninterrupted smash—bang! above my head.

Throwing on a rain coat over my *pajamas*, I went outside and up the ladder leading to the bridge-deck; and as head and shoulders rose above the deck level, a wall of hot, wind-borne rain struck me—rain so hot it felt almost scalding—that almost swept me off the ladder. If it had I should probably have become food for the fishes. I got to the upper deck just in time to see Captain Thomas get a crack on the head from a fragment of flying spar of the wreckage from the upper bridge—luckily a glancing blow that did no more damage than leave him groggy for a moment.

For the next fifteen minutes I was busy hugging a bridge stanchion, dodging flying wreckage and trying to breathe; for, driven by the violence of the wind, the rain came horizontally in such suffocatingly hot dense masses as nearly to stifle one.

It was the watch of Second Mate Isitt. Afterwards he told me that a few minutes before the storm broke he saw a particularly dense black cloud coming up upon us out of the southeast, where it had apparently been lying in ambush for us behind the northernmost headland of the Gulf of Guinea, an ambush so successful that even the barometer failed to detect it, for when Mate Isitt ran to the chart-room he found that the instrument showed no fall. But scarcely was he back on the bridge before the approaching cloud flashed into a solid mass of sheet lightning that covered the ship like a fiery canopy; and instantly thereafter, a wall of wind and rain hit the ship, heeled her over to the rail, swung her head at right angles to her course, ripped the heavy canvas awning of the upper bridge to tatters, bent and tore loose from their sockets the thick iron stanchions supporting it, made kindling wood of its heavy spars, and strewed the bridge and forward deck with a pounding tangle of wreckage.

How the mate and helmsman, who were directly beneath it, escaped injury, is a mystery. In twenty minutes the riot of wind and water had swept past us out to sea in search of easier game, leaving behind it a dead calm above but mountainous seas beneath, that played ball with us the rest of the night. Heaven help any wind-jammer it may have struck, for if caught as completely unwarned as were we, with all sails set, she and all her crew are likely to be still slowly settling through the dense darksome depths of the twenty-five hundred fathoms the chart showed thereabouts, and weeping wives and anxious underwriters will long be scanning the news columns that report all sea goings and comings—except arrivals in the port of sunken ships.

The second fall the elements have essayed to take out of us remains yet undecided. The fact is, I am now writing over a young volcano we are all hoping will not grow much older.

Two nights ago I was awakened half suffocated, to find my cabin full of strong sulphurous fumes; but fancying them brought in through my open portholes from the smoke-stack by a shift aft of the wind, I paid no further attention to them. But when the next morning I as usual turned out on deck to see the sun rise, a commotion aft of me attracted my attention, Looking, I saw the first mate, chief engineer, and a party of sailors, all so begrimed with sweat and coal dust one could scarcely pick officers from seamen, rapidly ripping off the cover of one of the midship hatches, while others were flying about connecting up the deck fire hose. This didn't look a bit good to me, and when, an instant later, off came the hatch and out poured thick volumes of smoke, I failed to observe that it looked any better.

When the hatch was removed, the men thrust the hose through it, and began deluging the burning bunker with water; for, luckily, it is only a bunker fire,—in a lower and comparatively small bunker.

The fire had been discovered early the day previous, and for nearly twenty-four hours officers and seamen had been fighting it from below, without any mention to their two passengers of its existence, fighting by tireless shovelling to reach his seat. And now they were on deck, attacking it from above, only because the heat and fumes below had become so overpowering they could no longer work there. But after an hour's ventilation through the hatch and a continuous downpour of water, the first mate again led his men below.

And so, the usual watches being divided into two-hour relays, the fight has gone on wearily but persistently, until now, the evening of the fourth day, the men are wan and haggard from the killing heat and foul air. In the engine-room in these latitudes the thermometer ranges from rarely under 108 degrees up to 130, and one has to stay down there only an hour, as I often have, until he is streaming with sweat as if he were in the unholiest heat of a Turkish bath. And as the burning bunker immediately adjoins the other end of the boiler room, to the heat of its own smouldering mass is added that of the fire boxes, until the temperature is probably close to 140 degrees.

While the fire is confined to the bunker where it started, we are in no particular danger; but if it reaches the bunker immediately above, it will have a free run to the after hold, where several thousand packages of case oil are stored. In the open waist above the oil are a score or more big tanks of gasoline, and, on the poop immediately aft of that, a quantity of dynamite and several thousand detonating caps. Thus if the fire ever gets aft, things are apt to happen a trifle quicker than they can be dodged.

To denizens of *terra firma*, the mere thought of being aboard a ship on fire in mid-sea—we are now five hundred miles from the little British island of Ascension and one thousand and eighty off the Congo (mainland) Coast—is nothing short of appalling. But here with us, in actual experience, it is taken by the officers of the ship as such a simple matter of course, in so far as they show or will admit, that we are even denied the privilege of a mild thrill of excitement.

In the meantime there is nothing for the Doctor and myself to do but sit about and guess whether it is to be a boost from the explosives, a simple grill, a descent to Davy Jones, an adventure while athirst and hungering in an open boat on the tossing South Atlantic, a successful run of the ship to the nearest land—or victory over the fire. I wonder which it will be!

If the worst comes to the worst, I intend to do for these pages what no one these last three weeks has done for me—commit them to a bottle, if I can find one aboard this ship, which is by no means certain. Indeed it is so uncertain I think I had best start hunting one right now.

★★★★★★

After nearly a twenty-four hours' search I've got it—a craft to bear these sheets, wide of hatch, generously broad and deep of hull, but destitute of aught of the stimulating aroma I had hoped might cheer them on their voyage—more than I have been cheered on mine. For the best I am able to procure for them is—a jam bottle!

While the doctor and I are not novices at golf, this is one "bunker" we are making so little headway getting out of, that both now seem likely to quit "down" to it.

I wonder when the little derelict, tiny and inconspicuous as a Portuguese man-of-war, may be picked up; I wonder when the sheets it bears may reach my publisher to whom it is consigned. Perhaps not for years—a score, two score; perhaps not until he himself, whom a few weeks ago I left in the lusty vigour of early manhood, is gathered to his fathers; perhaps not, therefore, until the writer has no publisher left and is himself no longer remembered.

The burning bunker is now a glowing furnace, the men worked down to mere shadows. Plainly the fire is getting the best of them and, what is even more discouraging, there is little more fight left in them.

First Mate Watson, who, almost without rest, has led the fight below since it started, says that another half-hour will—

194

CHAPTER 14

They Who Must Be Obeyed

Few mightier monarchs than Menelek II of Abyssinia ever swayed the destinies of a people. Throughout the vast territory of the Abyssinian highlands his individual will is law to some millions of subjects; law also to hordes of savage Mohammedan and pagan tribesmen without the confines of his kingdom. His court includes no councillors. Alone throughout the long years of his reign Menelek has dealt with all domestic and foreign affairs of state.

But now this last splendid survival of the feudal absolutism exercised and enjoyed by mediaeval rulers is about to disappear beneath encroaching waves of civilization, that do not long spare the picturesque. Cables from far-off Adis Ababa, Menelek's capital, bring news that he has formed a cabinet and published the appointment of Ministers of War, Finance, Justice, Foreign Affairs, and Commerce. And this change has come, not from the pressure of any party or faction within his kingdom, for such do not exist, but out of the fount of his own wisdom. So sound is this wisdom as to prove him a most worthy descendant of the sage Hebrew King whom Menelek claims as ancestor—if, indeed, more proofs were necessary than the statesmanlike way in which he has dealt with jealous diplomats, and the martial skill with which, at Adowa in 1896, he defeated the flower of the Italian army and won from Italy an honourable truce.

No existing royal house owns lineage so ancient as that claimed by Menelek II, Negus Negusti, "King of the Kings of Ethiopia, and Conquering Lion of Judah."

Old Abyssinian tradition has it that in the tenth century, B.C., early in her reign, Makeda, Queen of Sheba, paid a ceremonial visit to the Court of King Solomon, coming with her entire court and a magnificent retinue bearing royal gifts of frankincense and balm, gold and ivory and precious stones. Her gorgeous caravan was bright with the many-coloured plumes and silks of litters, blazing with the golden ornaments of elephant and camel caparisons, glittering with the glint of spears and bucklers.

That the two greatest souls of their time, so met, should fuse and blend is little to be wondered at. She of Sheba bore Solomon a son and called him Menelek, so the legend runs. Later the boy was twitted by playmates for that he had no father. In this annoyance the Queen sent an embassy to Solomon asking some act that should establish their son's royal paternity. Promptly Solomon returned the embassy bearing to Sheba's court in far southwest Arabia a royal decree declaring Menelek his son, and accompanied it by a son of each of the leaders of the twelve tribes of Israel, enjoined to serve as a sort of juvenile royal court to Menelek.

Whether or not the claim of Menelek II be true, that he himself is lineally descended from the son of Solomon and Sheba's Queen, certain it is that in race type Abyssinians are plainly come of sons of Israel, crossed and modified with Coptic, Hamite, and Ethiopian blood. To this day they cling closely as the most orthodox Hebrew, to some of the dearest Israelitish tenets, notably abstention from pork and from meat not killed by bleeding, observance of the Sabbath, and the rite of circumcision. Notwithstanding this the Abyssinians have been Christians since the fourth century of this era, when, only eight years after the great Constantine decreed the recognition of Christianity by the State, a proselytising monk came among them with a faith so strong, a heart so pure, and an eloquence so irresistible, that, singlehanded, he accomplished the conversion of the Abyssinian race.

Throughout the centuries the Abyssinians have held fast to their faith as first it was taught them. The great wave of Mohammedanism that swept up the Nile and across the Indian Ocean broke and parted the moment it struck the Abyssinian plateau. It completely surrounded, but never could mount the tableland.

Thus cut off for centuries from all other Christian Churches, the Abyssinian religion remains today but little changed. Could Paul or John return to earth, of all the Christian sects throughout the world, the forms and tenets of the Abyssinian Church would be the only ones they would find nearly all their own; for the ritual is older than that of either Rome or Moscow.

And remembering the Abyssinian folklore tale of the twelve sons of the chiefs of the twelve tribes of Israel sent by Solomon to Makeda

MENELEK II, NEGUS NEGUSTI, "KING OF THE KINGS OF
ETHIOPA, AND CONQUERING LION OF JUDAH"

as attendants on Menelek I, it is most curious and interesting to know that the heads of certain twelve Abyssinian families (none of whom are longer notables, some even the rudest ignorant herdsmen), and their forebears from time immemorial, have had and still possess inalienable right of audience with their monarch at any time they may ask it, even taking precedence over royalty itself. Indeed Mr. George Clerk, for the last five years assistant to Sir John Harrington, British Minister to the Court of Menelek, recently told me that he and other diplomats accredited to Adis Ababa, were not infrequently subjected to the annoyance of having an audience interrupted or delayed by the unannounced coming for a hearing of one of these favoured twelve.

Many of Menelek's judgments are masterpieces. Recently two brothers came before him, the younger with the plaint that the elder sought the larger and better part of certain property they had to divide. Promptly Menelek ordered the elder to describe fully the entire property and state what part he wanted for himself. It was done.

"And this," questioned Menelek, "you consider a just division of the property into two parts of equal value?"

"Yes, Negus," answered the elder.

"Then," decreed Menelek, "give your brother first choice!"

Over wide territory beyond the Abyssinian border, Menelek's power is as much feared and his will as much respected as among his own subjects. Of this there occurred recently a most dramatic proof.

Bordering Abyssinia on the east is the Danakil country. It adjoins the Province of Shoa, of which Menelek was Ras, or feudal King, before his accession to the Abyssinian throne. The Danakils are a savage pagan people of mixed Hamite (early Egyptian) and Ethiopian ancestry. They are perhaps the most tirelessly warlike race in all Africa. Often severely beaten by their Italian and Somali neighbours, they have never been subdued. Indeed slaughter may, in a way, be said to be a part of their religion, for it is the fetish every young warrior must provide for the worship of the woman of his choice before he may hope to win and have her. It is necessary that he should have killed royal game—lion, rhinoceros, or elephant—but not enough. Singlehanded he must kill a man and bring the maid a trophy of the slaughter before she will even consider him, and Danakil maids of spirit often demand some plurality of trophies. Thus the license for each Danakil mating is written in the life blood of some neighbouring tribesman; thus are the few poltroons in Danakil-land condemned to stay celibate.

Only Menelek's word do they heed; his might they dread.

Through the Danakil country, between Errer Gotto and Oder, not long ago travelled the caravan of William Northrup McMillan, conveying the sections of several steel boats with which he purposed navigating and exploring the Blue Nile from its source to Khartoom, a region that had never been traversed by white men. In the party was M. Dubois-Desaulle, a gay and reckless ex-officer of the French Foreign Legion who had long served in Algiers against raiding Arab sheiks. He harboured no fear of the unorganized wild tribesmen through whose country they were travelling. McMillan knew them better, however; he held his command under strict military discipline, marched in close order with scouts out, forbade straying from the column, and *zareba*-ed his night camps. For the march was a severe one and he had neither the time nor sufficient force to search for or to succour missing stragglers.

Urged with the rest never to go unarmed and to stay close with the caravan, Dubois-Desaulle's only reply was a laughing, "*Jamais! Jamais. Je ne porte pas des armes pour ces babouins! Je les ferai s'enfuir avec des batons! N'inquiètez pas de moi.*"

Interested in botany and entomology, holding the natives in utter contempt, repeatedly he strayed from the column for hours without even so much as a pistol by way of arms, until finally McMillan told him that if he again so strayed he would be placed under guard for the balance of march. But the very next day, riding a mule with the advance guard led by H. Morgan Brown, Dubois-Desaulle slipped unobserved into the bush, probably in pursuit of some winged wonder that had crossed his path.

Camp was made early in the afternoon on the banks of the Doha River, and a strong party, with *shikari* trackers, led by Brown, was sent out in search of the straggler. Night came on before they could pick up his trail, and nothing further could be done except to build signal fires on adjacent hills; but all without result. Anxiety for his safety crystallized into chill fear for his life, when the dull glow of the signal fires was suddenly extinguished by the next morning's sun; for the desert knows neither twilight nor dawn—the sun bursts up blood-red out of shrouding darkness like a rocket from its case, and at once it is day.

An hour later Brown's *shikaris* found the place where Dubois-Desaulle had strayed from the column, followed his trail through the bush hither and thither for two miles, to a point where he had found a native warrior seated beneath a tree. They read, with their unerring skill at "sign" lore, that there he had stood and talked for some time with the native, and then pressed on, rider and footman travelling side by side, till, within the shelter of especially dense surrounding bush, the footman had dropped behind the rider—for what dastardly assassin's purpose the next twenty steps revealed. There stark lay the body of gay Dubois-Desaulle, dropped from his mule without a struggle by a mortal spear-thrust in his back, the manner of his mutilation a Danakil's sign manual!

Immediately messengers were sent to the caravan bearing the news and asking reinforcements. At this time the indomitable chief, McMillan, was laid up with veldt sores on the legs, unable to walk or even to ride except in a litter. Promptly, however, he despatched Lieutenant Fairfax and William Marlow, with about thirty more men, to Brown's support, with orders never to quit till he got the murderer. By a forced march, Fairfax reached Brown at four in the afternoon.

When journeying in desert places and amid deadly perils, it is always an unusually terrible shock to lose one from among so few, and to be forced to lay him in unconsecrated ground remote from home and friends. So it was a sobbing, saddened trio that stood by while a grave was dug to receive all that was mortal of their gallant comrade. And within it they laid him, wrapped in the ample folds of an Abyssinian *tope*; stones were heaped above the grave—at least the four-footed beasts should not have a chance to rend him!—and three volleys were fired as a last honour to Dubois-Desaulle, ex-legionary of the Army of Algiers.

Tears dried, eyes hardened, jaws tightened, and away on the plain trail of the murderer marched the little column. Turning at the edge of the thick jungle for a last look back, the three noted an extraordinary circumstance that touched them deeply and made them feel that even the savage desert sympathized. A miniature whirlwind of the sort frequent in the desert was slowly circling the grave; and even as they looked it swung immediately over it and there stood for some moments, its tall dust column rising up into the zenith like the smoke of a funeral pyre! Then on they marched and there they left him, sure that by night lions would be roaring him a requiem not unfitting his wild spirit.

Just at dusk the party reached a large Danakil town into which the murderer's trail led, and camped before it.

Told that one of his men had killed their comrade and that they wanted him, Ali Gorah, the chief, was surly and insolent. He refused to give him up, said that he wished no war with them, but that if they

200

wanted any of his people they must fight for them. Then guards were set about the camp and the little command lay down to sleep within a spear's throw of thousands of Ali Gorah's wild Danakils. The night passed without alarms, and then conference was resumed. Fairfax cajoled and threatened, threatened summoning an army that would wipe Danakil's land off the map; but all to no purpose. The chief remained obdurate.

Early in the day a courier was sent to McMillan with the story of their plight and a request for supplies and more men. These were instantly sent, leaving McMillan himself well nigh helpless, fuming at his own enforced inaction, alone with the Marlow, his personal attendant, a handful of men, and a total of only two rifles, as the sole guard of the caravan for ten more anxious days.

Daily councils were held, always ending in mutual threats. Fairfax could make no progress, but he would not leave.

One day Ali Gorah lined up two thousand warriors in battle array before Fairfax's small command and ordered him to move off, under pain of instant attack. But there Fairfax stubbornly stayed, in the very face of the certainty that his command could not last ten minutes if the chief should actually order a charge. His dauntless courage won, and the war party was withdrawn.

In the meantime some of his Somalis had learned from the Danakils that the murderer's name was Mirach, and that he was the greatest warrior of the tribe, a man with trophies of all sorts of royal game and of no less than forty men to his matrimonial credit. By the eleventh day mutual irritation had nigh reached the fusing point. Fairfax had carefully trained a gun crew to handle a Colt machine-gun that McMillan was bringing as a present to Ras Makonnen, the victor of the field of Adowa, and debated with his mates the question of risking an attack.

Luckily, however, the previous day McMillan had bethought him of a letter of Menelek's he carried, a letter ordering all his subjects to lend the bearer any aid or succour he might need. This letter he sent by his Abyssinian headman to Mantoock, the nearest Abyssinian Ras and a sort of overlord of the Danakils, with request for his advice and aid. Promptly came Mantoock, with only one attendant, heard the story, begged McMillan to have no further care, and raced away for Ali Gorah's village, where happily he arrived in mid afternoon of the eleventh day, just as Fairfax was making dispositions for opening a finish fight.

"Disarmed and shackled, Mirach remained a sullen but defiant prisoner"

Mantoock's first act was to advise Fairfax to withdraw his command and rejoin the caravan; and, assured that Mirach would be brought away a prisoner, Fairfax assented and withdrew. Then Mantoock entered alone the village of Ali Gorah and there spent the night. What passed that night between the Christian and the pagan chiefs we do not know. Probably little was said; nothing more was needed, indeed, than the interpretation of the letter of the Negus and the exhibition of the royal seal it bore. Full well Ali Gorah knew the heavy penalty of disobedience.

So it happened that near noon of the twelfth day Mantoock brought Mirach into McMillan's camp, accompanied by thirty of his family and the headmen of the tribe, Mirach marching in fully armed with spears and shield, insolent and fearless.

Asked why he had done the deed, Mirach replied:

"I was resting in the shade. The *feringee* approached and asked me to guide him to the river. I told him to pass on and not to disturb me. Then he stayed and talked and talked till I got tired and told him not to tempt me further; for I had never yet had such a chance to kill a white man. Still he annoyed me with his foolish talk until, weary of it, I led him away into the thickets to his death and won trophies dear to Danakil's maidens."

Three camels, worth twenty dollars each, or a total of sixty dollars, is usual blood-money in Abyssinia. When that is paid and received, feuds among the tribesmen end, and murders are soon forgotten. But Mirach was so highly valued as a warrior by his people that they offered McMillan no less than three hundred camels for his life. They were dumbfounded when their offer was refused.

Disarmed and shackled, Mirach remained a sullen but defiant prisoner with the caravan for the next two weeks' march, when the crossing of the Hawash River brought them well into Abyssinian territory and made it safe to rush him forward, in the charge of a small escort, to Adis Ababa.

There he was tried beneath the sombre shade of the famous Judgment Tree, condemned, and two months later hanged in the market place: and there for days his grinning face and shrivelling carcass swung, a menacing proof to the wildest visiting tribesmen of them all of the vast power of the Negus Negusti.

CHAPTER 15

Djama Aout's Heroism

"Throughout Somaliland, among a race famous for their fearlessness, the name of Djama Aout is held a synonym for reckless courage. He did the bravest deed I ever saw, a deed heroic in its purpose, ferociously sage in its execution; the deed of a man bred of a race that knew no longer-range weapon than an *assegai*, trained from youth to fight and kill at arm's length or in hand grapple; a deed that, incidentally, saved my life."

The speaker was C. W. L. Bulpett, himself well qualified by personal experience to sit in judgment, as Court of Last Resort, on any act of courage; a man who, at forty, without training and on a heavy wager that he could not walk a mile, run a mile, and ride a mile, all in sixteen and a half minutes, finished the three miles in sixteen minutes and seven seconds; a man who, midway of a dinner at Greenwich, bet that he could swim the half-mile across the Thames and back in his evening clothes before the coffee was served, and did it; and who has crossed Africa from Khartoom to the Red Sea.

If more were needed to prove Mr. Bulpett's past-mastership in hardihood, it is perhaps sufficient to mention that he voluntarily got himself in the fix that needed Djama Aout's aid, although in telling the story he did not convey the impression that his own part in it was more than secondary and inconsequential.

"We were big-game hunting, lion and rhino preferred, along the border of Somaliland," he continued. "Besides the pony and camel men, we had four Somali *shikaris*, trained trackers, who knew the habits of beasts and read their tracks and signs like a book; men of a breed whose women will not give themselves as wives except to men who have scored kills of both royal game and men.

"*Sahib* McMillan's personal *shikari* was DJama Aout; mine, Abdi

"THROUGHOUT SOMALILAND, AMONG A RACE
FAMOUS FOR THEIR FEARLESSNESS, THE NAME OF
DJAMA AOUT IS HELD A SYNONYM FOR
RECKLESS COURAGE"

Dereh. At the time of this incident the *Sahib* had several lions to his credit, while I yet had none. So the *Sahib* kindly declared that, however and by whomsoever jumped, the try at the next lion should be mine. The section we were in was the usual 'lion country' of East Africa, wide stretches of dry, level plain with occasional low rolling hills, thinly timbered everywhere with the thorny mimosa, most of it low bush, some grown to small trees twenty or thirty feet in height.

"To cover a wider range of shooting, we one day decided to divide the camp, and I moved off about four miles and pitched my tent on a low hill, which left the old camp in clear view across the plain. Early the next morning I went out after eland and had an excellent morning's sport. Returned to camp shortly after noon, tired and dusty, I took a bath, got into *pajamas* and slippers, had my luncheon, and was sitting comfortably smoking within my tent, when one of my men hurried in to say a messenger was coming on a pony at top speed. Presently he arrived, with word from the *Sahib* that he had a big male lion at bay in a thicket bordering the river and urging me to hurry to him.

"This my first chance at lion, I seized my rifle, mounted a pony, without stopping to dress, and, followed by Abdi Dereh and another *shikari*, dashed away behind the messenger at my pony's best pace. Arrived, I found the *Sahib* and about a dozen men, *shikaris* and pony men, surrounding a dense mimosa thicket no more than thirty or forty yards in diameter. Nigh two-thirds of its circumference was bounded by a bend of a deep stream the lion was not likely to try to cross, which left a comparatively narrow front to guard against a charge.

"'Here you are, Don Carlos!' called the *Sahib*, as I jumped off my pony. 'Here's your lion in the bush. Up to you to get him out. Djama Aout and the rest will stay to help you while I go back and move the caravan to a new camp-site. No suggestion to make, except I scarcely think I'd go in the bush after him; too thick to see ten feet ahead of you,' and away he rode toward his camp.

"The situation was simple, even to a novice at the game of lion-shooting. With my line of shouting men forced to range themselves across the narrow land front of the thicket and no chance of his exit on the river front, only two lines of strategy remained: it was either fire the bush and drive him out upon us or enter the bush on hands and knees and creep about till I sighted him. The latter was well-nigh suicidal, for it was absolutely sure he would scent, hear, and locate me before I could see him, and thus would be almost complete master of the situation. Naturally, therefore, I first had the bush fired, as near to windward as the bend of the river permitted, and took a stand covering his probable line of exit from the thicket. But it was a failure—not enough dead wood to carry the fire through the bush and it soon flickered and died out. Thus nothing remained but the last alternative, and I took it.

"Dropping on hands and knees, I began to creep into the thicket. Soon my hands were bleeding from the dry mimosa thorns littering the ground, my back from the thorny boughs arching low above me. For some distance I could see no more than the length of my rifle before me or to right or left. Presently, when near the centre of the brush patch, Abdi Dereh next behind me, a second *shikari* behind him, and Djama Aout bringing up the rear, I caught a glimpse of the lion's hind quarters and tail, scarcely six feet ahead of me.

"I fired at once, most imprudently, for the exposure could not possibly afford a fatal shot. Instantly after the shot, the lion circled the dense clump immediately in front of me and charged me through a narrow opening. As he came, I gave him my second barrel from the hip—no time to aim—and in trying to spring aside out of his path, slipped in my loose slippers and fell flat on my back.

"Later we learned that my first shot had torn through his loins and my second had struck between neck and shoulder and ranged the entire length of his body. But even the terrible shock of two great .450 cordite-driven balls did not serve to stop him, and the very moment I hit the ground he lit diagonally across my body, his belly pressing mine, his hot breath burning my cheek, his fierce eyes glaring into mine.

"Though it seemed an age, the rest was a matter of seconds. Abdi Dereh, my rifle-bearer, was in the act of shoving the gun muzzle against the lion's ribs for a shot through the heart, when a shot from without the bush—we never learned by whom fired, probably by one of the pony men—broke his arm and knocked him flat. Then the second *shikari* sprang forward and bent to pick up the gun, when one stroke of the lion's great forepaw tore away most of the flesh from one side of his head and face, and laid him senseless.

"Freed for an instant from the attacks of my men, the lion turned to the prey held helpless beneath him, and with a fierce roar, was in the very act of advancing his cavernous mouth and gleaming fangs to seize me by the head, when in jumped Djama Aout to my succour. His only weapon was the *Sahib's* .38 Smith & Wesson self-cocking six-shooter. His was the quickest piece of sound thinking, shrewd acting, and desperate valour conceivable. I was staring death in the face—he knew it at a glance. Just within those enormous jaws, and all would be over with me. The light charge of the pistol, however placed, would be little more than a flea-bite on a monster already ripped laterally and longitudinally through and through by two great .450 cordite shells. Indeed the lion was not even gasping from his wounds; his great heart was beating strong and steady against mine. Of what avail a little pistol-ball, or six of them?

"All this must have raced through Djama Aout's brain in a second, in the very second *Shikari* Number Two was falling under the lion's blow. In another second he conceived a plan, absolutely the only one that possibly could have saved me.

"Just at the instant the lion turned and opened his jaws to seize and crush my head, forward sprang Djama Aout; within the lion's jaws and into his great yawning mouth Djama Aout thrust pistol, hand, and forearm, and, though the hard-driven teeth crunched cruelly through sinews and into bone, steadily pulled the trigger till the pistol's six loads were discharged down the lion's very throat!

"Shrinking from the shock of the shots, the lion released Djama Aout's mangled arm and freed me of his weight. Unhurt, even unscratched by the lion, I quickly swung myself up into the biggest mimosa near, a poor four feet from the ground, within easy reach of our enemy if he had not been too sick of his wounds to leap at me.

"Having fallen from the pain and shock of his wounded arm, Djama Aout rose, backed off a little distance, and stood at bay, the pistol clubbed in his left hand.

"While apparently sick unto death, the lion might muster strength for a last attack, so I called to Marlow, who, under orders, had waited without the thicket, bearing an elephant gun. Ignorant of whether or not the lion was even wounded, in the brave boy came, crept in range and fired a great eight-bore ball fair through the lion's heart.

"It was only a few hours until, working with knife and tweezers, the *Sahib* had all the mimosa thorns dug out of my back and legs, but it was many months before Djama Aout recovered partial use of his good right arm, and it may very well be generations before the story of his heroic deed ceases to be sung in Somali villages."

"Within the lion's jaws and into his great
yawning mouth Djama Aout thrust pistol, hand,
and forearm"

CHAPTER 16

A Modern Coeur-de-Lion

To seek to come to death grips with the King of Beasts, a man must himself be nothing short of lion-hearted. Such men there are, a few, men with an inborn lust of battle, a love of staking their own lives against the heaviest odds; men who, lacking a Crusader's cult or a country's need to cut and thrust for, go out among the savage denizens of the desert seeking opportunity to fight for their faith in their own strong arms and steady nerves; men who shrink from a laurel but treasure a trophy. William Northrup McMillan, a native of St. Louis, who has spent the last eight years in exploration of the Blue Nile and in travel through Abyssinia and British East Africa, is such a man.

A friend of Mr. McMillan has told me the following story of one of his hunting experiences. While I can only tell it in simple prose, the deed described deserves perpetuity in the stately metre of a saga.

The Jig-Jigga country, a province of Abyssinia lying near the border of British Somaliland and governed by Abdullah Dowa, an Arab sheik owing allegiance to King Menelek, is the best lion country in all Africa. Jig-Jigga is an arid plateau averaging 5,000 feet above sea level, poorly watered but generously grassed, sparsely timbered with the thorny mimosa (full brother to the Texas *mesquite*), and swarming everywhere with innumerable varieties of the wild game on which the lion preys and fattens—eland, oryx, hartebeest, gazelle, and zebra.

There are two ways of hunting lion. First, from the perfectly safe shelter of a *zareba*, a tightly enclosed hut built of thorny mimosa bows, with no opening but a narrow porthole for rifle fire. Within the *zareba* the hunter is shut in at nightfall by his *shikaris*, usually having one *shikari* with him, sometimes with a goat as a third companion and a lure for lion. An occasional bite of the goat's ear by sharp *shikari* teeth inspires shrill bleats sure to bring any lion lurking near in range of the hunter's rifle. At other times goat ears are spared, and the loudest-braying donkey of the caravan is picketed immediately in front of the *zareba's* porthole, his normal vocal activities stimulated by the occasional prod of a stick. Sometimes several weary sleepless nights are spent without result, but sooner or later, without the slightest sound hinting his approach, suddenly a great yellow body flashes out of the darkness and upon the cringing lure. For an instant there are the sinister sounds of savage snarls, rending flesh, cracking bones and screams of pain and fear, and then a dull red flash heralds the rifle's roar, and the tawny terror falls gasping his life out across his prey.

The second, and the only sportsmanlike way of lion-hunting, is by tracking him in the open. The pony men circle till they find a trail, follow it till close enough to the game to race ahead and bring it to bay, circle about it while a messenger brings up the *Sahib*, who dismounts and advances afoot to a combat wherein the echo of a misplaced shot may sound his own death-knell.

One morning while camped in the Jig-Jigga country, William Marlow, our *Sahib's* valet, was out with the pony men trailing a wounded oryx, while the *Sahib* himself was three miles away shooting eland. In mid forenoon Marlow's men struck the fresh track of two great male lions, plainly out on a hunting party of their own.

Instantly Marlow rushed a messenger away to fetch the *Sahib*, and he and the pony men then took the trail at a run. Within two hours the pony men succeeded in circling the quarry and stopping it in a mimosa thicket. Shortly thereafter, while they were circling and shouting about the thicket to prevent a charge before the *Sahib's* arrival, an incident occurred which proves alike the utter fearlessness and the marvellous knowledge of the game of the Somali. Suddenly out of the shadows of the thicket sprang one of the lions and launched himself like a thunderbolt upon one of the pony men, bearing horse and rider to the ground. Losing his spear in the fall and held fast by one leg beneath his horse, the rider was defenceless.

However, he seized a thorny stick and began beating the lion across the face, while the lion tore at the pony's flank and quarters. Then down from his horse sprang another pony man, and knowing he could not kill the lion with his spear quickly enough to save his companion, approached and crouched directly in front of the lion till his own face was scarcely two feet from the lion's, and there made such frightful grimaces and let off such shrill shrieks, that, frightened from his prey, the lion slunk snarling to the edge of the thicket.

Just at this moment the *Sahib* raced upon the scene, accompanied by his Secretary, H. Morgan Brown. In the run he had far outdistanced his gun-bearers. Marlow was unarmed and Brown carried nothing but a camera. Thus the *Sahib's* single-shot .577 rifle was the only effective weapon in the party, and for it he did not even have a single spare cartridge. The one little cylinder of brass within the chamber of his rifle, with the few grains of powder and nickeled lead it held, was the only certain safeguard of the group against death or mangling.

All this must have flashed across the *Sahib's* mind as he leaped from his pony and took stand in the open, sixty steps from where the lion stood roaring and savagely lashing his tail. A little back of the *Sahib* and to his left stood Brown with his camera, beside him Marlow.

Instantly, firm planted on his feet, the *Sahib* threw the rifle to his face for a steady standing shot. But quicker even than this act, instinctively, the furious King of Beasts had marked the giant bulk of the *Sahib* as the one foeman of the half-score round him worthy of his gleaming ivory weapons, and at him straight he charged the very instant the gun was levelled, coming in great bounds that tossed clouds of dust behind him, coming with hoarse roars at every bound, roars to shake nerves not made of steel and still the beating of the stoutest heart. On came the lion, and there stood the *Sahib*—on and yet on—till it must have seemed to his companions that the *Sahib* was frozen in his tracks.

But all the time a firm hand and a true eye held the bead of the rifle sight to close pursuit of the lion's every move, so held it till only a narrow sixteen yards separated man and beast. Then the *Sahib's* rifle cracked; and, with marvellous nerve, Brown snapped his camera a second later and caught the picture of the kill. Hitting the beast squarely in the forehead just at the take-on of a bound, the heavy .577 bullet cleaned out the lion's brain pan and killed him instantly, his body turning in mid-air and hitting the ground inert. A better rifle-shot would be impossible, and as good a camera snapshot has certainly never been made in the very face of instant, impending, deadly peril.

A half-hour later Lion Number Two, slower of resolution than his mate, fell to the *Sahib's* first shot, with a broken neck, while lashing himself into fit fury for a charge. This was more even than a royal kill; each of the lions was, in size, a record among Jig-Jigga hunters, the first measuring eleven feet one inch from tip of nose to tip of tail, the second eleven feet.

And then the party marched back to camp with the trophies, Djama Aout, the head *shikari*, chanting *paeans* to his *Sahib's* prowess, while his mates roared a hoarse Somali chorus, and all night long, by ancient law of *shikari*, the camp feasted, chanted, and danced, one sable saga-maker after another chanting his pride to serve so valiant a *Sahib*.

www.ingramcontent.com/pod-product-compliance
Lightning Source LLC
Chambersburg PA
CBHW032056080426
42733CB00006B/291